THE EUROPEAN U

General Editors: Neill Nugent, William E. Paterson, Vincent Wright

The European Union series is designed to provide an authoritative library on the European Union ranging from general introductory texts to definitive assessments of key institutions and actors, policies and policy processes, and the role of member states.

Books in the series are written by leading scholars in their fields and reflect the most up-to-date research and debate. Particular attention is paid to accessibility and clear presentation for a wide audience of students, practitioners and interested general readers.

The series consists of four major strands:

- general textbooks
- the major institutions and actors
- the main areas of policy
- the member states and the Union

Published titles

Desmond Dinan
Ever Closer Union? An Introduction to the European Community

Wyn Grant
The Common Agricultural Policy

Justin Greenwood
Representing Interests in the European Union

Alain Guyomarch, Howard Machin and Ella Ritchie
France in the European Union

Fiona Hayes-Renshaw and Helen Wallace
The Council of Ministers

Simon Hix and Christopher Lord
Political Parties in the European Union

Brigid Laffan
The Finances of the European Union

Janne Haaland Matláry
Energy Policy in the European Union

Neill Nugent
The Government and Politics of the European Union (Third Edition)

European Union Series
Series Standing Order
ISBN 0–333–71695–7 hardcover
ISBN 0–333–69352–3 paperback
(outside North America only)

You can receive future titles in this series as they are published by placing a standing order. Please contact your bookseller or, in the case of difficulty, write to us at the address below with your name and address, the title of the series and the ISBN quoted above.

Customer Services Department, Macmillan Distribution Ltd, Houndmills, Basingstoke, Hampshire RG21 6XS, England

France in the European Union

Alain Guyomarch
Howard Machin
and
Ella Ritchie

First published 1998 by
MACMILLAN PRESS LTD
Houndmills, Basingstoke, Hampshire RG21 6XS
and London
Companies and representatives
throughout the world

ISBN 0–333–59357–X hardcover
ISBN 0–333–59358–8 paperback

A catalogue record for this book is available
from the British Library.

10   9   8   7   6   5   4   3   2   1
07 06 05 04 03 02 01 00 99 98

Copy-edited and typeset by Povey–Edmondson
Tavistock and Rochdale, England

Printed in Hong Kong

 Published in the United States of America 1998 by
ST.MARTIN'S PRESS, INC.,
Scholarly and Reference Division
175 Fifth Avenue, New York, N.Y. 10010

ISBN 0–312–21267–4

To the memory of our friend, Peter Morris

Contents

vii

List of Tables

Abbreviations

CAP	Common Agricultural Policy
CERES	*Centre d'Etudes de Recherches, et d'Education Socialiste*
CI	Community Initiative
CFDT	*Confédération Française Démocratique du Travail*
CFSP	Common Foreign and Security Policy
CGT	*Confédération Générale du Travail*
CI	Community Initiative
CNJA	*Centre National des Jeunes Agriculteurs*
CNPF	*Conseil National du Patronat Français* (Leading Business Organization)
COPA	Confederation of Professional Agricultural Organizations
COREPER	Committee of Permanent Representatives
CSF	Community Support Framework
DATAR	*Délégation à l'Aménagement du Territorie et à l'Action Régionale*
EAGGF	European Agricultural Guidance and Guarantee Fund
EC	European Communities
ECJ	European Court of Justice
ECU	European Currency Unit
ECSC	European Coal and Steel Community
EDC	European Defence Community
EEA	European Economic Area
EEC	European Economic Community
EFTA	European Free Trade Association
EIB	European Investment Bank
EMI	European Monetary Institute
EMS	European Monetary System
EMU	Economic and Monetary Union
EP	European Parliament
EPC	European Political Co-operation
ERDF	European Regional Development Fund
ERM	Exchange Rate Mechanism
ESF	European Social Fund

ESC	Economic and Social Committee
ETUC	European Trades Union Confederation
EU	European Union
Euratom	European Atomic Energy Commission
Eurocorps	Multi-lateral European Force (grew from Franco-German brigade)
Eurogroup	European group within NATO
FD	*Force Démocrate* (Reformation of CDS in 1995)
FN	*Front National*
FNSEA	*Fédération Nationale des Syndicats d'Exploitants Agricoles*
G7	Group of 7. Leading industrial countries (USA, UK, France, Germany, Italy, Canada, Japan)
GATT	General Agreement on Tariffs and Trade
IEPG	Independent European Programme Group
IGC	Intergovernmental Conference
IMF	International Monetary Fund
IMP	Integrated Mediterranean Programmes
JHA	Justice and Home Affairs
MEP	Member of the European Parliament
MCA	Monetary Compensation Amount
MRG	*Mouvement des Radicaux de Gauche* (left-wing radicals)
MRP	*Mouvement Républicain Populaire* (Christian Democrat Party, Fourth Republic)
NATO	North Atlantic Treaty Organization
OECD	Organization for Economic Co-operation and Development
OEEC	Organization for European Economic Co-operation
OPEC	Organization of Petroleum Exporting Countries
PCF	*Parti Communiste Français*
PS	*Parti Socialiste* (French Socialist Party 1969–)
QMV	Qualified Majority Voting
RPR	*Rassemblement pour la République* (Gaullist Party, 1976–)
SCA	Special Committee on Agriculture
SEA	Single European Act
SEM	Single European Market
SFLO	*Section Français de l'internationale ouvrière* (French Socialist Party 1905–69)
SGCI	*Secrétariat Général du Comité Interministèriel* (Interministerial Committee on European Questions)
SOFRES	*Société Français d'Enquêtes par Sondage* (French Polling Organization)

TEU	Treaty on European Union
TEN	Trans European Network
UDF	*Union pour la Démocratie Française* (French centre-right federation 1978–)
UDR	*Union des Démocrates pour la République* (French Gaullist Party 1968–76)
UNICE	Union of Industries of the European Community
URC	*Union des Républicains et du Centre*
WEU	West European Union
WTO	World Trade Organization

Preface

The research for this book started with a shared curiosity by its three authors about how and to what extent, politics and policy-making in France has changed as a consequence of membership of the European Union. A second closely-linked question soon emerged – how have French politicians and officials contributed to building European institutions and to making common policies within those institutions?

Although many secondary sources provided some answers, notably about particular policy sectors, very few addressed these questions directly and none provided a comprehensive and up-to-date response. In seeking fuller answers, we turned first to many official documents – treaties, texts of law and directives, ministerial circulars and reports (parliamentary, ministerial and European Commission) and party documents. Then came a series of interviews and discussions – some 200 in all – with members of the staff of the SGCI, with many ministers, the prime minister and the president of the Republic, with senior officials in many ministries in Paris (notably with directors of the ministries of agriculture, transport and health) and in several Directions Générales of the Commission in Brussels. We also spoke to politicians, trade unionists and interest groups and business leaders.

The planning and writing of the book was very much a collective effort among the authors. However, we received a large amount of support and help from a number of people. We would like to acknowledge our thanks to our publisher, Steven Kennedy, who cajoled and encouraged us at the right times and to Vincent Wright, the series editor responsible for this book, who commented extensively and constructively on draft versions. Our thanks go also to two anonymous readers whose comments (and especially criticisms) were very helpful in the redrafting of this book. All three of us are teachers of both EU politics and French politics and we have benefited from discussions with many of our students about the content and arguments in the book. Our thanks too go to numerous colleagues and friends who have given advice, help and support during the writing of this book; we especially thank Phil Daniels, Isabelle Devautour, Sonia Mazey, Achilleas Mitsos, Jerôme Vignon and Tony Zito.

Collaborating on a book from two different institutions is not easy, but the task was greatly facilitated by the technical help and expertise of Marian Clark from LSE and Lesley Stanwix and Cath Aitken from Newcastle University. They patiently helped us to overcome the incompatibilities of electronic mail systems and word processing packages. Alain Guyomarch and Howard Machin acknowledge the support of the Staff Research Fund at LSE and Ella Ritchie acknowledges the support of the Staff Travel Fund and the Politics Department at Newcastle for secretarial and financial support.

Finally, we dedicate this book to our dear friend, Peter Morris, who died suddenly in 1997.

ALAIN GUYOMARCH
HOWARD MACHIN
ELLA RITCHIE

Introduction: France, the EU and the World

In 1988, when President Mitterrand made his New Year's Eve broadcast to the nation, his message seemed simple but was profoundly ambiguous: 'France is our homeland, but Europe is our future.' In the September 1992 referendum, faced with the simple choice of ratifying or rejecting the Maastricht Treaty, French citizens acted with similar ambiguity: just under 50 per cent of those who voted cast their votes against further European integration, but opinion polls revealed that the issues which preoccupied the voters at that time were as much domestic as European. Under President Chirac, as during previous presidencies, there remains much ambiguity and confusion about the impact and effects of membership of the European Union on France. The election of a socialist government in 1997 confirmed that the profound ambivalence among elites and voters alike about the costs and benefits of EU membership is still unresolved.

The aims of this book are to identify and analyse the main trends of change which that membership has brought. In this introductory chapter our goals are threefold: to explain the main research questions which underpin the entire book, to give a brief account of the development of the EU and its present institutional framework, and to outline the methodology and approach taken in the rest of this book. The subject of our research is a two-way dynamic process of change, since it involves France – both the state and the society – actively contributing to the construction of the EU, and, at the same time changing and adapting in numerous and significant ways as a consequence of membership of the EU. Hence, our research involves disaggregating what diplomats and politicians mean when they refer to 'France' and to 'French interests', which implies identifying the competing French interests involved in almost any sector of joint policy-making within the EU. Our focus is more on France than on

1

the EU, although this introduction does examine the development of the EU and its main institutional features after the Maastricht Treaty.

The first major research question which runs through this book concerns the changing nature and extent of the influence of French governments both over the design of EU institutions and in the formulation and implementation of common EU policies. The focus is not only on the goals, but also on the methods of successive governments, since the aim is to identify and analyse the elements of continuity, the trends of change and the ambiguities and inconsistencies of policy-making.

A second question is the extent to which membership of the European Union has brought about changes in French institutions, politics and policies. This question has many facets and includes consideration of how European integration has been perceived and debated in domestic politics. It is also important to distinguish changes which appear to be 'caused' by EU policies but which, in fact, result mainly from domestic politics and pressures. For example, as we argue in Chapter 7, the growing importance of regions within the EU policy process coincided with changes brought about by the decentralization reforms of the Mitterrand administration and by the privatization and deregulation of many state functions.

Thirdly, we seek to ascertain the extent to which EU membership allowed French governments greater influence over global trends than they would otherwise have exercised. The process of European integration did not take place in an international vacuum; from the start its development was conditioned by balance of power considerations in Western Europe, by US encouragement and support and by the Cold War divide of Europe. It also developed within the post-war international economic and financial systems: in 1944, the Bretton Woods Conference set up the International Monetary Fund (IMF) and the World Bank to help to stabilize international currencies, and in 1947 the General Agreements on Tariffs and Trade (GATT) was set up to facilitate free trade. Increasingly, and especially since 1989, France has not only been part of a European 'regional' economic and political structure but has also been integrated into a 'global' system. We must, therefore, identify those changes which reflect broader global trends and attempt to assess whether or not EU membership amplifies and accelerates their impact in France or whether the EU membership strengthens the capacity of French leaders to manage a political agenda which is increasingly influenced by external forces.

The Treaties of Paris in 1951 and Rome in 1957, the Single European Act (SEA) in 1986 and the Treaty on European Union (TEU) in 1992 not only built up institutions for joint policy-making, but also laid down four major policy goals: a common agricultural policy to increase production and support farmers' incomes, a customs union within the framework of the GATT process, a single integrated domestic market, and a single currency system based on non-inflationary monetary policy. Around these four core policy areas, many other policies were developed within the European institutions, among which environment, industry, research, regional development and common foreign and security policies are the most well known. All the core policies, except agriculture, led to moves away from traditional French macroeconomic approaches. The customs union undermined old protectionist practices, and the single market banned the use of the main tools of *dirigisme*, whereby the state guided the development of the economy. In turn, the single currency precluded inflationary stimulation and competitive devaluation.

Three changes are related to these policy shifts: a transfer of power from state to market, a sharing of responsibility between the French state and the EU structures, and a redistribution of power within state structures (both French and EU) from the political executive to quasi-judicial or autonomous agencies, for regulatory or monetary questions. We argue that in some areas the French government has lost considerable control over the policy agenda and the implementation of policy. In other areas, however, it has adapted to EU policy process and continues to structure and control policy-making.

In this context, a fourth major question is addressed: to what extent has the French government lost its capacity to monopolize representations on behalf of the whole of France in the EU policy processes? Following on this line of enquiry is a closely related question: does the notion of 'the national interest of France' still have much meaning?

The EU: development and institutions

Development

A detailed knowledge of the history, economics and institutions of the EU is not an essential prerequisite for reading this book; nor is a familiarity with theories of European integration and public policy-making. None the less, the main features of the evolution of European integration during the post-war period and the institutional arrangements at the present time are valuable contextual introductions to the major topics of our study. The foundations of the EU of today were laid during the early post-war years and many of the initiatives were taken by French leaders. Table I.1 presents the most important dates in the chronology of building the EU.

TABLE I.1

The development of the EU

1950	9 May	The Schuman declaration to establish the European Coal and Steel Community.
1951	18 April	Treaty of Paris signed by the Six creates the ECSC.
1952	27 May	Treaty establishing the European Defence Community is signed by the Six.
1954	30 August	French Parliament rejects the ratification of the EDC Treaty.
1955	1 June	Messina Conference – agreement to create an economic community.
1957	25 March	Treaties of Rome signed by the Six to create European Economic Community and European Atomic Energy Community.
1958	1 January	EEC and Euratom become operational.
1963	14 January	De Gaulle announces a veto on UK accession.
1965	8 April	The Merger treaty (operational in July 1967) is signed.
	Autumn	The policy of 'the empty chair' – non-cooperation by the French Government.
1966	27 January	The 'Luxembourg Compromise' is agreed.
1968	1 July	The customs union becomes fully operational.
1970	22 April	Luxembourg Treaty creates 'own resources' for the budget.
1972	24 March	The Six establish the 'snake' to stabilize exchange rate fluctuations.
1973	1 January	Denmark, Ireland and UK join the Community.
1979	13 March	European Monetary System is established.
	7–10 June	First direct elections to the European Parliament.
1981	1 January	Greece joins the Community.
1986	1 January	Spain and Portugal join the Community.
	17–28 February	Single European Act (operational 1 July 1987) is signed.
1990	3 October	Reunification of Germany.
1992	7 February	The Treaty on European Union is signed in Maastricht (operational 1 November 1993).
1993	1 January	Completion Date for the Single Market.
1995	1 January	Austria, Finland and Sweden join the EU.
1996	March	Inter Governmental Conference begins.
1997	June	Amsterdam Treaty is agreed.

Before considering the dynamics of that evolution, let us first note three distinctive aspects of the situation in France at the start of the European integration process. The first was the preoccupation of political leaders with the unresolved problem of territorial security. The traditional threat had been from Germany, but after 1945 French political leaders had to face a more complex conundrum involving Germany, the French Empire and the two emerging super-powers, the Soviet Union and the USA. In 1870–1, France had been invaded and defeated in the Franco-Prussian War. Two prosperous regions, Alsace and Lorraine, had been detached and incorporated into the German Empire. In subsequent decades, the French Empire was built up by the acquisition of colonies, notably in Africa and Indo-China, but the world-power status of France did not provide security in Europe. In 1914 the Germans invaded again and until 1918 the blood-letting of the First World War took place largely on French soil. In 1918, Alsace and Lorraine were returned to France, but the national sentiment of insecurity remained high, as the construction of the Maginot Line and the policies of European alliances and appeasement of Hitler testified. In 1940, however, the failure of those strategies was demonstrated when the Germans invaded and occupied France yet again. In 1945 Germany was defeated because both the USSR and the USA intervened. The occupation and division of Germany were only temporary solutions to the German threat to France. During the next decade, however, French perceptions of the security problem changed: all except the Communists argued that in Europe the biggest danger came from the Soviet Union. None the less, the idea of a re-armament of West Germany – to help counter the Soviet threat – raised old demons.

A second significant feature of the situation in France was the relative underdevelopment of the economy, in comparison to those of Germany and the UK. Although France experienced several periods of strong economic growth during most of the nineteenth and early twentieth centuries, the economy was overtaken by the more indus-trialized neighbours, and population growth was stagnant. In 1944, the total population, at 40 000 000, was only slightly greater than it had been in 1870. In 1944, over 25 per cent of the labour force was still involved in agriculture, and often in inefficient peasant farming. The manufacturing and service sectors were both small-scale and undynamic, and much capital and infrastructure had been destroyed during the Liberation from the German occupation. Most political leaders were convinced that to recover from the war-time destruction required not only reconstruction but also 'modernization' – rapid economic growth, industrialization and urbanization. The debates of the post-war period essentially concerned the methods of achieving growth, and one national characteristic of those arguments was that those who favoured large-scale state interventionism included not only the Communists and some Socialists, but also the nationalist right, including many Gaullists. On the left, there was a widespread belief that 'modernization' must include the creation of a welfare state, a view which was also shared by many Gaullists and almost all Christian Democrats.

The distinctive third aspect of the situation in France was the tradition of governmental and regime instability which continued until 1958. Between the Revolution of 1789 and the establishment of the Fifth Republic in 1958, there were no fewer than ten distinct regimes: four republics, three monarchies, two empires, and the Vichy 'state'. During the Third Republic, between 1870 and 1940, 119 governments fell. When France was liberated, the new political leaders designed a new constitution in the hope of eliminating such crippling instability. The Fourth Republic, however, fared no better than its predecessor: between 1946 and 1958 there were 25 governments, of which only one lasted more than a year, and two lasted less than one week. Surprisingly, in these conditions, governments were able to mobilize majorities in parliament for the ratification of the two first and most innovative European integration treaties, those of Paris in 1951 and of Rome in 1957. The Fourth Republic fell in the context of the disintegration of the French Empire and the revolt in Algeria, which was formally part of France. De Gaulle became the last prime minister of that regime, but his price for accepting the responsibility of resolving the Algerian imbroglio was the establishment of a Fifth Republic. The new Constitution innovated by introducing elements of presidentialism and of constitutional review, but the major change was the reinforcement of the executive in relation to the legislature.

Paradoxically, and despite some major set-backs, these inauspicious circumstances proved quite fertile ground for cultivating the first European institutions. The EU grew from small seedlings which blossomed only decades after their planting. Initially, European integration concerned only a limited number of policy domains in a small group of countries. The first decision to make joint domestic policies for market regulation and international trade concerned only two industrial sectors, coal and steel, although their symbolic importance, as the bases of the armaments industry, was important. The 'Schuman Declaration' (May 1950), a speech by the French foreign minister, largely inspired by Jean Monnet, led to the establishment of the European Coal and Steel Community (ECSC). Six states, the Benelux partners, France, Italy and Germany, signed the Paris Treaty creating that first European Community a year later.

Within a year, as the result of another French government initiative, a further treaty to create a second Community had been proposed and signed, but it was never to be ratified. The policy sector concerned, defence, was too sensitive. The surrender of sovereignty involved in merging most of the French armed forces into a European army proved too dramatic for French leaders and public opinion. In 1954, the French parliament rejected the bill to ratify the treaty: the European Defence Community (EDC) was aborted. Thus, this French initiative for further European integration suffered a major set-back at French hands. In place of the EDC, a loose international co-ordinating agency, the West European Union (WEU) was established.

In 1955, however, the governments of the six ECSC member states again began talks, at Messina, about further joint policy-making. From those negotiations came the two Rome Treaties signed in 1957, which established the European Economic Community (EEC) and the European Atomic Energy Community (Euratom). The EEC Treaty provided for a customs union and a common internal market for almost all economic sectors, including agriculture, while the Euratom Treaty concerned the joint development of atomic energy for peaceful purposes. The process of achieving the treaty goals, however, was deliberately slowly phased over 12 years. The first measures to create the Common Agricultural Policy (CAP) were decided only in 1962, and the customs union, with no duties on intra-Community trade and a common external tariff, became operational in July 1968. The complex arrangements for the budget of the Community required a new treaty, signed in 1970, to establish a formula for 'own resources' to pay the expenses of the common policies.

The growth of common policies beyond the CAP and trade was a laborious process. The treaty goals of creating common fishing and transport policies proved especially difficult to achieve. Gradually consensus built up for 'structural policies' designed to spread the benefits of the customs union to deprived groups, and notably to the unemployed and to poorer regions. The two main instruments used were the European Social Fund (ESF) and the European Regional Development Fund (ERDF), although small parts of the agriculture and fisheries funds were also spent on these 'solidarity' objectives.

Initially, exchange-rate fluctuations were rare and caused few problems; the devaluation of the franc in 1969, however, heralded a period of considerable instability, especially after the end of the Bretton Woods dollar convertibility in 1971. A first attempt to create a zone of exchange rate stability by limiting the margin of fluctuation between EEC currencies to 2.25 per cent was established in April 1972, but this monetary 'Snake', as it became known, was not a success. A second, revamped version, 'the Snake in the Tunnel', also failed. In March 1979 a more structured scheme for monetary co-operation, the European Monetary System (EMS), with a carefully contrived Exchange Rate Mechanism (ERM), replaced the 'Snake'. By the 1980s there was a growing realization among member state leaders of the need for collective action to make the EC more competitive internally. In practice, little had been done to achieve the second goal set down in Article 3a of the EEC Treaty – the elimination of non-tariff barriers 'of all other measures having equivalent effect' to customs duties and quotas. This was a key factor in the major extension of Community responsibilities under the 1986 SEA. Once the SEA became operational, in July 1987, European institutions were empowered to abolish all non-tariff barriers impeding intra-Community trade, and were instructed to do so before 1993. Thus the 'four freedoms' of movement of persons, goods, services and capital, set down as vague objectives in the Rome Treaty were to be made effective. This 'completion of the internal market' was to be complemented by common environmental and research policies. The SEA gave the Council of Ministers powers for foreign policy co-ordination, in a process known as European Political Co-operation. It also defined 'social and economic cohesion' (harmonious development across the EU) as a treaty goal, and in February 1988 the member state governments decided to double the expenditure on structural policies.

In Maastricht in 1992, the TEU was signed with key provisions to create Economic and Monetary Union (EMU) – a single currency with an autonomous central bank system – by 1999. The TEU also included provisions for European citizenship, for some common social policies and for intergovernmental co-ordination of justice and home affairs. Finally, the TEU established a cohesion fund to accelerate economic development in the four poorest member states, Greece,

Ireland, Portugal and Spain. After more than a year of negotiations in the Intergovernmental Conference (IGC), the European Council Meeting at Amsterdam in June 1997 further agreed a limited package of reforms on employment, social policy, common foreign and security policy and co-decision.

This growth of the policy competencies of European institutions has been paralleled by the growth in the membership of what is now the EU. De Gaulle vetoed the UK's first and second attempts to join the Community in 1963 and 1967. In 1969, however, once de Gaulle had resigned and Pompidou had been elected, the governments of all six member states agreed to the enlargement of the Community; the UK, Ireland and Denmark joined the Community in January 1973. The next accession treaty, signed in 1979, concerned Greece, which became a member state in 1981. Then, a similar treaty, signed in 1985, brought in Spain and Portugal in 1986. After the fall of the Berlin Wall in November 1989, East Germany joined the Community in a unique way, by merging into the Federal Republic of Germany in October 1990. Finally, by accession treaties in 1994, Austria, Finland and Sweden joined the EU in January 1995. In mid-1997, however, with applications from 11 European states awaiting consideration, it is clear that the enlargement of EU membership is far from complete. None the less, the waves of enlargement have already increased the population of the EU by 170 million citizens.

The expansion of policy competencies and of membership of the EU has been matched by a series of institutional reforms. Initially, the treaties created separate executive agencies for the three Communities (the ECSC, the EEC and EURATOM), although other institutions were shared. Only in 1965 was a merger treaty signed, and the basis of the present institutional framework dates from July 1967 when that treaty became operational. The Treaty of Rome laid down that the Communities should move to majority voting in many policy areas by 1967. However, in 1966 the French government forced the 'Luxembourg Compromise' on to the Community; this was an arrangement whereby majority voting in the Council of Ministers was not used when any member state government argued that its vital national interest was at stake (see Chapter 1). From this point, intergovernmentalism became dominant within the policy-making process. A more positive step was taken in 1969, when the Luxembourg Treaty set up a system of 'own resources' to fund the Community budget. In 1976, agreement was reached on the direct election of the European Parliament (EP), and the first elections were held in June 1979.

A major reform came with the SEA in 1987, when the system of majority voting in the Council was extended to cover the internal market programme, and the influence of the EP over legislation was increased by the introduction of the 'co-operation' procedure. Finally, the TEU further extended the use of majority voting and gave new power to the Parliament in the 'co-decision procedure'. That treaty also established the structure of intergovernmental 'pillars' for decision-making in common foreign and security policy and justice and home affairs. In short, a series of complex institutional structures has been established at the European level through slow processes of institutional reform and the accretion of powers at the EU level.

The institutions

These institutional structures created by the treaties are responsible for making laws, budgets, executive decisions, judicial rulings and other policy measures for the goals laid down in the treaties by the methods defined in those same texts. There are four main institutions, the Council, the Commission, the EP and the Court of Justice (ECJ), and three minor bodies, the Court of Auditors, the Economic and Social Committee and the Committee of Regions. The roles played by these bodies vary considerably according to the different policy domains. Since the TEU became operational in 1993, the EU has three separate but inter-related frameworks for decision-making – known as 'pillars' – for different areas of policy.

The first and most important 'pillar' is the Community structure, which is responsible for most economic and trade policies. The second and third 'pillars' deal with common foreign and security policy (CFSP) and justice and home affairs (JHA) respectively. In the Community 'pillar' the Commission takes the lead in policy-making, while an increasing number of decisions is taken by majority voting and powers are shared between the four major institutions. In the second and 'third pillars', member state governments are the main initiators of policy, and unanimity between governments is the rule. Hence, here, the role of the Commission is limited and the influence of the ECJ, the EP and the minor institutions is negligible. In practice, the policy output of the second and third 'pillars' has been small, so it is useful to concentrate our discussion on the Community framework, which is still based on the principles laid down in the Paris and Rome Treaties.

The Council the main law-making institution, consists of the ministers from each of the member states who have responsibility for the policy area being discussed at any particular meeting. In the Community 'pillar' all legislation is initiated by the Commission, but the adoption of legislation is decided either by the Council alone (in some policy areas) or shared by joint decision of the Council and the EP (in areas specified in the SEA and TEU). These two bodies also share control over the EU budget.

Many legislative decisions in the Council are taken by qualified majority vote (QMV), when at least 62 votes out of a total of 87 are required; for such votes France, Spain, Germany, Italy and the UK have ten votes each, Belgium Greece, the Netherlands and Portugal have five, Austria and Sweden have four, Denmark, Finland and Ireland have three and Luxembourg has two. Unanimity is still required to adopt international agreements (which are negotiated by the Commission), to change the treaties, to admit new member states or to adopt measures of great importance, such as tax.

At least twice a year the heads of government of the member states (and the French President) meet with the President of the Commission as the 'European Council', a body with no legislative power, but which sets the agenda for the EU and sorts out unresolved problems. The presidency of the Council rotates between the member states every six months; ministers from the country holding the presidency chair all meetings of the Council and its head of government presides the European Council (see Table I.2).

TABLE I.2

French presidencies of the Council of Ministers

1 January–30 June 1959
1 January–30 June 1962
1 January–30 June 1965
1 January–30 June 1968
1 January–30 June 1971
1 July–31 December 1974
1 January–30 June 1970
1 January–30 June 1984
1 July–31 December 1989
1 January–30 June 1995
[1 July–31 December 2000]

Sources: Bulletin of the European Economic Community; General Report on the Activities of the European Communities.

Much of the decision making in the Council is negotiated in advance by the Committee of Permanent Representatives of the member states (COREPER), aided by specialist working parties of senior civil servants from the member state ministries. The work of organizing the meetings of all the 'levels' of member state representatives, from the European Council down to the working parties, with all the preparation of committee papers in all the working languages of the EU is carried out by the general secretariat of the Council, located in the huge Justus Lipsius building in Brussels, where most meetings are held.

The Commission, as the executive agency of the EU, has wide-ranging responsibility for the implementation of the treaties. It has the right and duty of initiating legislation in areas laid down in, and for the goals defined by, the treaties. It prepares all legislative proposals and intervenes at all stages of the legislative process to facilitate agreement within the Council or between the Council and the EP. Although it does not perform direct implementation duties (the task of the ministries and agencies in the member states), it has the responsibility of supervising the execution of EU laws ('regulations' or 'directives') and policies. In this role, it has considerable executive responsibilities, many delegated to it by the Council, and it takes many executive 'decisions', with the force of law, for the EU. It can also bring cases to the ECJ when respect for EU law is in question.

Since January 1995 the Commission has consisted of 20 members (two each for France, Germany, Italy, Spain and the UK and one for each of the others) chosen, for coincident five-year terms, by agreement between the member state governments. The member state governments together also choose the president of the Commission. In theory, the whole Commission can be forced to resign by a censure motion in the EP, although this is extremely unlikely. In practice, the effectiveness of the Commission depends not only on the political skills of its members, but also on the work of its staff, about 18 000 in number, who are organized into 26 'directorates general' in Brussels and Luxembourg. In preparing legislative projects and supervising the implementation of common policies the Commission staff work in close contact and co-operation both with COREPER, with the civil servants of the relevant ministries and agencies in the member states and with experts from all parts of the EU.

The European Parliament, elected by direct universal suffrage every five years, attempts to ensure democratic accountability of EU policy-making and plays a role in some but not all legislation. The 626 Members of the European Parliament (MEPs) meet for a few days each month in plenary sessions in Strasbourg, but most work is done in Brussels in the 20 committees and the political groups. The nomadic life of MEPs is further complicated by the fact that much of the secretariat is based in Luxembourg and a few sessions of parliament are held there each year. Although relatively feeble compared to parliaments in most of the member states, the EP has the last word on 'non-compulsory' expenditure in the budget and can block legislative proposals in policy areas where the 'co-decision' process, created by the TEU, applies.

The European Court of Justice (ECJ), last but by no means least of the major institutions, is responsible for ensuring compliance with EU law in all parts of the EU and for resolving disputes over interpretation of the treaties. The ECJ comprises 15 judges and 9 advocates-general, who are chosen by agreement between the member state governments for a six-year term. Cases are brought by EU institutions, or member state governments or by individuals or firms directly affected by particular laws or decisions. If questions concerning the validity or interpretation of any EU treaty or legal instrument are raised in cases before any national court (at any level), that court may, under Article 177 of the EEC Treaty refer to the ECJ for preliminary advice. Since 1989 a Court of First Instance assists the ECJ by dealing with many disputes concerning the Commission and individuals or firms. Over time the ECJ has become a significant force for integration within the EU.

It is hardly surprising that this slow process of competence accretion at the EU level and the matching growth of membership and complication of institutions and procedures within the EU framework has stimulated numerous and far-reaching debates about the nature of the institutions, the characteristics of the processes (both of European integration in general and policy-making in specific domains) and the desirability of such changes. While the last of these debates is outside the scope of this study, the first two have influenced the choices of research questions and approaches taken.

France in the EU: the approaches of this study

Chapter 1 directly addresses the question of the changing nature and influence of French governments over the institutional and policy evolution of the EU by analysing that evolution from several different angles. The first approach is to identify the long-term goals which were pursued over time by the different governments in power, especially at the critical stages of institutional development or policy change. A second approach is to analyse the particular strategies adopted and the modifications of those strategies over time. From both these approaches it becomes clear that even if French governmental influence at some moments, on some institutions and on certain policy packages was considerable, the general record is mixed. French politicians were sometime pushed to concede more to their partners than they desired, while at other times the behaviour of just one other member state government could frustrate French plans. What also emerges is that French governments became increasingly reactive, rather than proactive, as the European integration process gained a momentum of its own and as the policy parameters were changed by external forces in the international environment. By the mid-1990s, France, although still a key player, was no longer the main force in determining the political agenda of the EU.

Chapters 2 and 3 analyse the extent to which membership of the EU has changed French state institutions and politics. Chapter 2 focuses on the state machinery, not only at the very top where there has been a presidentialization of policy-making in European affairs and joint foreign relations, but also on the ministries, Parliament and the courts. Much of this analysis concerns the co-ordination of inputs into the processes of EU policy-making, but problems of implementation are also considered. What emerges is that until the 1980s successive French governments were much more preoccupied with influencing decision making in Brussels than in applying the policies which they had helped to shape.

Chapter 3 turns to the complex problem of how European integration has been dealt with in domestic politics, both by the parties and by public opinion. We identify a dominant, vaguely pro-European, consensus in the centre of the political spectrum which has only been consistently challenged by the French Communist Party and more recently the *Front National* (FN). However, we argue that this consensus has masked a number of diverging views on European policies and institutions among and within the main political parties.

In the late 1990s it appeared that this consensus within the major parties about the benefits of European integration for France is increasingly fragile. Leaders are sensitive to the growing wariness of the French public about the European project. The uncertainty of many in the political elite about the development of strong institutions at the EU level strikes a chord with a public which is hesitant about accruing more power at that level. We consider the dynamics of shifts in public opinion over European issues, and examine whether French voters are becoming more functional and policy-specific in their attitudes, and whether the symbolic significance of national sovereignty is declining.

The next section of the book considers the changes in policies and policy-making in a number of significant sectors. Instead of attempting to provide a superficial coverage of the entire range of EU policies, we have picked a number of key policy sectors. Chapter 4 examines both the contribution of French policy-makers to, and the impact in France of, the gradual evolution towards a common foreign and security policy. We argue that for much of the period French governments were able to pursue an independent foreign and security policy and at the same time exert a key role in the limited development of the EU's own policy. However, as the potential for the EU to develop its own security policy has grown since the early 1990s, it is becoming increasingly more difficult for France to sustain an independent role.

Chapter 5 analyses the formulation and evolution of the CAP and the linked domestic policies by which French agriculture has been transformed since 1958. Here we are concerned with a complex policy package which is in part redistributive and in part regulatory. Chapter 6 considers competition, trade and monetary policies, and the often difficult processes of dismantling the traditional system of state aid and protectionism. In both these chapters the changing attitudes and behaviour of the main policy actors are also examined to assess whether joint European lobbying and other pressure politics techniques applied to EU institutions are co-existing with, or even replacing, traditional nationally-focused tactics.

In Chapter 7 the subject is the adaptation of regional and local governments in France, in the context of both European regional development policies and the waves of domestic decentralization, especially in the 1980s. Finally, Chapter 8, focuses on the policy adjustments – in border controls, immigration and policing, in employment conditions and educational qualifications, and in social protection structures – necessary for the free movement of persons. Throughout these sectors we stress the interrelationship between policy-making at the European and the domestic levels. We argue that even highly integrated sectors, such as agriculture, may retain national characteristics, especially in the processes of policy implementation.

In all these case studies of policy adaptation we seek to identify both domestic roots of changes which appear to have European inspirations and those policy modifications which reflect broader global trends. We also seek to identify how global trends interlink with French policy processes. Finally, we seek to reveal whether or not EU membership increases the capacity of French governments to influence the impact of global trends, or rather, whether EU membership merely amplifies and accelerates the impact of global trends in France.

In conclusion, we consider the overall record of all the moves associated with EU membership away from traditional French macroeconomic policy practices. It is difficult to dispute that, within the EU framework, a transfer of power from state to market has occurred. There has also been a redistribution of power within existing state structures from the political executive to the finance ministry, quasi-judicial regulatory bodies and, more recently, to the autonomous Bank of France. At the same time, at the EU level, the sharing of responsibility between the French state and the EU structures has been rebalanced in favour of joint actions decided in Brussels. All these questions bring us back to our starting point: the extent to which the French government is losing its monopoly to represent the whole of France in the EU policy processes, and the remaining significance of the concept of a single French 'national interest'. As French citizens and groups acquire a second identity as Europeans, they also identify a new power centre in the EU institutions. The EU does open up new possibilities for groups and political actors to exercise power. However, for those used to the simplicity of a system which was often caricatured for its unlimited presidential power, its over-centralized structures, its *dirigiste* and protectionist mechanism and policies, understanding and operating in a multi-level system, even if partly French-created, remains difficult.

1

The French Contribution to Building the EU

During almost five decades of European construction, successive French governments have played a key role in fashioning EU institutions, policy processes and policies. For most of the period French governments have been attempting to achieve national objectives within the European arena by trying to ensure that policy and institutional developments are in line with French priorities. It has not always been possible to identify clearly what aims they were pursuing. On occasions narrow national objectives were deliberately obscured by idealistic European rhetoric and public statements of goals have sometimes been not merely diplomatic but misleading. French governments have not always achieved what they wanted in Brussels; none the less, they have often confused their partners by passing off defeats as victories. Governments, of course, are not the only influence on the institutional development of the EU; writers and thinkers, pressure groups and even large firms are able to influence public opinion and policy-makers both in France and in other member states. In this chapter, our focus is on the work of governments; we both identify elements of continuity and periods of change, and distinguish reality from what governments boast about their own achievements.

Some French contributions are easy to identify. The Schuman Plan, named after France's foreign minister, but initiated by Jean Monnet, led to the creation of the ECSC in the Treaty of Paris in April 1951. In March 1957, the Guy Mollet government signed the Treaty of Rome creating the EEC and Euratom. Under President Pompidou, a major step was taken at the 1969 Hague Summit – to enlarge membership of the EEC by including Britain, Denmark and

Ireland. Nine years later, Valéry Giscard d'Estaing, with Roy Jenkins and Helmut Schmidt, co-founded the EMS. During the 1980s, Jacques Delors and François Mitterrand strongly contributed to shaping and pushing through the SEA and later the TEU. Some major French initiatives, however, were unsuccessful: in the 1950s, the Pleven Plan for creating common European foreign and defence policies proved abortive. Similarly, in 1962, under de Gaulle's presidency, a new French initiative for foreign policy co-ordination, the Fouchet Plan, also failed.

Nor have French contributions to the EU's development always been positive; some have slowed down European integration. In August 1954, it was the French National Assembly which killed off the EDC, proposed in the Pleven Plan. In 1962 and 1967, de Gaulle blocked enlargement of the membership of the EEC, and in 1965, he prevented the move to majority voting in the Council of Ministers, as foreseen in the Treaty of Rome. Under his successors, Pompidou and Giscard d'Estaing, the record of French governments in transposing European directives into French law and in respecting rulings of the ECJ were but modest. Even the Mitterrand governments balked at decisions of the Commission on competition policy – to the point of provoking resignation threats from its President, Jacques Delors.

It is clear, then, that if French governments have been key actors in building the EU, their record is less than consistently positive. Some French leaders have initiated key institutional and policy developments, while others have been responsible for some of the major problems and set-backs in the integration process. Moreover, as the results of the 1992 referendum on the TEU and subsequent debates about the GATT negotiations and the value of the franc demonstrated, elite and mass attitudes to European integration may historically have been largely positive, but they have become increasingly divided. Some sections of French society remain hostile to the basic ideas of European integration. How, then, can we explain this mixed record?

The contributions made by successive governments of France have reflected both domestic and external stimuli and constraints. In the first two sections of this chapter, we examine the ambiguous, sometimes contradictory, nature of governmental objectives, and how both goals and strategies have evolved over time, as leaders and circumstances changed. In the third section, our focus is on the institutional momentum gained by the EU itself, which increasingly obliges French rulers to respond. In general French governments have been less than enthusiastic about the strengthening of the EU's institutions; however, they have often had to support the institutional development of the EU because of wider policy goals which they were trying to achieve. In the fourth section, we analyse the international vulnerability of France and of the entire EU. All member states have been forced to react to changes such as the collapse of stable exchange rates in 1971, or the oil price rises of 1973 and 1979, although they have not always done so in unison. To conclude, we stress two themes which underpin this whole examination of the input of French governments to the process of European integration:

1. the attitudes and policies of French rulers towards the EU and its evolution remain inconsistent.
2. the roles played by French governments in European integration are both proactive and reactive, as the EU extends its competence and influence and as international circumstances change.

Governmental strategies, politics and Europe: 1945–69

European strategies have changed as governments with different views have succeeded one another, but such successions are not the only source of apparent contradictions in policy development. The different goals and ideas of various presidents, prime ministers and ministers are one important factor in explaining policy inconsistencies, but French rulers have also been influenced by the need to win domestic support for their European policies – from coalition partners in parliament and voters, but also from major firms and pressure groups concerned with those policies.

In 1945 almost all political leaders in France envisaged some form of European integration both as an *ideal* – an end in its own right – and as an *instrument* – a means for achieving other objectives, which were often less than idealistic. The ideal was that of replacing intermittent bloody warfare on the European continent by peaceful, tolerant co-operation for the benefit of all (Milward, 1992, pp. 325–7; Monnet, 1976, pp. 319–20). The major goal was to undermine the destructive force of competing nationalism by creating strong common interests and some sense of a shared identity. Consensus among politicians on this ideal has been very wide and continuous, and all have appreciated that amicable co-existence with Germany was crucial.

The other French objectives, for which European integration was primarily instrumental, were numerous and diverse. One was that of exploiting integration as a means to catch up, and if possible to overtake, more industrialized neighbours. In general, these 'national interest' objectives mainly concerned Germany, although here goals have changed considerably as the passage of time healed bitter memories of war and occupation. Thus, in 1945, the main aim was to contain Germany or to 'tie Germany down'. Later, with the Cold War, Marshall Aid and reconstruction, the aim of French policy-makers was to make West Germany, under the control of the Western Alliance, contribute to the defence of Western Europe against the threat of Soviet imperialism. Even later, when the extent of the German 'economic miracle' became apparent, the main aim was to bind France economically to West Germany, so as to share all the benefits of Germany's success. The metaphors employed have been those of 'hitching the French wagon to the German locomotive' or 'making German industry pay for the modernization of French agriculture' (Gillingham, 1991, pp. 297–8). Such explicit nationalist objectives, however, are rarely admitted in idealistic official speeches and writings; only hints, in coded diplomatic language, can be detected.

At the start of the Fourth Republic, the views of political leaders as to what sort of Europe should be constructed varied considerably. The Communist Party, with a specific view of economics and politics, saw capitalism as the breeding ground of fascism, and advocated close, peaceful European co-operation – under Soviet leadership, with Stalinist economics. The Communists, however, were only part of the governing coalition until May 1947, by which time none of the main steps in European construction had been taken. Public declarations of the leaders of most other political parties, however, stressed that peace, liberty and prosperity were the ideals of French policy for Europe. To defend against a resurgence of fascism or a take-over by Stalinist communism, joint policies were needed to define and protect liberties and to prevent economic crises of the kind in which totalitarian movements had flourished during the 1920s and 1930s. State action was required to reconstruct the war torn economy and thus rebuild prosperity, but the protectionism of the past was rejected as a major source of tension and conflict of neighbours. A stable peace in Europe required co-operation, convergence and common action to replace nation states' conflicting defence and foreign policies.

J

The translation of this shared ideal into *institutions*, however, was a source of bitter controversy. For General de Gaulle, head of the provisional government until January 1946, his supporters in the RPF (the Gaullist Party), and for some independents, radicals and socialists, the ideal institutional pattern was a framework for co-operation between sovereign nation states. De Gaulle himself believed that any attempt to tamper with nation states as sovereign actors was doomed. Nevertheless, he did think that European nation states should exercise sovereignty to co-operate with one another in specific areas and to make policies jointly by means of loose intergovernmental arrangements. De Gaulle thus recognized some limited community of interests and identity among European states; hence co-operative, or even confederal, functional bodies to make common policies by unanimous agreement were acceptable. In short, he advocated '*l'Europe des Etats*' (de Gaulle, 1970a, pp. 171–210).

Outside the Gaullist movement, however, many disagreed profoundly with his view. An integrationist position was taken by Jean Monnet and many Christian Democrats in complete opposition to de Gaulle's thinking. The integrationists argued that merging the European states, with a single economy, united armed forces, a single currency and a single foreign policy would reduce destructive nationalism, banish the risks of war, poverty and totalitarianism and promote peace, prosperity and liberty. French leaders also disagreed about the appropriate *dimensions* for the new Europe. Most federalists saw that a workable merger would be possible only between states with shared liberal democratic practices, market-based economies and similar standards of living. In the immediate post-war context, that implied the exclusion of communist Eastern Europe and the authoritarian states of Southern Europe. Britain, Switzerland and the Scandinavian states, however, were seen as natural constituents, even if their governments did not realize it.

In marked contrast was the scale of de Gaulle's confederalist vision. He rejected the small Europe of the federalists, and instead envisaged co-operation between all the states of the continent, 'from the Atlantic to the Urals'. He believed that communism and authoritarianism were both merely transitory phenomena. He also held that Europeans should regulate their own international affairs, with no interference from a super-power, albeit a friendly one such as the USA, and the implication was that European states should co-operate together in defence. De Gaulle, however, distinguished between his ideals for the long term and the practical possibilities for immediate action: until the demise of communism and authoritarianism, effective co-operation would be possible only among the liberal, West European states.

Political leaders were also divided on the *method* for constructing Europe. In the immediate post-war period, a 'bottom up', cautious approach, was taken, with intergovernmental co-operation in specific functional areas. Thus, in the economic domain, the Ramadier government accepted Marshall Aid and membership of the loose, co-operative inter-governmental body, the OEEC. In a similar approach for defence, the Dunkirk Treaty with Britain in 1947, the 1948 Brussels Treaty (extending the Dunkirk arrangements to the Benelux states) and the 1949 Washington Treaty establishing NATO were all inter-governmental. So too, in the field of civil liberties, was the Council of Europe, which the Marie government helped to found in May 1949.

An alternative method was that of sectoral integration which would lead eventually to a supranational organization. Here, the existence of independent nation states was recognized, but only as the starting point of a process from which a federal form of government would eventually evolve. Integration was conceived as a dynamic process which involved bringing ever more policy sectors into structures for joint decision-making and policy implementation. Supranational integration demanded substantial institutional improvements on the structures for intergovernmental co-operation. These included regular majority voting (rather than unanimity among member states), a central, autonomous agency for policy initiation and supervision of implementation (rather than a simple secretariat) and a supreme court (rather than an arbitration tribunal).

This method was adopted partly in reaction to disappointment over the poor performance of the Council of Europe. Indeed, Spaak, its first general secretary, had resigned in despair at its powerlessness. Equally, the OEEC was not seen to have had a significant policy impact, despite its positive role in building contacts and exchanging information. Sectoral integration was suggested by Jean Monnet, then head of the French economic planning commissariat in France, as a politically acceptable road to federalism. In May 1950, Robert Schuman, then foreign minister, announced his 'Plan' of what was to become the ECSC. Like Monnet's planning commissariat in France, the ECSC was to deal with a limited number of crucial economic sectors. Equally, the core of the ECSC was to be a small but highly qualified task force, the High Authority, composed of civil service technocrats (rather than politicians or bureaucrats). Its tasks were to be those of initiating policies and persuading the different member states to accept its solutions. The ECSC Treaty was easily ratified in the National Assembly, despite criticisms from Communists and Gaullists.

There was also a third method, that of 'top down', constitutional federalism, based on the idea that a major constitutional change was required to establish a 'United States of Europe'. This approach was adopted in Pleven's EDC. Although the EDC Treaty was signed in Paris in May 1952, its rejection by the French National Assembly in August 1954 by a combination of Gaullists and Communists (and a minority of anti-European centre–left deputies) aborted the project. A proposal for a European Political Community as a complement to the EDC never even reached the treaty stage. Although the common defence policy of the EDC seemed a logical progression from the ECSC idea of a common market for the products at the base of defence industries, the treaty went far beyond simply extending integration to another sector. EDC implied a dramatic curtailing, if not a renunciation, by the member states of their independent roles in world politics. The institutional similarity between the ECSC and the EDC was misleading, since the EDC and the projected European Political Community represented a first stage in a plan to build a federal Europe.

The crucial problem which remained when the National Assembly rejected the EDC Treaty was that of rearming Germany. The solution, a loose intergovernmental defence organization to supervise the new German armed forces, came from the British Conservative government led by Anthony Eden. The government of Pierre Mendès-France rapidly accepted this proposal, and in October 1954, the 6 members of the ECSC and Britain signed a treaty creating the WEU.

After such a frustrating débâcle, it was hardly surprising that subsequent governments of the Fourth Republic adopted more cautious methods. In June 1955, French representatives took part in major discussions on further European construction, on the initiative of the Benelux governments. At the Messina Conference, the foreign ministers of the ECSC countries set up a joint committee, chaired by Spaak, to undertake interlinked studies of sectors suitable for integration. Influenced by the French government's interest in atomic energy, the committee report of April 1956 proposed the setting up of both a multi-sector European Economic Community (EEC), or Common Market, and a separate European Atomic Energy Community (Euratom). The outcome was the March 1957 Treaties of Rome, which were easily ratified by the National Assembly, partly as a consequence of the absence of federal aspirations. In January 1958, the EEC came into operation.

Five months later, however, the Fourth Republic faced the Algerian crisis and de Gaulle returned to power. In October 1958 the Constitution of the Fifth Republic was adopted by referendum. Although that constitution admitted the superiority of treaties over domestic law (in Article 55), de Gaulle made no secret of his dislike of the supranationalism of the ECSC and the EEC. His ultimate vision remained confederal in shape and continental in scale. None the less, he believed that the six-member composition of the EEC was realistic, since economic co-operation was only possible between states with similar economic structures. For de Gaulle, economic incompatibility made the UK, with its small efficient agricultural sector and distinctive financial system inappropriate for EEC membership, as did the undesirable tendency of British governments, whether Conservative or Labour, to consider the 'special relationship' with the USA to be of far greater importance than any European linkage.

De Gaulle appreciated that European co-operation in the form of the EEC had considerable advantages for France. Indeed, under French leadership, a united Europe could transform the two-bloc division of the world. European co-operation would thus enable France both to remain part of the Western bloc and to retain its independent foreign policy. This was all the more important for de Gaulle as the French Empire soon disappeared. In short, Europe was the means by which de Gaulle sought both to retain a role of international leadership and to build up a lucrative French export trade in weapons (de Gaulle, 1970b).

None the less, the institutional arrangements of the EEC remained a source of irritation to de Gaulle. In 1962 he attempted to change them. He offered to increase the policy scope of the Treaty of Rome to include foreign policy in exchange for a reduction of the role and influence of the Commission. The Six established a commission led by Christian Fouchet to study these proposals. The negotiations revealed a great deal about de Gaulle's ideas, notably that he sought to marginalize the influence of the Commission and to exclude Great Britain permanently from membership. When de Gaulle's intentions became clear, only the German government remained interested and the scheme proposed under the Fouchet Plan collapsed (Jouve, 1967; Dinan, 1994, pp. 48–54).

De Gaulle's hostility towards supranationalism was again demonstrated in 1965, when France assumed the presidency of the Council of Ministers. At that time, according to the treaty terms, the use of majority voting in the Council should have been extended. Given the number of disputes unresolved in the Council and in particular the problem of finding an acceptable system of paying for the CAP, de Gaulle decided that France would not take part in further meetings without a formal acceptance by other governments that a 'national interest veto' would be admitted. De Gaulle made it clear that each government – not the Community institutions – should determine how its 'national interest' was defined. This French-provoked crisis was resolved only in January 1966 when the other five governments refused to make any formal amendment to the treaty but accepted *de facto* – but not *de jure* – de Gaulle's main demand for a veto. The 1966 'Luxembourg Compromise' was thus an informal deal. It none the less set new parameters closer to de Gaulle's European ideal (Kolodziej, 1974).

De Gaulle's anti-integrationist policies did not go unchallenged within France. Until the Algerian War ended in 1962, tensions between the parties over Europe were generally contained, but soon after the signature of the Evian agreements in April 1962, the five Christian Democrat (MRP) ministers resigned in protest after de Gaulle ridiculed the EEC in the infamous '*volapuk* speech' (on 15 May). Jean Lecanuet, the Christian Democrat leader, went on to challenge de Gaulle in the first presidential election in 1965. In the months after the 'Luxembourg Compromise' there were hints of a change of heart about Britain joining the EC (Banbridge and Teasdale, 1995, pp. 308–15). In 1967, however, Lecanuet's supporters, reorganized as the *Centre Démocrate*, made a poor showing in the general election, leaving de Gaulle uninhibited to veto the second British membership application. His position was further strengthened by the single party majority gained by the Gaullists in the 1968 general elections.

In early 1969, de Gaulle's hostility to British entry remained strong, as the controversy of the Soames affair revealed. The 'Soames affair' was an open dispute between the French and the British governments over the exact nature of a private discussion between de Gaulle and the British ambassador in Paris, Sir Christopher Soames. Prime Minister Harold Wilson claimed that de Gaulle had suggested a deal to let Britain into the EC providing Britain agreed to help to reduce the supranational aspects of the EC and to co-operate in defence matters. De Gaulle denied that any such suggestions had been made. The whole affair merely demonstrated the high level of dispute between the two governments (Banbridge and Teasdale, 1995, pp. 412–13).

Soon, however, de Gaulle was again facing the electorate in his referendum on the reform of the regions and the Senate, and his centrist, pro-integration enemies proved firm defenders of the Senate. On 27 April 1969, the NO vote triumphed, and de Gaulle resigned.

Governmental strategies, politics and Europe: 1969–97

After de Gaulle resigned, his former prime minister, Pompidou, was elected president. Although he promised both 'continuity' and 'change' in European policy, it was soon clear that, even with the same parliamentary majority, the personal preferences of the new president were changing French policy towards the EEC: he was not opposed to British entry, and at the Hague Summit of December 1969, he agreed to several measures to reinforce Community institutions. These included a project to create an economic and monetary union by 1980, and the development of 'political co-operation' (in the field of foreign policy). Pompidou's pragmatic conservatism marked a shift from de Gaulle's principled opposition to supranationalism. He took a cautious and unhurried approach to push for a 'twin track' approach of intergovernmental co-operation in new policy areas and a revival of the dynamics of the Community. Pompidou also initiated a major change in the legitimation of European integration, by holding the 1972 referendum on the treaty for the accession of Denmark, Ireland and the UK. Ironically, his predecessor, who had used referenda on the Constitution and on Algerian independence, never gave the electorate the opportunity to judge his approach to European questions.

In party and coalition politics, Pompidou's promise to support British membership contributed significantly to his winning support from many of the opposition centrists, as well as from Giscard d'Estaing's Independent Republicans, although it irritated a few die-hard Gaullists. The use of a referendum to legitimate the accession treaty and the large majority YES vote silenced criticisms from within the Gaullist ranks. The referendum also had a bonus effect of splitting the opposition, since the Socialists, (who mainly favoured enlargement) opted for abstention, while the Communists, (whose hostility to European integration remained undiminished), campaigned for a 'No' vote. The development of Pompidou's European policy was however, cut short by his illness and death.

In May 1974, when elected to the presidency, Valéry Giscard d'Estaing made no secret of his firm belief in European integration, but never clearly articulated what kind of Europe he hoped to construct. After leaving the presidency, he explained that he had sought to contribute in four areas. One was that of continuing the enlargement of EC membership – by bringing in Greece and preparing the way for Spain and Portugal. A second was that of making both EC and intergovernmental decision-making work better by institutionalizing meetings of heads of government and state as the European Council. His third area of action was that of monetary policy, since he sought, after the 1971 exchange rate crisis, to resurrect the Hague Summit plans for monetary union. When, despite his efforts, the 'Snake' collapsed, he pushed hard for the creation of the EMS. Finally, he pressed ahead the long-delayed election of the EP by direct suffrage (Frears, 1981).

His declared enthusiasm for Europe in the 1974 presidential election campaign helped to persuade those centrists still in opposition to join the governing coalition. Lecanuet himself became minister of justice. Subsequently, the president faced major coalition problems, but of a very different nature from those of his predecessor. Many in the Gaullist party fundamentally distrusted his European intentions. It is simultaneous attempts to win over and to weaken the Gaullist party provoked great irritation, and contributed to pushing the Gaullist leader, Chirac, to resign from office as prime minister in 1976.

Raymond Barre, a non-Gaullist and a former European Commissioner (the author of a report arguing for greater integration) succeeded Chirac. Despite the congruence in views between the president and his prime minister, European policies remained a source of contention between the Giscardians and Gaullists within the governing coalition. Barre had to use the 'question of confidence' device (Article 49/3 of the Constitution) to get the law providing for the first direct election of the European Parliament passed by the National Assembly. When the first European elections were held in 1979, the Gaullists refused an alliance with the Giscardians, and fought as a separate nationalist list led by Debré, the former prime minister and arch-critic of the EEC. So ferocious was the Gaullist hostility that a system of rotation in office for Gaullist members of the EP was established to prevent 'contagion' from federalists. The European issue was only one of a series of divisive issues between the parties, but it weakened the coalition and undermined the authority of the president. In this way it contributed to his defeat in the 1981 presidential election.

The new occupant of the Elysée Palace, François Mitterrand, had favoured European integration since the 1950s. His ideas had evolved considerably by 1981. His aim of transforming the EC into a federation reflected his assumption about the permanent nature of the East–West divide. His ideas evolved further after the events of the late 1980s in Eastern Europe. He developed a 'concentric circles' vision of Europe, with confederal co-operation on the continental scale around a federation of the EC core of advanced liberal democracies (Favier and Martin-Roland, 1990, pp. 362–85). He also envisaged association links at intermediate levels for states wishing to participate in some of the core activities of the federation. His vision was not anti-American, but he assumed that some withdrawal of US forces from Europe would inevitably follow the ending of the Cold War and thus Europeans would have to take almost entire responsibility for their own defence.

None the less, the approach taken by Mitterrand was ambivalent. Like other French presidents he wanted a strong Europe without giving too much power to the EU institutions. He sometimes criticized the 'democratic deficit', but did little to give more power to Parliament. Although his discourse was often federal, many of his strategies were intergovernmental. Mitterrand achieved a great deal, particularly after 1984. The presence of an exceptionally talented political ally, Delors, at the helm of the Commission, was a crucial factor. He also had three other assets which both Pompidou and Giscard d'Estaing lacked: longevity in office, the support of a loyal parliamentary majority, except during the period of *cohabitation*, and a friendly partner in the German Chancellor, Kohl.

Once elected to the presidency in 1981, Mitterrand had to face rather unusual coalition and party problems. The overall majority of his Socialists in the National Assembly meant the new president had to make few concessions to his lukewarm Communist allies. The Communists stayed in government only until 1984, and he ignored their hostility to Europe with impunity. The greater difficulty for Mitterrand arose from within the ranks of the Socialist party and in particular from Jean-Pierre Chevènement and his faction (then called CERES, but later renamed *Socialisme et République*). The dispute over the 1983 devaluation (within the EMS as Mauroy and Delors insisted or outside, as Chevènement argued) led to the resignation of the CERES leader. But the breach was not long and he returned to government in 1984. From their débâcle in the 1984 European elections to the 1986 parliamentary elections, the Socialists closed ranks in the hope of regaining popularity.

The first period of *cohabitation* (or power sharing between a Socialist president and a prime minister and government from the centre-right majority in parliament), from 1986 to 1988, was marked by great, but usually non-public, tensions between the president and prime minister about responsibility for European policy-making, but relatively few major disputes about the actual policies. During the years in opposition since 1981 Chirac seemed to have won over a majority of the Gaullists to his own pragmatic view of European integration and of market economics. He favoured the suppression of non-tariff barriers in the single market programme and accepted that majority voting in the Council was essential for that programme to be completed. His UDF coalition partners were even more pro-integration than he was, and both Gaullists and centrists sought to differentiate themselves from the National Front on the extreme right (Shonfield, 1986; Machin, 1989).

The re-election of Mitterrand in 1988, albeit with minority support in the National Assembly, led to the separation of the centrists from the UDF to form a distinct parliamentary group, the UDC. On European questions, the Socialist governments of Rocard, Cresson and Bérégovoy could all rely on the UDC, either for external support or for sympathetic abstention. Furthermore, after the Maastricht negotiations, Mitterrand found he had the support of much of the rest of the UDF as well as of the UDC, so that in 1992 the required revision of the Constitution was possible through the mechanism of the Congress of both houses of parliament at Versailles, without any need for a referendum. If the great majority of the political elite was, by 1992, sufficiently pro-European to favour ratification of the TEU, some remained anxious that the gap between politicians and citizens revealed in the Danish referendum might also exist in France. In the event, the referendum debate exposed major cleavages among both the electorate and parties (see below, Chapter 3). However, when they came to vote on 20 September 1992, French electors did not revert to the earlier pattern of blocking European integration, although the margin of the 'Yes' victory (one per cent) was very narrow.

The European issue had little significance in the 1993 parliamentary elections but the new government, led by Balladur, soon found that its European policies would not be spared from criticisms within its own ranks. Like its predecessor, whose policy objectives it shared, the Balladur government had to deal with the preparations for EMU and the negotiation of the GATT agreement. While this meant that relations between the government and president were smooth during this second period of *cohabitation*, it irritated many anti-Maastricht campaigners within the centre-right. If the December 1993 GATT deal was a public relations success in France for Balladur and his ministers, the continuing high unemployment was widely viewed as a consequence of continuing the *'franc fort'* policy. Balladur's implementation of the TEU commitment to give autonomy to the Bank of France provoked renewed criticism. In the June 1994 European Parliament elections, the centre-right coalition partners could not reach agreement to present a common list. De Villiers, a maverick centre–right deputy, even led an anti-integration list, and won 12.3 per cent of the vote. The results indicated that part of the elite and a substantial section of the mass electorate seemed profoundly suspicious about further integration (J. Smith, 1995).

By autumn 1994, the campaign for the 1995 presidential election was under way. Balladur started as the favourite, but in November opinion polls showed that popular support was snowballing for Delors. His decision not to stand prepared the way for the eventual victory of Chirac. The issue of Europe did not feature very highly in the election campaign and in practice, little separated Chirac, Balladur and Jospin on the main European issues, such as EMU (see Chapter 3). After Chirac's election in May, Juppé became prime minister and Chirac's first acts and speeches indicated that there was little difference in his European policies from those of Balladur and Mitterrand. His campaign idea of a referendum on the single currency has been replaced by a vague proposal of a referendum on the institutional changes adopted in the 1996 Intergovernmental Conference. That change, however, does not imply that a more negative approach has been adopted. Chirac expressed his willingness to extend majority voting in the council, to give more power to the EP and to reform the Commission so that each member state would no longer appoint one or two of its members.

The election in 1997 of a centre-left majority and the formation of Jospin's government did not lead to a major shift in French positions, except in one respect. Whereas Chirac and Juppé had made clear their willingness to make tough spending cuts so as to meet the Maastricht convergence criteria on time, Jospin and his colleagues stated their intention of creating jobs, even if the result was that the convergence criterion on public deficits was not fully respected.

Since de Gaulle, French political elites themselves share some of the responsibility for the continuing popular suspicions of European integration expressed in the large 1992 'No' vote and subsequent opinion polls. All leaders, including de Gaulle, have found it useful to use the EU as a convenient scapegoat for unpopular policies. Most recent governments have expressed some criticisms of joint European policies, almost as if they had not themselves actively participated in the decision-making process. Such ambivalent attitudes merely reinforce nationalist and sectoral criticisms of the whole EU structure. In this way the governments which contribute to building the EU edifice ensure that it does not develop a legitimacy comparable to that of the French political system.

Institutional momentum in the EU

French policy-making towards Europe has involved not only taking initiatives but also, and increasingly, responding to the dynamics of the integration process itself. French ministers helped to draft the treaties which defined areas of competence in which Community institutions were responsible for making joint policies to attain defined goals. Since its creation, the EU has not only built up an *acquis communautaire* of established policies and methods of reaching agreements, but also created a momentum of bringing new areas into joint policy-making or extending the 'competence' of the EU and institutional reform to improve policy-making. Over the years an ever larger number of policy areas have been brought into the competence of EU institutions for joint decisions. Policy 'spill-over' has in part occurred in the way foreseen by the neo-functionalist theorists. In the 1990s the central elements of the EU political system, the Commission and the ECJ, have been recognized as the spokespersons for the EU as a whole. The institutional development of the EU has posed particular problems for those French governments that are generally reluctant to agree to power being transferred to supranational institutions. Increasingly, however, within the enlarged EU with its shifting balance of power, French governments are cast in the role of reacting to initiatives, rather than proposing their own schemes for change.

The central aim of the ECSC (noted in Article 1 of the Treaty and elaborated in Article 4) was the creation of a 'common market' for the two core industrial sectors, coal and steel, without customs or quotas, subsidies, restricted practices, discriminatory policies or other non-tariff barriers. This involved ministers of the Six deciding together on major policy measures as the Council of Ministers. A distinctive feature of the system, however, was that the Council was allowed to act only on the proposal of its executive agency, the 'High Authority' (later merged into the 'Commission'). That Authority was attributed responsibility for some executive decisions. Two other Community institutions were also important: the Court of Justice with unchallengeable authority to resolve disputes between member states or between Community institutions; and the parliamentary Assembly to advise and supervise the Council and High Authority. The system had many elements of 'supranationality'. One was that for many decisions the Council decisions did not require unanimity. Another was the power of the Court. Finally, the treaty included a commitment (in Article 86) that all member states would take the necessary legal measures to transpose ECSC legal acts into national law and to implement them.

The EEC and Euratom reproduced many features of the ECSC, but the policy competence was much wider. The Council of Ministers had similar powers to its ECSC equivalent and the Court of Justice and parliamentary Assembly were institutions common to the three communities. In 1967, the High Authority was merged into the less powerful Commission of the EEC. Although the Commission retained the sole right of initiative and responsibility for supervising implementation, virtually all secondary legislation was to be decided by the Council. The Treaties of Rome provided for a twelve-year transition period, in three four-year phases, and set down the principles of the customs union, and of common agricultural, transport, energy, and external economic relations policies. The content, rules and structures of all those policies, however, had to be decided in the Community structures, and the essential secondary legislation had to be agreed by the Council (usually by unanimity in the first phases). Many EC laws had then to be transposed into national law within the member states, and implemented.

The build-up of a considerable *acquis communautaire* of joint policies and agreed decision-making methods took place during de Gaulle's presidency. The key sector for de Gaulle was agriculture, and the complex structures of the CAP and particularly its price support mechanisms, were built up with considerable French governmental input. De Gaulle and his ministers were ruthless in the pursuit of what they saw as the national interest of France, and at times disrupted all progress which was not on their terms. They also played an active role in the construction of the Customs Union, and in setting the rules for the Community budget. Only in 1962 was the CAP fully elaborated. The customs union was completed in July 1968. Financial arrangements and refining inter-institutional operations (notably merging the High Authority and Commissions in the Merger Treaty of 1967) were only agreed after long months of negotiations.

De Gaulle postponed the enlargement of the Community, but after his resignation membership was extended to 9, then to 12 and most recently to 15 member states. Each enlargement brought problems of policy and institutional adaptations for the Community as well as for new members. Unanimity in the Council was increasingly difficult to achieve. The costs of the CAP were not only escalating but also borne disproportionately unfairly by one member state; the consequences were the reform of the policy and the budget process. New member states brought new policy priorities and the agenda of policy-making was modified. The ability of the governments of old member states such as France to determine the nature and outcome of policy choices was increasingly constrained.

The implementation of the treaties was far from complete when de Gaulle resigned. In particular, the treaty goals of creating the 'four freedoms' of movement of goods, services, capital and persons within a common market implied developing a free trade area into a real 'internal market'. That step was taken with the SEA in 1987, when the EC progressed from harmonizing external tariff barriers to dismantling internal non-tariff barriers. To achieve the basic idea of the EC of fair competition between firms in a single market required a legislative package of almost 300 measures, and all member states agreed that qualified majority voting in the Council (rather than unanimity, the practice since the Luxembourg Compromise) was essential to complete that package. For France, the SEA meant that traditional *dirigiste* practices, such as backing 'national champion' firms with cheap loans and public contracts, or subsidizing a massive public sector, had, slowly and reluctantly, to be given up. Furthermore, the freedom of movement of persons and equal access to employment policies mean that the French government is obliged to open up public sector and administration jobs to other EU nationals.

The TEU of 1993 had a particular resonance in France as it affected not only the state's control over traditional core functions but also raised constitutional issues. To ensure the stability and integrity of the single market, the TEU programmed the shift from the system of fixed exchange rates (the Exchange Rate Mechanism, or ERM, within the European Monetary System, or EMS) by a phased evolution to a single currency, a single monetary policy for the EU and an integrated central bank system (EMU). To achieve a more effective integration of external economic relations (a Community responsibility from the start) with foreign and security policy the TEU established an intergovernmental framework for making common foreign and security policy (CFSP) a 'second pillar' of the EU, closely linked with but legally distinct from the 'Community' framework. The TEU also recognized that suppression of one constraint on free movements, border controls (which the French government had accepted in the Schengen Agreement even before the single market programme) implied close collaboration between police forces and judicial authorities; hence an intergovernmental 'third pillar' for making common policies on justice and home affairs (JHA) was created. Finally, the TEU established a 'European citizenship' and gave nationals of one EU member state, but resident in another, the right to vote in local and European elections.

The TEU, by placing foreign and security policy and justice and home affairs in separate, intergovernmental pillars, distinct from the Community pillar, was responding to the pressure from many member states to limit co-operation in these areas to intergovernmental agreements. However, the introduction of 'European citizenship' and the measures in the TEU to ensure that the institutional momentum of the EU would continue, greatly concern opponents of supranationalism. Not only is EMU phased in steps until the single currency is introduced in 1999, but the holding of the Intergovernmental Conference in 1996 to examine desirable institutional changes was written into the treaty. The Amsterdam Treaty signed in 1997, stipulated that a major institutional reform of the EU should take place before further enlargement. In short, French governments are being drawn much further into EU institutional development and joint policy-making than expected when the Treaties of Paris and Rome were signed. With enlargement to as many as 26 member states on the agenda for 2000 and beyond, there is little prospect that the institutional momentum will stop.

International constraints

The behaviour of French governments has been constrained not only by the internal dynamics of the EU but also by the evolution of the international situation. The influence of other European leaders and their aspirations has been one international limitation on French European policies. Another has been the evolution of the overall strategic situation, and especially East–West relations. In post-Cold War Europe it is no longer logical or feasible for French governments to pursue unilateral action, and alternative policies have had to be considered. None the less, the international situation is not always a constraint; 'windows of opportunity' for the European policies of French leaders are sometimes opened by events abroad.

The Cold War, which excluded East European states from receiving Marshall Aid, or joining NATO, the ECSC and the EEC, both established limits within which European co-operation was possible and made the presence of US forces in Europe essential. Even de Gaulle did not question the desirability of the Western Alliance; what he opposed was the domination of that alliance by the US government, and the acceptance of that supremacy by British, German and Italian leaders alike. However, successive US presidents encouraged and supported European integration. Until the 1970s, the political situation in some European states also set limits on the extent of European integration. Although Portugal, Greece and Spain sided with the West in the Cold War, the existence of dictatorships and the backward nature of their economies meant that they were not considered for membership of the EEC. After years of economic growth and the departure of the dictators these states became eligible for EC membership, although their demands for help to upgrade their economies have placed heavy financial burdens on the Community budget.

In the early 1950s, however, among the liberal democracies in Western Europe, the situation seemed propitious for plans of integration. Italy, with a liberal constitution, had a Christian Democrat government under de Gasperi which shared many of the ideas of French Christian Democrats about European Union. So, too, did Adenauer's Christian Democrat-led coalition in the newly constituted West Germany. The establishment of the Federal Republic in itself created pressures for integration. In the first place, co-operation was essential to determine the future of the Saarland which had been placed under French control at the end of the war but which was claimed by Germany.

The second pressure arose from the need to find an acceptable means of rearming West Germany to contribute to the defence of Western Europe. The US administration insisted that it could no longer afford to replace the Germans in the defence of the West, but the idea of a remilitarized Germany scared many in France. Even French ministers feared that an independent Germany with its own armed forces would again endanger French security. Thus the Pleven Plan was drafted as a response to US pressure for the rearmament of Germany. Despite the support of the German government, the EDC proved unacceptable to the French Parliament. Ironically, the compromise of a loose West European Union, proposed by the British government and including Britain as a member, was the outcome – a result very different from the original French idea.

During the 1950s, British governments proved a constant obstacle to the achievement of French leaders' European goals. British hostility to joining anything with supranational powers prevented the development of bodies uniting all liberal West European states. British leaders continued to see their country as a world power, with an empire, a 'special relationship' with the leading superpower, and no need for involvement in building a new European union. After 1951, British Conservative governments admitted only the need for freer trade within Europe, and sought to achieve this by creating a loose intergovernmental group, the European Free Trade Association (EFTA), as a rival to the EEC. Thus, although French and other European leaders wanted Britain to be a co-founder of the ECSC and EC, British leaders were simply not interested. Ironically, by the time that the British government changed its mind, de Gaulle was already in power and determined to keep Britain out. That, too, had serious consequences. The relations between France and the other five EEC member states, which still wanted Britain to join, remained extremely tense until 1969 when de Gaulle resigned.

Another major international constraint has been the evolution of the international monetary system. The collapse of the stable exchange rate structure created at Bretton Woods significantly influenced both the pace and policies of European integration. In 1969, the impact of exchange rate instability was felt in France and throughout the Community. Although de Gaulle had refused a devaluation after the run on the franc during the 'events' of May 1968, Pompidou decided to devalue in 1969. However, as he wished to preserve all the benefits of the CAP, he agreed to establish, as a temporary measure, a special, distinct system of currency exchange for agriculture – the 'green franc'. The following year the mark revalued and a 'green mark' appeared. In subsequent years a further four 'green currencies' were created for similar reasons. With the 'green currencies', monetary compensation amounts (MCAs) were established to reimburse importers and to charge exporters from devaluing countries like France. The objective was to give the devaluing or revaluing state the domestic benefit of its exchange rate change, but to prevent a distortion of trade between member states as a consequence of the lower or higher prices resulting from the creation of the 'green currency'.

International pressures were also largely responsible for the fiasco of the first attempt at moving towards monetary union in the EEC, 'the Snake in the Tunnel'. The Snake, a system for keeping exchange rate of member currencies close to each other while maintaining their joint value to the dollar, was established in February 1971, as a key element in the plan to achieve EMU by 1980, following the Barre and Werner reports. In August 1971 the monetary crisis which followed the end of convertibility of the dollar dealt the death blow to that first 'Snake'. A second 'Snake' was set up in April 1972 but with little more success than its predecessor. The first oil price crisis came in 1973, and after intense speculative pressure, Pompidou was forced to withdraw the franc in January 1974. In July 1975, Giscard d'Estaing attempted to rejoin the second Snake but again had to withdraw in early 1976. The sad experience of the 'Snake' was also to have a longer-term effect: it partly explained Britain's reluctance to take part in the ERM of the EMS in 1979.

These failures of participation in the 'Snake' made subsequent French governments concerned that the EMS should succeed. This meant that Mitterrand found himself in a particularly difficult situation as early as 1982. The revaluation policies developed by his new government, without the increased trade on which they were promised, exacerbated pressure on the franc (which had already been under speculative attack before the 1981 presidential election). In

July 1982 and again in March 1983, Mitterrand faced stark choices: one option was to devalue on terms agreed by other states within the EMS (which meant an end to reflation); the alternative was to withdraw from the EMS – which might have destroyed that system. Despite the cost, Mitterrand chose the first option, thus preserving the EMS and avoiding the diminution of French influence within the Community.

International pressures, and particularly the OPEC price rises of 1973 and 1979, also had a negative effect on European integration, since the possibilities for European leaders to develop their joint policy activities were greatly limited by the 'stagflation' of their economies in the late 1970s. With high rates of inflation and the rapid growth of unemployment, governments became increasingly cautious, especially as many large enterprises, both public and private, came close to collapse. All governments were drawn into providing financial aid to some industries and creating other non-tariff barriers, including national safety specifications and preferential procurement policies. These protectionist, market-fragmenting tactics meant a pause in the movement towards a 'single market', whatever the integrationist sentiments of Giscard d'Estaing (George, 1991).

International pressures and opportunities were very different in the 1980s, facilitating the work of Mitterrand and Delors by providing an opportunity for European institutional development. The bitter disputes over the British budget contribution allowed Mitterrand to isolate British ministers from traditional friends (in the Dutch and Belgian governments) and from anti-integrationist allies (the Danes and the Greeks). Chancellor Kohl's subsequent willingness to leave Britain behind by signing a new treaty between the other 11 member states, provided a pressure point on Mrs Thatcher, who was horrified at the prospect of seeing the creation of a strongly supranationalist 'inner core', which she could not influence. The 1984 Fontainebleau summit, at the end of the French presidency of the Community, was a turning point. Mitterrand, working closely with Kohl, negotiated a broad deal with Thatcher, covering the British budget contribution and the relaunch of the integration process. Indeed, Thatcher's commitment to market economics provided an opportunity to deepen the Community. Delors, the compromise choice of Mitterrand and Thatcher as new president of the Commission, found common ground with Lord Cockfield (Thatcher's chosen Commissioner) on the programme to remove all non-tariff barriers. Mitterrand and Delors appreciated that Mrs Thatcher would also accept something which she would otherwise block – majority voting in the Council – as the sole practical means of achieving the goal of a single market. Indeed, no one could dispute the impossibility of getting unanimity in the Council to adopt 279 directives before the deadline of 31 December 1992. The French leaders effectively exploited the British leader's hopes and fears during the negotiations for the SEA, and again during the 1988 budget reform debates (Taylor, 1989).

A very different international pressure for change appeared in the late 1980s, in the form of *perestroika*. First, this dramatic change of policy by the Soviet Union made possible the reunification of Germany in 1990. That change gave extra impetus to French leaders to keep the German government involved in deepening European integration but also made domestic economic management more difficult because of the high interest rates of the Bundesbank. At the same time, the Nordic countries which had hitherto stayed out of the EC for reasons of neutrality, and Austria, which had hitherto been vetoed from joining by the Soviet Union, all felt free to join and a new wave of enlargement began in 1993. The East European former Communist states all set out to return to market economics and liberal democracy, but for this they sought technical and financial aid from Western Europe and close links with the EC.

The new governments of states geographically closest to the EU have all asked to join. Though many French leaders have serious worries about the likely impact of the membership of Hungary, Poland and the Czech and Slovak republics on EU finances, policies and policy-making (notably on structural funds, agriculture, textiles, steel, and immigration) it is difficult to forget the promises of the past. Thus, while, for the first time since 1945, de Gaulle's idea of Europe from the Atlantic to the Urals has become a practical possibility, Chirac, Jospin and other European leaders have to face problems undreamt of a decade earlier.

As part of the EU the options and strategies of French governments have also been limited by domestic political changes in other European states. Elections in other member states may lead to shifting alliances within the EU and hence modify the influence of French leaders. De Gaulle and Adenauer had a firm mutual respect, as did Pompidou and Heath, Giscard d'Estaing and Schmidt, and Mitterrand and Kohl, despite partisan and ideological differences. However, even reliable friends are subject to domestic pressures, which sometimes inhibit policy co-operation. Certainly Kohl's pursuit of a rapid reunification of Germany, and insistence that the

European Central Bank should be autonomous, did not coincide with Mitterrand's ideas on these subjects. In contrast, de Gaulle had little respect for the Benelux and Italian politicians who did not see the wisdom of his idea to replace the EEC by a loose confederation under French leadership. Between de Gaulle and Wilson a profound mutual suspicion soon developed. Pompidou and Brandt were not easy partners, and Mitterrand found it difficult to work closely with Schmidt, despite their ideological affinity. Like other European leaders, Mitterrand often found it difficult to work with Thatcher, and the accession of Major in 1990 was welcomed. Chirac never managed to establish the excellent relationship that his predecessor had with Chancellor Kohl. Chirac and Major initially worked well together, but after the 1996 BSE crisis relations deteriorated. Indeed, French leaders shared the relief among other European political elites when Blair was elected in 1997.

However, even when personality problems have existed, real collaboration has generally been possible when domestic policy preferences converge. Mitterrand's wish to push forward European integration aligned easily with Thatcher's desire to abolish non-tariff barriers in a single market. Similarly, both agreed in opposing increased powers for the European Parliament during the Maastricht negotiations (Moravcsik, 1993).

Conclusion

From the first two sections of this chapter, which explored the complex nature of goals behind governments' pursuit of Community construction, it emerges that most French governments have viewed the EU as both an ideal in its own right and as an instrument for achieving other objectives. The idealistic goal was a peaceful, prosperous, liberal and democratic Europe, based on tolerant co-existence and mutually beneficial co-operation and interdependency between states. The instrumental goals, however, were less noble, notably in relation to Germany. Initially, the goal was to contain Germany, then to make West Germany pay for the defence of Western Europe, then to link France economically to West Germany, thereby to share all the benefits of its economic success. Other goals in EU construction concerned relations with the rest of the world and especially the USA. A united Europe was to provide a means both of resisting the two-bloc division of world politics and the subjugation of French foreign policy to American leadership and of remaining part of the Western bloc and NATO alliance. Furthermore, as the French Empire disintegrated, Europe provided the means to retain a role of international leadership and of developing the armaments industry.

Alternations between periods of attempting to accelerate integration and of trying to prevent enlargement or the strengthening of the Community do not merely reflect changes of governments or presidents, or the evolution of elite thinking. All post-war government policies have sought to marry European idealism of different degrees of intensity among some elites with a strongly nationalist tradition in public opinion. Changing international circumstances and opportunities have not been neglected. Both intellectual attitudes and mass public opinion changed over time, partly as a consequence of learning from and reacting to events. Furthermore, the EC joint policy-making process itself became useful to all governments, including those of de Gaulle. It provided a convenient scapegoat to blame for essential but unpopular modernizing policies, and a means of introducing such policies without immediate parliamentary or media scrutiny.

Under de Gaulle, French governments were often tough partners, and at times threatened to destroy the Community itself if they could not have their own way. None the less, de Gaulle failed to sabotage the Community or even to achieve a formal amendment of the treaties. Subsequent governments were not always successful in negotiations in Brussels. As the scope and complexity of EU politics has grown, French leaders have had to deal with a policy agenda which they increasingly do not control. The increase in majority voting has meant that the capacity for all member states to block decisions has been reduced. The gradual growth of joint policy-making in the EU may have been acceptable to most, but not all, political elites, but hostile parties, interest groups and sections of the public could only be ignored at great risk.

French contributions to the development of the EU institutions have been many and varied. There has been no single great or dominant vision, but rather successive leaders have followed different strategies and have sometimes even changed their minds. Nor has there been a single or agreed definition of a French 'national interest'.

On the contrary, different governments have given different priorities to the various interests competing to influence policy-making. If the varied discourses have often been grandiloquent, practices have been much more pragmatic.

2

Adapting the State Machine

In all EU member states, the institutions of government have been adapted to deal with European policy-making on both the 'input' side of initiatives and policies, and the 'output' side of implementing the decisions and policing implementation. This chapter explores a paradoxical aspect of the adaptation of French institutions to these processes. On the one hand, an effective, multi-layered structure was quickly established for co-ordinating inputs into EU policy-making systems. On the other hand, however, the implementation of EU policies – by respecting agreed rules or by transposing directives quickly and accurately into French law and then implementing them – was, until the late 1980s, largely left to existing mechanisms. With no clear structure responsible for implementation, the record of performance was poor. If some of that inadequacy in implementation resulted from internal politics, much was a consequence of bureaucratic and legal obstructionism from within the state machine.

Adapting the state machinery to deal with making and implementing European policies has been complicated by two factors. First, the EU has a hybrid political system; in some policy areas it acts as an international organization, whereas in others it behaves as a federal government. The second factor is that, as discussed in Chapter 1, present EU institutional arrangements result from several phases of incremental development. These changes led to institutional adaptation within the French decision-making processes. The Maastricht Treaty, for example, imposed one major institutional change in France, that of making the Bank of France autonomous from governmental control, in preparation for it to become part of the

European Central Bank System for the single currency. The legislation in France to implement that change is discussed in Chapter 6.

The first four sections of this chapter analyse how co-ordination of European policy in France is carried out by a number of distinct but closely related institutions. As the range of EC policy-making grew after 1958, more and more branches of the state became involved in the preparatory stages. During the Fifth Republic, the presidency has always been involved. Although the Treaties of Paris and Rome did not provide for the direct participation of either president or prime minister in the institutions of the Community, enlargements and treaty changes have required intergovernmental conferences, where the president has led the French delegation. The creation of the European Council, and the grafting of that body on to the Community structures by the SEA, meant regular presidential involvement in top-level agenda setting and crisis resolution. France is the only member of the EU represented by its head of state at the European Council. The president is always involved in sorting out interministerial disputes before those meetings, along with the prime minister in his roles as head of government and budget arbitrator. In periods of *cohabitation* the prime minister shares the task of overall co-ordination with the head of state.

The foreign affairs and finance ministries play a key role in setting parameters of French positions in Community policy negotiations. Foreign affairs claims a traditional monopoly on all international questions, and its minister sits in the EU's General Affairs Council. As all European policies cost money to tax payers and affect economic policies, the finance ministry also claims an overview. However, the prime minister, as the acknowledged budget arbitrator, is also involved in all Community decisions with budgetary implications. Given the financial importance and complexity of the CAP, the agriculture ministry is also one of the most frequent actors in Brussels negotiations. All domestic spending ministries – transport, industry, social affairs, environment, health, education and even culture – are concerned with some European questions, and many issues cross-cut the competence of ministries. As most policy details are negotiated at levels below that of the Council of Ministers, in Council working parties headed by the committees of permanent representatives, at COREPER 1 and COREPER 2, and at the Special Committee on Agriculture, most of the detailed preparatory work is done by civil servants rather than ministers or their advisers. On the input side, disagreements between ministries in Paris inevitably arise over the best negotiating positions to be adopted and the compromises which are acceptable. Therefore, interministerial co-ordination, and arbitration when consensus cannot be reached by discussion, are essential elements of preparing co-ordinated European policies.

A specialized administrative agency, the General Secretariat of the Interministerial Committee on European Questions (*Secrétariat Général du Comité Interministèriel* or SGCI), is responsible for co-ordinating French inputs into Community policy-making. Under the supervision of the prime minister's staff, and working closely with the president's advisers, the SGCI is also the crucial link between the French permanent representative and his staff in Brussels and all the domestic ministries concerned. Of all the major institutions, the French Parliament has adapted least to the EU framework. Like most of its counterparts it still has no significant impact on the making of EU policy and only a limited role in the scrutiny of EU legislation.

The final two sections of this chapter examine the implementation of agreed European policies in France. The transposition of European laws into French law usually requires the co-ordinated action of several ministries, but only recently, after decades of poor implementation performance, has a structure of co-ordination been created. The judicial system, responsible for the enforcement of European legislation, has also a mixed record. Some courts accommodated to the reality of a European legal order slowly and reluctantly. The contrast with the impressive institutional adaptation on the input side is very marked.

The presidentialization of European policy-making after 1958

On 1 January 1958, the Treaty of Rome became operational. Six months later, after a major crisis in Algeria had brought France close to civil war, de Gaulle was invested as prime minister by the National Assembly. De Gaulle's price for accepting office was that a new Constitution would be adopted and that he would become president of the new Fifth Republic.

The new Constitution greatly reinforced the executive in relation to the Assembly, but retained the principle of parliamentary government. It did not institutionalize presidential government, but allocated to the presidency a limited number of powers in foreign and defence questions. None the less, the unlimited parliamentary sovereignty of the Fourth Republic gave way to a regime characterized by executive domination and effective presidentialism. De Gaulle exploited the continuing Algerian war to 'presidentialize' the system. He chose a deferential ally, Debré, as prime minister, safe in the knowledge that the Assembly would not censure the government as long as the Algerian crisis continued. He also established the presidency as the seat of foreign policy-making. A 'technician', Couve de Murville, became foreign minister, and the prime minister and other members of the government were marginalized in foreign affairs decisions.

Since 1962, the extent and nature of the policy role played by the presidency depends not only on the personality of the incumbent, but also on the balance of political forces in parliament. The president has a constitutional role in foreign policy but his or her influence over other policy-making largely depends on the ability to control a majority in the National Assembly. A 'presidential majority' may be inherited (the case of Pompidou in 1969 and Chirac in 1995) or it may be created by a general election victory after a presidential dissolution, as in 1981. It may consist of only one party (for example, Socialists between 1984 and 1986), although a coalition is more normal in French multi-party political competition. If the coalition-building efforts of the president fail, he must accept the prime minister imposed by a hostile majority, as Mitterrand was obliged to do in 1986 and again in 1993 when the centre–right coalition won the elections, and Chirac was also forced to do in 1997 when the Socialists emerged on the largest party in the new National Assembly. In such *cohabitation* periods, the president's foreign policy role remains largely unaffected.

As the 1958 Constitution provided for parliamentary government, no executive office was created for the president, and the development of a significant co-ordinating role for presidential advisers only developed over time. Administrative and consultative tasks remain the responsibility of the ministries, with central services and agencies of co-ordination in the prime minister's office. The prime minister is given the role of co-ordinating the work of the ministers, overseeing relations between government and parliament and arbitrating between ministers in budget disputes. The general secretariat of the government, which organizes meetings of the council of ministers and programmes Government activities, remains under the prime minister's authority. In theory, the French presidency appears to be institutionally weak, with no direct control of the machinery of government.

In practice, however, the president's indirect control of governmental decision making is achieved mainly by influence over the composition of the government and discussions with the prime minister and individual ministers, either in private interviews or in 'limited councils' (*conseils restreints*). Chirac, like his predecessors, uses the council of ministers each Wednesday as a brief formal meeting for the exchange of information and official approval of choices made elsewhere. Except for the three periods of *cohabitation*, presidents have dealt directly with the general secretary of the government to set the programme for ministerial work. The task of preparing the president with sufficient information, advice and analysis for meetings with ministers, falls on the presidential advisers, in the general secretariat of the presidency. Presidential advisers 'shadow' the work of the government, following and evaluating the work of ministers, and suggesting alternative policies.

Since the outset of the Fifth Republic, almost all politicians have accepted presidential leadership in foreign affairs. The foreign affairs minister is normally chosen by the president, and even during *cohabitation* the choices of Raimond (1986) and Juppé (1993) had the agreement of Mitterrand. In 1997 Chirac approved the appointment of Védrine. Under de Gaulle, major EEC questions were almost entirely presidential responsibilities. Under his successors, however, EU questions have remained 'presidential' only when they have concerned solving crises, enlargements of membership or changes in competence and institutions. All the presidents, however, have also occasionally intervened in details of ongoing Community policies. The extent of such involvement is a matter of personal choice and political circumstances. A crisis with international implications (a currency crisis is a good example) will almost always provoke detailed presidential decision-making. Presidential interventions also vary over time. Mitterrand, for example, appears to have been most interventionist in 1982–4, in 1989 and in 1991–2. There are no set rules, or rather the president sets and changes the rules at will.

The European policy role of the president has always included responsibility for deciding positions on major issues of institutional development. It was de Gaulle who both fixed the details of the Fouchet Plan and blocked negotiations for the enlargement of the Communities in 1963 and again in 1967. In 1965, it was de Gaulle who took the decision to boycott EC institutions in opposition to the introduction of majority voting. Subsequently, while Couve de Murville, as foreign minister, negotiated the Luxembourg Compromise, de Gaulle determined the parameters of that deal. In July 1969, it was Pompidou who cancelled his predecessor's veto on enlargement. In 1974, Giscard d'Estaing agreed to direct elections to the EP and to institutionalize meetings of heads of government (or of the state) as the European Council. Mitterrand took the decisions to remain within the EMS in the devaluation crisis of March 1983 and to adopt the SEA and single market programme in 1985. In 1989, when France held the EC presidency, all major initiatives came from Mitterrand. In 1991, Mitterrand himself led the negotiations at Maastricht and decided to hold the referendum on the TEU in 1992. In 1996, Chirac decided on the main lines of French input into the Intergovernmental Conference. The president's advisers always prepare the papers for meetings of the European Council or of the Group of 7. (The Group of Seven leading industrial countries USA, Canada, Japan, France, Germany, Italy and the UK.) In such major policy questions' presidential initiatives and decisions are expected and accepted by the prime minister and other ministers.

If de Gaulle had no wish to direct the administrative machine, he did intend to dominate some areas of policy-making. For this purpose, he assembled at the Elysée a small staff of advisers to provide him with ideas, research, and constant information about the work of the ministers, and to 'represent' the presidency in inter-ministerial committees. With the government's compliance, de Gaulle 'borrowed' a number of posts from various ministries so that his advisers could be full-time and salaried. Under de Gaulle the Elysée staff remained discreet and small, never more than 40 in number. Of its four units – the Military Household, the *cabinet*, the general secretariat for French Community and Malagasy Affairs and the general secretariat of the Presidency of the Republic – only the last included advisers on Europe. Their task was to keep the president informed and advised about all policy developments concerning Europe (S. Cohen, 1980). When Pompidou became president in 1969, each adviser or assistant was asked to 'cover' a much smaller, well-defined area of governmental action, such as the EC. However, in the last years of Pompidou's presidency, during his debilitating illness, members of his staff appeared to take decisions on his behalf, over the heads of ministers. Critics noted that France appeared to be governed by the Elysée staff, rather than by the government (Chaban-Delmas, 1975).

After his election, Giscard d'Estaing attempted to revert to the model of a discreet, self-effacing Elysée staff. He reduced the size of the secretariat and gave strict instructions that the staff's function was to advise him, not to overrule ministers. Giscard d'Estaing was personally involved in decisions about changes in EC institutions (notably the direct elections to the European Parliament) and in major policies (including the move from 'the Snake' to the EMS). In these areas he counted on his advisers, especially during the first two years when Chirac, his prime minister, led a party deeply suspicious of the president's European plans. Indeed, on the issue of direct elections to the Parliament, the prime minister and government were informed only after he had taken the decisions. However, his second prime minister, Raymond Barre, an ex-Commissioner, had considerable influence on European questions.

Once elected in 1981, Mitterrand replaced all presidential advisers, and reorganized the work pattern of the Elysée and ordered his personal staff to leave governing to the government. He created a small special advice 'cell', led by Jacques Attali, the *conseiller spécial du Président*. Mitterrand did not treat his staff members as a team, but rather as individuals, and sometimes asked two or three advisers to consider the same problem at the same time, without consulting one another. On major European questions, the president consulted the general secretary (Bianco, later Védrine), his special adviser (Attali, later Lauvergeon) and his European specialist (Machin, 1994). The first special adviser on European matters, Elisabeth Guigou, soon gained particular influence at the Elysée. Initially, her role was to advise on international economic policies, but she became the European specialist when the reform of the EC budget, and later the single market programme, were core policy problems. At the same time she was appointed as general secretary of the SGCI (see below) which gave her a complete overview of all aspects of European policy-making. When elevated to ministerial status in 1989, she continued to act as an unofficial presidential adviser, although the task of following the work of the SGCI was taken over by Caroline de Margerie, her official replacement at the Elysée.

In 1986, during the period of *cohabitation*, Chirac became prime minister, and the flow of governmental files to the Elysée on domestic matters dried up at once. Only Bianco was authorized by Mitterrand to have direct dealings with ministers or the head of government. European questions were acknowledged by both the president and his prime minister to straddle domestic and foreign policies. They agreed that co-ordination between the presidential and prime ministerial staffs was essential. Attali and Guigou were involved in policy co-ordination efforts with Yves-Thibault de Silguy and Emmanuel Rodocanachi from Chirac's staff, and their relations were often tense.

In 1988, when Mitterrand was re-elected, the work-pattern at the Elysée returned to normal, and with it the European policy process. In 1993, when the second *cohabitation* began with Balladur, relations between the president and prime minister, and their staffs' were considerably smoother. On the main issues, GATT and EMU, there was a broad consensus, personal relations were warmer and as the president became weakened by his illness, his activities were reduced.

When Chirac became president in May 1995, he immediately replaced the entire Elysée staff of advisers. The new general secretary, Dominique de Villepin, had previously worked for Juppé when he was minister of foreign affairs. So too had both Pierre Ménat, the new European affairs adviser and Bernard Emié, the second foreign affairs adviser. In short, Chirac's presidency began with an advisory team which symbolized the approach he shared with prime minister Juppé, and a continuity of Juppé's policy as foreign affairs minister in the Balladur government. That symbolism, however, became much weaker after the election of the centre-left majority in 1997. Indeed Jospin made it very clear, as Chirac himself had done in 1986 to Mitterrand, that the constitution gave the prime minister full responsibility for all the 'joint domestic' side of EU policy-making.

Throughout the Fifth Republic, however, there have been two constant constraints on the role of presidential advisers, even those concerned with European policies. One is the need to placate the prime minister and ministers by allowing them sufficient freedom of action for political credibility and personal self-esteem. In practice this means that presidential advisers must work very closely with the prime minister's European adviser. The second major constraint is the limited resources of the Elysée. Each minister has a *cabinet* of eight, plus all resources of his or her ministry for just one policy area. In contrast, the small staff of the Elysée attempts to cover all policy areas (Schifres and Sarazin, 1985).

The prime minister and interministerial co-ordination

The prime minister has a personal staff, the *cabinet*, to assist in his or her work, to help prepare, co-ordinate and execute government policy, to give political advice and to carry out certain administrative and managerial tasks. In this respect this *cabinet* is similar to ministerial *cabinets*, but as there are no official texts which set its numbers, structure, or functions, the size of the prime ministerial *cabinet* has always been noticeably larger than any ministerial team. In general, one adviser (*chargé de mission*) shadows the work of each ministerial department. The foreign affairs and European advisers, however, have a delicate task, since they both follow all activities in the 'presidential sector' to keep the prime minister informed (especially as the president is often negligent in this respect), and to supervise the work of the SGCI.

Other *cabinet* members are also involved when a bill must be prepared, which is necessary for each treaty ratification. Here, advisers participate in all the preparatory processes, up to the *conseils restreints*, chaired by the president, at which the final text of the bill is drafted for approval at the Council of Ministers. Once a bill has been adopted officially at the Council, the prime minister's advisers manage its passage through parliament, working in close contact with the leaders of the majority party or coalition, helping to negotiate solutions to disputes over amendments and also advising the prime minister on procedure. The prime minister is also assisted by the general secretary of the government, who plays a central role in the policy preparation in many areas, and keeps records of all meetings, including discussions in committees.

In practice, the roles played by the president, prime minister and their advisers in deciding European negotiating positions have been closely tied since 1958. However, co-ordination problems may arise when the president decides to intervene, with broad lines of policy development or minor details, in routine matters which are normally dealt with by the prime minister or the SGCI. Though the existence of a presidential majority in parliament (except between 1986 and 1988, and 1993 and 1995 and from 1997) allows the president to intervene in any policy area, such interventions may interrupt established patterns of policy preparation. In theory, conflicts could arise between the prime minister and president; in practice, anyone who agrees to become prime minister under a president with a parliamentary majority knows that opposition to the president may precipitate his or her own departure. The president cannot constitutionally dismiss a prime minister, but can effectively force him or her to resign, as Chaban Delmas, Chirac, Rocard and Cresson all experienced.

During periods of *cohabitation*, as noted above, European policy-making is shared, and disputed, between the president and prime minister (Mesnier, 1990). In 1986, the president claimed that European matters were 'foreign affairs', and hence, his responsibility. He had prepared for conflict by appointing his adviser from the Elysée, Guigou, as general secretary of the SGCI and François Scheer, a politically-sympathetic diplomat, as permanent representative in Brussels. When the new government was appointed, Mitterrand insisted that the post of foreign minister be given to someone acceptable to himself. Although Jean-Bernard Raimond, previously the ambassador in Moscow, was the compromise choice, the new minister showed little respect for the Fifth Republic's tradition of deference to the president in foreign affairs, and consulted him formally only once a week. Raimond, however, showed little interest in European topics.

The prime minister, in contrast, faced a conundrum over European policy. Article 20 of the Constitution clearly gave him a role to play, but Chirac made no secret of his ambition to become president in 1988, and hence had no wish to diminish presidential authority in foreign policy. None the less, as a candidate for the presidency, Chirac also wished to demonstrate his stature as an international statesman. On arrival at the Hotel Matignon, Chirac created a diplomatic 'cell' within his *cabinet* under François Bujon de l'Estang, and instructed the foreign affairs ministry to cease all direct communication with the Elysée. In most areas of foreign policy, the main links between the prime minister and president were informal discussions between Bujon d'Estang and Maurice Ulrich (Chirac's chief of staff), and Bianco, Attali and Vedrine.

On EC questions, however, the situation was more complex, since Chirac claimed that many ongoing policies were 'domestic' and thus mainly within the government's competence. Chirac, instead of the foreign minister, insisted on accompanying the president at meetings of the European Council and playing an active role in negotiations at those meetings. To limit the flow of information to, and hence the influence of, the president, the prime minister decided to change the pattern of co-ordinating work. No formal meetings of the interministerial committee on Community affairs were held – since Guigou would have had the right to attend as general secretary. Instead, some matters were settled by informal meetings of ministers to which she was not invited. François Scheer was also excluded from these meetings, and at some COREPER negotiations French representation were left with virtually no instructions.

During this period, co-ordination was facilitated by an informal network of officials chaired by Pierre de Boissieu, head of the economic co-operation service in the foreign affairs ministry. Members of this group included Attali, Guigou and Scheer, de Silguy and Rodocanachi from Chirac's staff, Claude Villain, chief of staff of Balladur, then finance minister, and Bernard Vial, from the ministry of agriculture, all of whom knew each other. The economic co-operation service, unlike the SGCI, was a politically neutral meeting place. Whereas the SGCI continued to deal with ongoing administrative co-ordination, this informal group settled matters disputed by the president and prime minister. Between 1993 and 1995, under Balladur's premiership, the situation was much less tense, reflecting the generally less conflictual character of the second *cohabitation*. Mitterrand was generally willing to leave policy decisions in the hands of Balladur and foreign minister Juppé, whose views on Europe were very close to his own.

After his election as president, Chirac took the lead on major European questions, although there was close collaboration with the foreign affairs minister, de Charette. The surprise election of June 1997, however, inaugurated a third period of *cohabitation*. Hubert Védrine, a career diplomat who had advised Mitterrand for most of his fourteen-year presidency, was the compromise choice of Jospin and Chirac for the foreign affairs ministry. The Jospin government soon made it clear that, unlike its predecessors, it gave a very high priority to reducing unemployment even if the consequence were to be overshooting the public deficit requirement of the Maastricht Treaty. The start of the third period of *cohabitation* suggested that it would not work as smoothly as the Balladur–Mitterrand *cohabitation* had done and that conflict would inevitably emerge in the arena of European policy.

The ministries and interministerial co-ordination in the SGCI

Within almost all ministries, adaptations have been made to deal with the growing volume of European questions. According to Carnelutti, in 1989 more than 500 civil servants were actively involved in Brussels negotiations, while several thousand were concerned with the transposition of directives and their application within France (Carnelutti, 1989). In general, four kinds of changes have been adopted in the ministries: the creation of specialist European services, the designation of experts to participate in working parties in Brussels, the training of civil servants to deal with European questions, and the secondment of officials to the staffs of the Commission, the Council, or the Permanent Representation. Each ministry has been free to organize its own internal 'Europeanization programme', although several colloquia, seminars and short courses have been organized for the civil service as a whole by the civil service division (*Direction Générale de l'Administration et de la Fonction Publique*) in the prime minister's office.

Most ministries have established units to co-ordinate activities of the main 'divisions' (*directions*) which deal with European questions. In the most active ministries – foreign affairs, economics and finance, and agriculture – each major division has a specialist European service. Such units not only follow all aspects of the relevant policy processes through the Commission–Council–COREPER dialogue, but also deal with the minister's *cabinet* and the SGCI, make suggestions to the SGCI about suitable experts for appointment to committees and working parties in Brussels, and organize training courses for colleagues. Ministries with fewer European contacts have more embryonic structures, with one international service for the whole ministry.

The SGCI was created by decree in 1948 to overcome traditional rivalries between the foreign affairs and finance ministries over responsibility for international economic relations. The committee was chaired by the prime minister, but the secretariat worked closely with the finance ministry, and the general secretary was a senior civil servant from that ministry. The committee and secretariat initially had the task of preparing instructions for French representatives in the negotiations about the use of Marshall Aid within the OEEC. Although Marshall Aid came to an end in the early 1950s, the SGCI has continued the work of liaison with the OECD (which replaced the OEEC in 1960). Since 1945, European economic co-operation has been recognized as interministerial in character, but initially the dominant ministry was finance, not foreign affairs (Grosser, 1984).

When the ECSC was established in 1951, the interministerial committee and secretariat assumed the tasks of ensuring coherent French positions within Community negotiations. The minister of Industry, representing France on the ECSC council of ministers, became a member of the committee. The ECSC council of ministers established a co-ordination committee (known as COCOR), composed of national civil servants, responsible for co-ordinating the work of the High Authority with that of national administrative services. The assistant general secretary of the SGCI was chosen as French representative on COCOR. In 1954, the chair of the interministerial committee and administrative responsibility for the SGCI were given to the minister of finance. Thus, in the ECSC, policy-making was largely the responsibility of domestic, technical ministries, with foreign affairs playing a relatively minor role.

This pattern was modified after the ratification of the Treaty of Rome, when the competence of the interministerial committee and SGCI was enlarged to include interministerial co-ordination for negotiations in the EEC and Euratom. The prime minister officially assumed the chair of the committee, but the SGCI remained administratively linked to the finance ministry. The role of the SGCI grew considerably after 1958, as detailed discussions for core policies and in particular, for the customs union and the CAP, proved long and complex. In Brussels, COREPER became a crucial institution in EEC policy-making, as it took on much of the detailed preparatory negotiations of the Council which was rapidly assessing itself as the dominant policy-making body. De Gaulle was determined to ensure that the EEC remained an 'international organization', in which France's 'national interest' was represented. Hence, the job of permanent representative was given to an ambassador from the *Quai d'Orsay*, replacing the finance ministry official who had sat on COCOR in the ECSC.

To allow the permanent representative, or relevant minister, to take clear positions on behalf of France, in Brussels, the SGCI was reinforced in its role of co-ordinating ministerial stances in Paris. It was made the sole liaison agency between ministers, their officials and the Commission, and the information office on European matters for the whole government. In early 1959 prime minister Debré instructed his government that all communications with the Commission must pass through the office of the general secretary of the SGCI. His successor, Pompidou, in 1965 reminded his ministerial colleagues, that to maintain coherent governmental action in the EEC, the SGCI monopoly of communications with European institutions must be respected in all circumstances. As the scope of EEC policy-making extended, successive prime ministers have reminded ministers and civil servants of this essential co-ordinating role of the SGCI; the most recent text came from Balladur in 1994: 'In respect of Community matters, the positions that French representatives express in these EU institutions is decided after interministerial co-ordination by the SGCI under the authority of the prime minister' (*'Circulaire du 21 mars 1994 relative aux relations entre les administrations françaises et les institutions de l'Union Européenne'*).

The fact that successive prime ministers have found it necessary repeatedly to remind their colleagues and officials of the co-ordinating role of the SGCI suggests that traditions of ministerial autonomy and competition have not died out.

In addition to its functions of communication and co-ordination, the SGCI gradually acquired a role of arbitration in administrative matters. This was both a reflection of the reputation of its officials as 'honest brokers' with no ministry interests, and of the authority of the prime minister. The secretariat itself remained small and its formal powers limited. No attempts were made to transform it into a ministry for Europe. Experiments placing the SGCI under the responsibility of other ministers – the finance ministry in 1954 or the junior minister (*Ministre délégué*) for European Affairs between 1981 and 1984 – undermined its effectiveness.

Although located near the finance ministry at the *Quai Bercy*, some distance from the Elysée and Matignon, the SGCI is not cut off from the main agencies of governmental co-ordination, the prime minister's *cabinet* and the general secretariats of the government and of the presidency. Contacts are frequent between senior SGCI and the European advisers of the president and prime minister. Most general secretaries have combined their responsibilities at the SGCI with those of policy adviser to the prime minister or the president. One, Bernard, was a member of Pompidou's staff at Matignon, and followed him to the Elysée in 1969. Guigou, the main policy adviser on Europe to Mitterrand between 1982 and 1990, was also, as mentioned above, general secretary at the SGCI between 1985 and 1990.

In the 1990s, as during the 1950s, the SGCI has remained a small, distinctive unit, with a clearly defined area of competence (Carnelutti, 1988). Its 160 staff are grouped into a number of policy-area 'sectors' and a special 'sector' which deals with the internal administration and co-ordination of the secretariat. At the head of the SGCI, the general secretary is assisted by two assistant general secretaries. The SGCI structure has been adapted over the years as EU competence has grown, but it has never exactly matched either the ministerial division of competence in France or the distribution of tasks between general directorates in Brussels. Within this structure, five sectors are of special importance. The first deals with economic and financial questions including the Community budget. Two other crucial sectors deal with agricultural policy questions, one primarily with the price support system and the other with structural policy. Agriculture still receives almost half of all EU funds and is more regulated than any other EU policy area and hence requires more meetings in Brussels. Moreover, meetings of the Council of Ministers of Agriculture are prepared by the Special Committee on Agriculture (SCA), rather than by COREPER, and the two heads of sectors at the SGCI alternate as the French representative on that committee. The fourth key sector deals with all juridical and institutional issues and provides other sectors with advice on legal points. It is responsible for interministerial co-ordination about French cases before the ECJ. Finally, the internal administration and co-ordination sector is responsible for documentation, archives and information services to the ministries.

Among the other sectors of the SGCI, seven deal with specific EU policy areas:

1. industrial and environmental policy; social policy
2. education and culture.
3. research
4. trade
5. regional and transport policy
6. energy
7. Mediterranean affairs and development aid.

One sector covers communications with French members of the EP, the ESC and the Committee of Regions. Another sector co-ordinates French activities at the OECD. Since November 1993, when the TEU became operational, a new post of co-ordinator deals with the third pillar responsibilities of justice and home affairs. In 1994, the prime minister made the SGCI responsible for dealing with the Schengen Agreement and Dublin Convention, for contacts with the European Court of Audit, and for providing information to the French parliament. The success of the SGCI depends on effective support services, which include documentation, an information service, a computing team and 20 other staff in personnel, supplies, mail sorting and delivery.

The senior staff of the SGCI are characterized by mobility. Between 1948 and 1995, there were 15 general secretaries. Only one, Bernard, stayed for 10 years (1967–77), and three others held the post for five years, but the others remained in office for three years or less. A similar mobility is seen among the sector heads, where the average posting lasts two and a half years. This level of mobility does not imply that the SGCI suffers from periodic disruption, since it is rare for several senior posts to change hands simultaneously. A major element of continuity is provided by the assistants in the sectors, since, on average, an assistant stays for five years. This turnover means that the SGCI plays an informal but important role of training senior civil servants on their way to top posts in various ministries and that high flyers actively seek posts at the secretariat. Partly as a result, the SGCI has a good reputation, its staff often gain promotion on leaving, and they are replaced by equally bright and ambitious civil servants. The present system has the advantage of training people in EU affairs who can move throughout the administration and even take posts as advisers in ministers' *cabinets*.

The general secretary is appointed by decree in the council of ministers on the proposal of the prime minister. The Assistant General Secretaries and the head of sectors are usually chosen from professional corps within ministries appropriate to their duties at the SGCI. There are many candidates, in part because all category A civil servants have a mobility obligation to work for two years outside their own corps. Vacancies are communicated informally, person to person, and enquiries about the qualities of candidates are equally informal. The general secretary conducts the interviews and makes the final choices.

The competence of those in senior posts at the SGCI has won widespread respect. The professional origins of these post-holders give some indication of their competence. Eight of the 15 general secretaries between 1948 and 1995 came from the finance inspectorate (*Inspection des Finances*), and one from the Council of State (*Conseil d'Etat*). Of the 25 holders of the post of assistant general secretary, 10 came from the finance inspectorate, nine from the corps of mining engineers (*Ingénieurs des mines*), and five from the diplomatic service. Most are graduates of the prestigious National Administration School (*Ecole Nationale d'Administration* or ENA) or the *Ecole Polytechnique*. Almost all the general secretaries had previously worked as ministerial advisers before appointment to head the SGCI. Their careers after leaving the SGCI are also indicative of their competence. Schweitzer became head of the IMF, Delouvrier the first prefect of the Paris region and later, chairman of the French Electricity Corporation (*Electricité de France*) and Dromer managing director of the National Bank of Paris (BNP). Ortoli and Guigou became ministers.

The basic task of the SGCI is to provide negotiating briefs for France's permanent representation in Brussels or for ministers at different meetings of the Council. As the European Commission initiates policies, the work of the SGCI is largely responsive to that body. When the Commission proposes any new directive, a response from the French government is required in subsequent negotiations, in a working party, at COREPER Council or at the Council. The SGCI provides both the communication link between Brussels and the ministries in Paris and the mechanism for ensuring that the instructions given to whoever negotiates in Brussels for France have the full authority of the Government. The SGCI has to persuade the ministries and ministers to come to agreement and to do so in time for Brussels negotiations, the times and dates of which it does not control. SGCI staff seek to create consensus and to bring the various administrative actors to accept common positions. If disagreements persist then arbitration may be necessary to impose a solution in time for the Brussels meeting. The SGCI itself can provide acceptable arbitration of low-level conflicts, especially over purely administrative matters. For more important interministerial disagreements the prime minister is responsible for arbitration.

Normally, a proposal for a directive is sent by the Commission to the permanent representative, who transmits it by fax to the SGCI (an exception to the rule that all correspondence from ambassadors abroad passes through the foreign affairs ministry). The appropriate SGCI sector head then communicates it to the ministries concerned and requests their written observations. In some cases, the replies reveal few major disputes and the sector head is able to secure by telephone the agreement of all concerned on a common text for an instruction. In many cases, however, a meeting of representatives from the ministries is necessary to ensure agreement on the response. When potential conflicts are thus identified, one task of the SGCI staff is to take informal soundings, often by telephone, to find if an acceptable compromise can be reached. In 1992, there were on average five conflict-resolution meetings a day at the SGCI. Normally, ministerial representatives are civil servants from relevant divisions. In most meetings, agreement is reached, so a simple minute, drafted by the SGCI sector head, becomes the instruction communicated to the permanent representative in Brussels as the French negotiating position. Where no common position is agreed, the dispute is referred to a higher level for further efforts of co-ordination, or eventually for arbitration. First, the general secretary attempts to find a compromise solution. If this fails, the dispute is referred to the prime minister's *cabinet*. In practice, the European adviser in the *cabinet* is usually responsible for dealing with such problems, and only rarely does the prime minister arbitrate in person.

The SGCI does not perform all the work of co-ordinating European policy-making. The delegation of responsibility for co-ordinating many elements of agricultural policy developed during the 1970s as the CAP became increasingly complex, with several specific funds and services, each with a management committee, meeting almost weekly in Brussels. For these routine matters, however, the SGCI leaves the task of finding agreed positions to the ministry of agriculture, the 'lead' ministry. At a very different level, the co-ordination of French negotiating positions within the CFSP and JHA 'pillars' are primarily the work of the foreign affairs and Interior ministries, although the SGCI is kept closely informed. If, however, a policy under discussion in the second or third pillars involves expenditure or is closely connected with a Community policy, it is the task of the SGCI to co-ordinate ministerial inputs.

The system is far from being fixed and inflexible. The SGCI, however, has not attempted to colonize all European co-ordination but has decentralized much routine work to ministries, and deliberately tried to stay small so that there is no problem of co-ordinating co-ordinators. None the less, the expansion of EU activities after the TEU and the prime minister's circular of March 1994 have given the SGCI a vast area of competence and a highly complex and sensitive task of co-ordination.

The French parliament in search of a European role

The Treaty of Rome transferred responsibility for legislation from national parliaments to Community institutions, and in particular to the Council, creating a 'democratic deficit' as there is little effective control over Council decisions, either by member state parliaments or the EP. In ratifying the treaties, national parliaments gave up legislative control, while the SEA and TEU gave the EP only limited influence over legislation. The democratic deficit has been exacerbated by two factors:

- the secrecy of the decision-making process in the Council (and particularly the crucial preparatory stages in COREPER and the working parties);
- the increasing use of qualified majority voting (QMV) as a means of adopting European laws, since the SEA was passed.

When QMV is used, governments can easily find themselves in a minority on issues. This means that they may be forced to implement policies which they have not supported. The increasing use of QMV has made the issue of member states' control over the policy-making process more important. As all member states are parliamentary democracies, the absence of transparency and parliamentary accountability is no minor problem, and various attempts have been made to develop parliamentary 'scrutiny' by domestic parliaments to compensate for this loss. In France, however, the change of regime in 1958 led to a weakening of parliament, and it was not until the late 1970s that some institutional means for parliamentary scrutiny were established.

The law ratifying the Treaty of Rome, passed in the last months of the Fourth Republic, provided one means for parliament to obtain information about EC policy-making – by obliging the government to give it an annual report on all measures, at national and European levels, to apply the treaty. The change of regime in 1958, however, brought in a government generally suspicious of parliament, and a president who saw no place for such scrutiny in 'foreign affairs'. De Gaulle was especially hostile to parliamentary influence over European policy-making, since he knew that many of the parliamentarians were pro-integrationist. Thus, during the early years of Community development, parliament received little information from the government. The only channel for information about what was taking place in Brussels and Strasbourg was through deputies and senators who held 'dual mandates'. Those 35 members of parliament chosen to represent their party groups in the EP, could, through this double membership, keep themselves and their colleagues in Paris informed about Community policies discussed in Strasbourg. Unfortunately, the EP itself was often ill-informed about what was decided in the Council–Commission dialogue. Furthermore, the number of representatives was small – only 35 including 11 senators.

Finally, the accumulation of mandates left representatives little time for either job, especially as many were also active in local government. Indeed, a high level of absenteeism marked most meetings of the EP.

These institutional arrangements changed in 1979 when the EP was directly elected and its membership increased. Henceforth, France elected 81 Euro-Deputies. Dual mandates were not explicitly prohibited, although they became rarer, especially after the 1985 French law limiting the accumulation of elected offices. In 1994, the number of seats allocated to France was increased to 89. With the first election of the Members of the European Parliament (MEPs), 'Parliamentary Delegations for the European Communities' were created in both the Senate and the National Assembly. Parliamentary debates over these delegations, however, revealed a gulf between the demands of Gaullists and Communists who wanted to create powerful parliamentary committees, and the government and most of the Senate who wished only to improve the information flow to parliamentarians. The government's wishes prevailed, and the task allotted to the delegations was to monitor European legislation and to keep parliament informed. Each delegation was composed of 18 members, chosen from the parliamentary groups in proportion to their strengths. An incompatibility rule prevented MEPs from joining these delegations.

In 1990, these arrangements were modified, after complaints about the ineffectiveness of the delegations. Their memberships were doubled, the incompatibility rule excluding MEPs was abolished, and provision was made for all standing committees to be represented. The delegations' role is to discuss draft directives and regulations which fall within parliament's sphere of legislation. The government was made responsible for providing information, passing documents about proposed European laws, and answering questions. In 1991, the Assembly delegation held 17 hearings, while its Senatorial counterpart held 15, and reports of these hearings were published. Every three weeks, the delegations publish a selection of important European documents for the use of standing committees; and every six months, they draft a balance-sheet of the achievements of the previous presidency. The delegation of the National Assembly has been especially active: from its establishment in 1979 to the summer of 1992 it met, on average, 20 times a year and published 332 reports. The delegations also make visits to Community institutions and participate in the bi-annual joint meetings of the committees on EC matters of all member states. However, their main role is a technical and administrative one – to collect and disseminate information to the standing committees of parliament.

The 1992 modification of the French Constitution which allowed the ratification of the TEU included provisions to enhance the role of parliament in EU policy-making. In particular, the government is required to transmit to parliament all proposals from the Commission for EU legislation which concern matters falling within the law making competence of parliament (according to Article 34 of the Constitution). The goal is to allow parliament to express its views before government ministers take part in a legislative decisions in the EU council of ministers. In practice, this involves not only the parliament, but also the highest administrative court, the Council of State, in its advisory capacity, to determine which Commission proposals fall within the scope of Article 34. Virtually all initiatives from the Commission are classified by the Council of State: between 1992 and 1996 it examined 2000 proposals, and deemed 44 per cent to be within the Article's scope. Since 1992 parliament has thus had the chance to influence French inputs for negotiations on almost 900 Commission initiatives. As yet there is no detailed study of the influence of parliament on French negotiating positions, but it is clear that parliament has been much better informed about EU activity since 1992.

The transposition of European law into French law

Integration within the EU framework has involved two types of legislation:

- treaties
- secondary legislation, made by the EU institutions.

The founding treaties of 1951 and 1957, amended by the SEA and TEU, created the political, administrative and judicial institutions of the EU for making secondary legislation. In the member states the treaties were ratified by statutes which thus constitute 'primary' European legislation, in the form of 'enabling acts'. The legal texts produced within EU institutions are, therefore, a special kind of joint delegated legislation. This European 'secondary legislation' is generally of two types:

- *regulations* which determine both ends and means, usually in a specific policy area, and are directly applicable in member states; and
- *directives* which determine objectives but leave the choice of means to member-state governments.

Directives usually require transposition into national law before becoming operational, either by parliamentary statute or by domestic delegated legislation. The transposition of directives into domestic law by member-state governments is carried out under the scrutiny of the European Commission, which may challenge measures it considers inappropriate before the European Court of Justice. In some cases pre-existing domestic laws must be changed, in others, notably concerning competition in the single market, they must be abrogated.

In France, the 1958 Constitution, by limiting the law-making competence of parliament and enlarging the scope of delegated legislation through Articles 34 and 37, facilitated the task of transposition, as the majority of directives do not require statutory legislation for transposition into French law (Ligot, 1990). Most transposition work is carried out within the executive by adopting 'decrees'. Thus, if the 'democratic deficit' seems greater in France than elsewhere, the cause is not only the Treaty of Rome, but also the Fifth Republic Constitution.

In practice, the SGCI, the Council of State and the general secretariat of the government ensure that the transposition process takes place smoothly and without delay. Two prime-ministerial circulars, in January 1990 and July 1992, set the rules which currently apply. The 1992 circular followed the revision of the Constitution in June 1992 for the ratification of the TEU. That revision, however, did little to reduce the democratic deficit, but did provide scope for reducing the 'juridical deficit' (Guillaume, 1992).

In theory, the problems of transposing directives into French law should be foreseen at the negotiation stage of the policy. The SGCI informs all relevant ministries and the Council of State of Commission proposals for directives and asks for preparatory studies, including lists of modifications or additions to legal texts resulting from the adoption of the directive. An adviser is appointed from the Council of State to help the ministries involved. Once a directive is adopted, the SGCI communicates the text to the general secretariat of the government and the ministries, and indicates the 'lead ministry' for the transposition. Each ministry must respond within three months and propose a time-table for the legal changes it deems necessary. As 30 per cent of all directives typically concern agriculture, the agriculture ministry plays a special transposition role, and has created a cell purely for transposition work. At the end of the three-month period, the SGCI and general secretariat of the government convene a meeting to agree on the necessary legal modifications and to programme the adoption of the directives. The Council of State advises which measures require statute law and checks the legality of the texts drafted in the ministries before they go to parliament. Where decrees are needed, it advises on the texts submitted to the council of ministers. In all cases, the ministries are required to consult the Commission before the French law or decree is made, a rule which the Council of State vigorously polices.

This pattern was established in the 1990s in response to repeated criticisms of long delay in transposition during the first decades of the EC. The Treaty of Rome provided (under Article 169) for the Commission to verify that the necessary transpositions have been made, but also to ensure that the terms and conditions of a directive are accurately transcribed in the national law. Initially, the Commission simply serves notice on the government of the recalcitrant member state that a directive has not been transposed or applied, or that the transposition is inaccurate. This triggers a debate with that government, and often inspires it to act or to modify earlier decisions. If, however, the government takes no action, or gives an unsatisfactory response, the Commission may refer the case to the ECJ.

Until the late 1980s, France was one of four member states most in dispute with the Commission over the transposition, implementation and general respect of European laws. In 1984, France was the worst offender, and the Commission served 92 notices on France for all forms of non-respect (25 more than on Italy, and 58 more than on the UK) and made 14 referrals of France to the ECJ (Italy was referred 12 times and the UK only 4 times). The changes of the late 1980s were clearly effective: by 1991, France had moved up to fourth place in the league table of respecters and appliers of European law.

The courts and the implementation of Community law

If ultimate responsibility for ensuring that European law is accurately transposed and applied in member-states lies with the ECJ, many disputes concerning individuals, firms or groups affected by European laws are dealt with in the courts of member states. The Treaty of Rome provided a means for national courts to obtain the advice of the ECJ before reaching judgments (under Article 177), thus ensuring the coherence of national and European legal systems. EU law does not cover the full range of subjects in any member state's domestic law, but overlaps in many areas. Demarcation disputes are, therefore, inevitable, given the wide treaty goals of creating a customs union and a common market with free movement of persons, capital and services.

The authors of the Treaty of Rome were diplomatic in phrasing the articles covering the precedence of Community law over domestic law:

> The member states take all necessary general or specific measures for the execution of obligations arising from the present Treaty or resulting from the acts of Community institutions. They assist the Community in achieving its objectives and refrain from all measures likely to prevent the achievement of the goals of the present Treaty. (Article 5)

The terms describing the role of the Court of Justice are equally vague:

> The Court of Justice ensures respect for the law in the interpretation and application of the present Treaty. (Article 164)

For the Community to function effectively, all member states have to accept the primacy of Community law. Any possibility for the government or legal authorities of member states to block or modify the application of Community law would have allowed member states to opt out of policies at their discretion. Hence in the very first cases concerning the hierarchy of Community and national laws, the ECJ strongly asserted the primacy of Community law. In the Costa *v.* ENEL case of 1964, it ruled:

> By creating a Community of limited duration, with its own institutions, its own legal personality, its own legal right of representation at the international level, and more particularly, real powers stemming from a limitation of sovereignty, or a transfer of powers from their states to the Community, the member states

have limited their sovereign rights, albeit within restricted fields, and have thus created a body of law which binds both their individual citizens and themselves.

In the Simmenthal *v.* Commission case in 1978, its ruling was even more precise:

> Every national court must, in a case within its jurisdiction, apply Community law in its entirety and protect rights which that law confers on individuals, and must accordingly set aside any provision of national law which may conflict with it, whether prior or subsequent to the Community rule.

Inevitably, conflicts have arisen in the domestic courts of most member states, including France, over this supremacy of Community law. One distinctive feature in France was that the period of the building up of legislation from the Community coincided with the time when the established domestic hierarchy of legal norms was itself changing as a consequence of the change of regime in 1958.

The constitutional change in 1958 marked a real shift in French law. The Constitution of the Fourth Republic recognized the supremacy of parliament, and Article 91 created a constitutional committee to examine whether new laws implied revision of the Constitution. In short, if that Constitution set down 'rules of the game', those rules were changeable. The most recent statutes always had precedence over their predecessors. The 1958 Constitution, however, established a whole new hierarchy of laws. At the summit was constitutional law and Title 7 created a new body, the Constitutional Council, to decide whether laws voted by parliament were constitutional. The council could annul clauses, or indeed an entire law, if it judged it unconstitutional. Furthermore, the Constitution set limits on the domain of law-making by parliament (Article 34). Finally, Article 55 classified treaties in an intermediate category, between constitutional law and statute law, stipulating that treaties were to have priority over national law, although the Constitution did not make clear how Article 55 was to be enforced.

The council was very slow to show any teeth in its role of constitutional review, and it was not until 16 July 1971 that it annulled any law. Its inability to intervene resulted partly from the definition of its role, and partly from the fact that it could only rule on those laws which were referred to it, and until 1974, only the president, the prime minister and the presidents of the two houses of parliament had the right to make referrals. In 1974, however, the Constitution was amended to allow any group of 60 deputies or senators to refer laws to the council. The consequence of the amendment has been a rapid growth of constitutional review cases at the council.

In two of these cases, however, the council has given rulings that it is incompetent to deal with challenges to constitutionality based on Article 55, of laws which are contrary to treaties. In the first case, concerning the 1975 law legalizing abortion (the decision 74-54-DC, 15 January 1975), it ruled that it was not competent to control the principle of the legal primacy of treaties; the fact that a law is contrary to a treaty is not in itself sufficient grounds for judging it contrary to the Constitution. This judgment provoked some controversy, since it implied that the highest constitutional authority in France had chosen to ignore an article of the Constitution. Many jurists disagreed, and argued that the logic of Article 55 was that treaties should be recognized as having 'constitutional value' (Vedel and Delvolvé, 1990, p. 68). In a subsequent decision, however, the council, consulted on the constitutionality of the 1986 law on entry and residency of foreigners (decision 86-216-DC, 3 September 1986) clearly announced that its own incapacity to enforce respect for Article 55 did not mean that French authorities could ignore the precedence of treaties over statute laws; rather, it expected that other 'appropriate institutions' would ensure that Article 55 was respected.

The council, however, did have a role to play in ensuring that the Constitution did not conflict with the European treaties. Hence, in 1976, Giscard d'Estaing requested the Council's preliminary advice on the constitutionality of the decision of the council of ministers of the Community to establish direct elections to the EP. Later, the Council was asked by Mitterrand to give preliminary advice about the constitutionality of the SEA and the TEU, before the bills for their ratification were presented. In the first two cases, its positive opinions effectively prevented any referral by critics of the ratification bills to the Constitutional Council. In the last case, it provided details of how the Constitution should be changed to allow the ratification to take place. The government responded by calling the Versailles Congress of both houses of parliament in late June 1992 to change the Constitution, as prescribed, ahead of the treaty ratification by referendum in September.

There are two appropriate institutions which the Constitutional Council expects to play a key role in ensuring respect for European laws: the Court of Cassation (*Cour de Cassation*), the supreme court for all criminal and civil cases, and the Council of State, in its judicial role as the supreme court for all cases over state actions and decisions within the domain of administrative law. The latter is of particular importance, given its responsibility for judging the legality of all delegated legislation made by the executive. Furthermore, as noted above, the 1958 Constitution increased the government's competence to make delegated legislation. Actions taken by public authorities under all forms of delegated legislation may be challenged on the grounds of legality at the Council of State.

Initially, the Council of State and the Court of Cassation took very different approaches. In a celebrated decision in 1975, concerning the firm Cafés Jacques Vabre, the Court of Cassation accepted both its own competence to reach judgments in this area and the primacy of the EEC Treaty over national law. Indeed, it ruled that: 'the legal order created by the EEC Treaty is directly applicable to the nationals of member states and is binding on their tribunals and courts'.

The Council of State, however, in 1968 (in the case of the *Syndicat général des fabricants de semoule*) reached a very different conclusion: that its own competence did not extend to making rulings on conflicts between international law and domestic law (despite Article 55). It therefore determined that in this conflict between an EC regulation and a subsequent French law it could not over-rule the law voted by parliament. Thus in practice, the key judicial body in France which might have been expected to enforce respect for the Treaty of Rome ruled that it had no authority so to do. Again, in 1979, it ruled that the administrative judge did not possess jurisdiction to appraise the constitutionality and the conformity of a law with a treaty (22 October 1979, in the case of the *Union Démocratique du Travail*).

It took the Council of State many years explicitly to reverse its decision, a reversal that was achieved only as a consequence of a series of small steps relating to particular cases. One step was its ruling in the Cohn Bendit case which provided individuals with several legal methods for obtaining the application of Community directives, and notably for challenging the legality of national secondary legislation taken to implement a directive. In December 1981, in the case of the *Syndicat National de la Chaussure*, it ruled that the priority of the EC Treaty over an earlier decree must be enforced and in 1982 (the case of the *Conseil de Paris; ordre des experts comptable*) it admitted the precedence of the EC Treaty over a previously enacted law. Then in two cases in 1984, the council acknowledged the precedence of EC directives over subsequent French decrees (the case of the *Confédération Nationale des Sociétés de Protection des Animaux de France* and the *Fédération Française des Sociétés de Protection de la Nature*).

The next step was the Danielou case in 1987, by which the precedence of an EEC regulation over a previously enacted law was upheld. Then on 20 October 1989 came the Nicolo case, where the legal superiority of the EC Treaty over a subsequent law was recognized. Almost at the same time, in the Alitalia case, the Council of State acknowledged that a directive prevails over an earlier French decree. Finally, in 1990, it reversed its 1968 decision by admitting and thus enforcing the pre-eminence of an EC regulation over a subsequent law (the Boisdet case, 24 September 1990).

In theory, however, this process of aligning French administrative law with European law has neither raised EC law to the status of constitutional law nor has it denied national sovereignty. Some lawyers point out that whereas the Constitutional Council can annul a law, the Council of State simply suspends or removes its effects, and they conclude that if France decided to leave the EU all such suspended legislation would immediately become applicable (unless of course it had been changed by parliament). In practice, however, this theory has no immediate effects.

Conclusions

Over almost five decades since the Treaty of Paris, few institutions of government in France have escaped some modification to deal with European policy processes. The political executive, parliament, the administration and the courts have all been affected by processes of Europeanization, but the French record of institutional adaptation is patchy. In many ways this reflects the ambiguity of governmental approaches to making and implementing European policies. De Gaulle's insistence that the EEC was merely an international organization has left a legacy, despite the development of 'joint domestic' policies in many areas. The growth of Community competence and intergovernmental agreements between the 15, the development from European political co-operation to common foreign and security policy, the adoption of QMV in the council of ministers, the recognition of the European Council in the SEA, and the provisions for EMU and the 'third pillar' in the TEU have all inspired waves of institutional modifications.

The co-ordination of French inputs into EU negotiations is a multi-layered process which works when all the actors know who is responsible for what. Presidential co-ordination and arbitration deal with institutional developments, international policies, and intergovernmental co-operation between the 15. The prime minister may be called upon to resolve Community matters which have not been sorted out through the SGCI. The SGCI deals with established, ongoing Community policies, from annual farm price reviews to complex competition directives.

The processes of institutional adaptation to deal with EU membership have brought about shifts in the balance of power within the French state. These shifts of power, however, are complex and constantly evolving. Parliament, for example, whose influence on the treaties was considerable under the Fourth Republic, has had virtually no say in European policy-making since 1958, although the 1992 constitutional changes offer the possibility of playing a more active role. The courts, in contrast, and in particular the Council of State, after initially refusing to participate in the Europeanization process, have recently carved themselves an influential position. Ironically, they have achieved this by admitting the existence of an EU legal order, and thus have contributed to the legitimation of the ECJ. Attempts to identify institutional 'winners' and 'losers' are thus misleading.

Although institutional adaptation is far more coherent and effective on the input side than on the output side, the multi-layered distribution of roles does not always work in practice. The president sometimes 'calls up' files which would normally be dealt with at lower levels, and may then impose decisions, thereby curtailing normal processes of conflict resolution. prime ministers may sometimes refer decision on Community matters to the president to ensure that there is no conflict between what is decided within the Community and what is decided intergovernmentally. In rare cases ministers may ask the president to intervene. In normal circumstances, however, the imposition of decisions on Community matters is exceptional; the great majority of positions for negotiations in Brussels are agreed in interministerial discussions under the SGCI. Finally, the key French actors in Brussels have remained the foreign affairs minister, the permanent representative and his deputy, all diplomats, trained to find compromises, while most of those in Paris who co-ordinate negotiating positions for the Brussels team are from 'domestic' ministries, whose goals are to find best practices and policies. The match between the two does not always work.

3

Parties and Public Opinion

The European dimension has become increasingly important in the organization and articulation of political interests in the domestic arenas of the member states of the European Union. While the growth of transnational parties and interest groups has been much slower than some of the founding fathers of the Community had anticipated, the scope and reach of EU legislation mean that it is now impossible for political leaders and parties to ignore the European dimension. In France this increasing Europeanization has meant that parties and leaders have not only had to define their positions on European issues more clearly but also had to make a strategic shift in the way they try to appeal to the electorate. This adaptation has been difficult, particularly for right-wing parties, which traditionally have used the concept of a strong and independent France as a rallying cry. The increasing politicization of the European issue has also polarized public attitudes towards the EU; this in turn has renewed inter-and-intra party debate. Furthermore, the issue of the future development of the EU has increasingly divided parties since the early 1990s and the issue has the potential to cause a new cleavage in the party system (Guyomarch, 1995). This chapter assesses the ways in which the European issue has become much more important for parties and for public opinion since the mid-1980s. It then analyses party positions on Europe and considers the extent and nature of public debate over the European issue and the implications of these changes for party politics.

The party debate over Europe

The issue of France's role in the process of European integration has varied in its importance for political parties during the post-war period. In the early 1950s there was considerable inter-party conflict over France's membership of the ECSC, the proposed EDC and the setting up of the EEC. However, once the shape of the EEC and its institutions had been established, the issue of Europe became a more tacit one. With the exception of the French Communist Party (PCF) most parties broadly accepted the dominant Gaullist view that membership of the EEC brought considerable economic, political and strategic benefits to France. There were some policy differences among the parties about how the EEC should develop, with the centrists favouring the most rapid and far-reaching extension of Community competences and the development of strong Community institutions and the conservatives expressing reluctance about transferring political sovereignty to European bodies. The European issue became important in the early 1960s and central in the first direct election of the presidency in 1965 when Jean Lecanuet, a Christian Democrat, challenged de Gaulle largely on the issue of de Gaulle's nationalistic stance towards Europe. However, membership of the EC was widely viewed by the public as being beneficial to France, so there was little electoral advantage to be gained by parties in opposing the Community.

From the mid-1980s the European issue has become increasingly significant for domestic parties. The pace of integration and the increasing scope and importance of EU policies in areas such as trade, economic policy, industrial policy, regional policy, immigration and the environment have meant that parties can no longer afford to ignore the European dimension in their programmes. The question of Europe has become a 'position issue' among the parties. Butler and Stokes [1969] used their term 'position issue', on which parties may appeal to rival bodies of voters, in contrast to 'valence issues' where there is one body of opinion on values and goals. (See also the discussion in Campbell H. *et al.* (1969).) The European issue has increasingly shaped the internal dynamics of the major parties and has affected alliance strategy between them. As parties have taken increasingly public stances on the EU, the traditional, but largely tacit, differences among and within them over Europe have come to the surface. Parties can be divided along two axes:

- between those which favour a weaker intergovernmental Europe and those which want a more politically integrated Europe;
- between those which want a free market, deregulated Europe and those which would prefer an interventionist and protectionist EU. (Gamble [1993] broadly uses this distinction in his analysis of attitudes towards Europe in the British Conservative Party.)

There are a number of interrelated reasons for the heightened level of party debate over Europe in the 1980s and 1990s. Firstly, the growing salience of Europe as an issue of partisan divide is to a large extent due to the renewed impetus in European integration since the mid-1980s. The adoption of the SEA in 1987 made important changes to the Community's decision-making procedures and laid out a programme for the completion of the Single European Market (SEM). The moves towards the completion of the internal market by the end of 1992 gave rise to pressures for further integration in the fields of economic and monetary policy, with proposals being put forward for the introduction of a single currency as a necessary complement to the internal market. At the same time, the 'social dimension' of the Community was reinforced in order to counter some of the negative effects of the single market (Mutimer 1989); proposals were made under the Social Charter to develop a Community Social Policy and to restructure and reinforce the cohesion fund.

The internal market programme, based on the removal of all fiscal, physical and technical barriers to trade, threatened traditional French *dirigisme* and protectionism by opening up French financial markets. Although these policies were in line with some of the neo-liberal economic reforms which had already been made both by the Mitterrand presidency and the Chirac government, their range and scope proved disconcerting for parties which were used to operating in a political system where the state had historically played a key role in the regulation of the market and in directing industrial policy. The extension of Community competences in economic and social policy stimulated a public debate in France between, and within, right and left about whether the Community should develop into a large free market or whether it should be regulatory and protectionist. These differences appeared clearly in the 1994 Euro-elections: the official Socialist list, the Communists, the dissident Socialist (Tapie) list and the Greens all argued that the EU should fund public investment programmes; the UDF–RPR list favoured a market solution by proposing that the EU should introduce legislation to reduce the cost of employing people for firms; extreme nationalists such as the *Front National* wanted French markets to be protected at all costs.

A second reason for the growing salience of the European issue in French politics was the challenge to the European security framework in the post-1989 period. The collapse of the Eastern bloc regimes in 1989 and the subsequent unification of Germany gave an added impetus to the integration process. The new defence and security questions confronting Europe following the end of the second Cold War led to demands for Europe to move forward in developing its own common foreign and security policy. As will be seen in Chapter 4, German unification and its implications for both France and Europe became a key issue in French political debates. By the end of the 1980s, Community enlargement was once again on the agenda, with applications from the EFTA states and from Central and East European states, and domestic political elites had to position themselves on this issue. In the 1994 Euro-elections most parties favoured enlargement to Central and Eastern Europe, although the more federalist groupings, such as Tapie's list and the *Parti Socialiste*, were concerned that the proposed widening of the EU should not slow down its political development. Predictably, the only party to oppose any form of enlargement was the *Front National*, which was fearful about the decline of French 'cultural distinctiveness' within a wider Europe and about the likely increase in immigration. Though public opinion in France also welcomed enlargement, there were some fears that in an enlarged EU the role of Germany would be enhanced while France would risk a relative weakening of its position.

The extension of the EC policy competences and the prospect of enlargement produced a renewed impetus at the end of the 1980s for political reform of the EC's institutions (Nugent, 1993). There was considerable pressure to increase the powers of the EP in order to counter the growing democratic deficit and to enhance the role of the European Commission in order to maintain the pace and scope of the integration process. The nature of the EC institutional and political development was an issue which had considerable potential for creating divisions in France between those political forces which favoured a more supranational Community and those wishing to retain the Gaullist view of a '*Europe des Etats*'. These partisan divisions on the EU's institutional development emerged clearly in the 1994 elections to the EP. The most federalist list, that of Tapie, championed a substantial increase in the powers of the EP and the direct election of a president of the EU; the Socialists supported greater powers for the EP and an extension of qualified majority voting in the Council of Ministers. The official UDF–RPR list favoured a more intergovernmental approach with slightly increased powers being given to the EP (to be counter-balanced by more control of the EP by the French National Assembly) and proposals that the European Commission should be jointly controlled by the EP, the European Council and the Council of Ministers. This list was outflanked by the nationalist list, *Union pour la France*, led by the UDF dissident, Philippe de Villiers, which favoured the EU as a loose association of states which would not threaten the primacy of the French Parliament. The Communists and the *Front National* shared this perspective on institutional development and vigorously opposed any further powers being granted to the EP.

Another reason for the increasing politicization of the European issue at a national level was that the arena for debating the European issue had become more public. By 1995, four direct elections to the EP had taken place and these had become institutionalized in the French electoral cycle. As in the other member states, Euro-elections became an arena for testing the strength of national parties and domestic governments. In the French case Euro-elections are often strongly influenced by the presidential context: for instance, the 1994 campaign was a pre-run for possible contenders for the 1995 presidential elections. The poor performance of the Socialist Party list under the leadership of Michel Rocard was one of the contributory factors in ending Rocard's chances of becoming a future presidential candidate and it also precipitated his removal from the post of secretary general of the party.

Although national issues tended to be the decisive factor in the outcome of Euro-elections, each party contesting the elections has to delineate its position on European issues. The party lists presented at Euro-elections tend to mirror national alliances, but they also can reflect divisions within those alliances (see Table 3.1). For example, the UDF–RPR list presented at the 1984, 1989 and 1994 EP elections reflected the coalition strategy of the conservatives during that period. At the same time, splinter groups from within the coalition exploited the opportunity presented by the Euro-elections to mount a challenge to their rivals. The centrist CDS fielded a separate list in 1989, under Simone Veil, and the nationalist faction headed by de Villiers capitalized on their near victory in the 1992 Maastricht Referendum campaign and stood as a separate party list in the 1994 Euro-

TABLE 3.1

Results of votes in Euro-elections in France 1979–94

Results in percentages	1979(1)	1984(2)	1989(3)	1994(4)
Communists	20.42	11.20	8.12	6.88
Socialists and Left Wing	23.42	24.17	23.61	29.06
Radicals			(Tapie List 12.03)	
Gaullists	16.24	UDF-RPR 42.73		Villiers(4) 25.58
Giscardiens	27.87		28.87 Veil-Centrist 8.42	12.33
Extreme Right		11.07	11.73	10.51
Extreme Left	3.06	3.73	2.02	2.70
Ecologists	4.38	3.42	10.59	Les Verts 2.95 / Génération-Ecologie 2.01
Others (including CPNT(5))	4.65	3.71	6.57 (CPNT 4.13)	7.90 (CPNT 3.95)

(1) Figures from Julian Crandall Hollick, 'The European Election in France: A Masked Ball for 1981', *Parliamentary Affairs*, vol. 32, no. 4, p. 467.

(2) Figures adapted from Jean and Monica Charlot, 'France', *Electoral Studies*, vol. 3, no. 3, December 1984, p. 277.

(3) Figures adapted from *Le Monde*, 15 June 1994.

(4) De Villiers stood on a nationalist ticket: *Majorité pour une autre Europe*.

(5) CPNT stands for *Chasse, Pêche, Nature et Tradition*.

elections. The system of proportional representation used in France for the Euro-elections often makes this 'go-it-alone' strategy pay off. It also means that EP elections facilitate the entry of new parties into the political system. For example, the *Front National* used the 1984 Euro-election to consolidate the electoral success it had achieved in the previous year in local elections and to legitimize itself as a national party. The Greens also used the 1989 and 1994 EP elections as a sounding board for their policies and to build their credibility; unfortunately for the Greens, splits over attitudes to the EU contributed to dissent within the movement and led to two lists, *Les Verts* and *Génération Ecologie*, standing for the 1994 election.

Once elected, parties in the EP are highly fragmented, with the six French party lists represented in eight European groupings. This fragmentation is particularly evident on the right where, following the 1994 elections, 14 Gaullists, along with the Irish Fianna Fáil, Greek nationalists and Portuguese centrists formed the European Democratic Alliance group in the EP. The 13 UDF MEPS (largely from the CDS) participate along with other Christian Democrats in the European People's Party, and one UDF member sits in the Liberal Democrat and Reformist group. De Villiers' *Autre Europe* group, which included Sir James Goldsmith, has joined forces with four Danish anti-marketeers and two Dutch members to form the 'Europe of the Nations' group. Members of Le Pen's 'Europe of the Right' group, established after the 1989 elections, did not find enough support to form a parliamentary group and sat as independents. On the left, the Communists sat with their Spanish, Greek, Italian and Portuguese counterparts in the Confederal Group of the European United Left, and the 15 Socialists formed part of the largest Party of European Socialists grouping. Bernard Tapie's Radical Alliance, which gained an impressive 13 members, combined with two Scottish Nationalists, two Italian radicals, and one Flemish and one Spanish regionalist to form a new group, the European Radical Alliance. This group supports moving towards a federal Europe and is part of the 'progressive left'; however, for strategic reasons it wishes to remain distinct from the socialist grouping.

The *potential* role for party groups within the EU has become greater because the EP has steadily been accruing powers (Jacobs *et al.*, 1995). Initially, these were in the area of budgetary control, but since the SEA the EP has become more closely involved in the decision-making process within the EU. The new co-operation procedure gave the EP more powers in the legislative process, by providing it with the opportunity of a second reading of Council legislation. This was further strengthened under the TEU's co-decision procedure, which gave the EP the right to modify policy initiatives coming from the European Commission where these modifications were supported by a majority of members of the EP. The effect of these two procedures has been to draw the EP more centrally into the policy-making process of the EU, and, since the early 1990s, there has been a greater degree of inter-institutional bargaining, both between the European Commission and the EP and to ensure that policy initiatives are not rejected by the EP. All this has meant that the party groups in the EP are becoming more closely involved in the policy-making process. It is possible that in the future party activity in the EP may become an increasingly important factor in shaping domestic alliances.

The final factor which helped to crystallize party positions on Europe was the public debate in France over the adoption of the Treaty on European Union. The decision by President Mitterrand to put the Maastricht Treaty to a national referendum in September 1992 led to an intense level of conflict both within and among the parties. Mitterrand's key motive in calling the referendum was to expose divisions on the right over the issue of further integration and to bolster his own personal standing, but the referendum campaign took on its own momentum and triggered one of the first real debates in France on European integration. As Meunier-Aitsahalia and Ross (1993, p. 57) commented, 'it clarified the controversy between the economic and political nature of the EC, and provided for a moment of collective reflection on the issues of identity and belonging'.

For the first time since the discussions over the setting up of the EDC in 1952–4, French parties were able to seize the opportunity to shape the debate about the future of Europe. Most importantly, the referendum campaign brought into sharp focus the differences between, on the one hand, the 'integrationalists', consisting of a large part of the Socialist Party, the majority of the UDF and around half of the RPR, who supported the strengthening of the political powers of the EU and its institutions; and, on the other, the 'nationalists' consisting of the *Front National*, the PCF, a considerable minority of the RPR, and a few dissident UDF MPs who wanted to ensure that the powers of the EU would be curtailed and that it would continue to be a '*Europe des patries*'. The debate polarized public opinion and created lasting and bitter divisions within the parties over future European strategy. The issue of Europe remained at the heart of political debate in 1993 during the negotiations of the GATT Round, and in the 1994 Euro-election campaign. However, the European issue did not figure prominently in the 1995 presidential election campaign, in part because two of the leading contenders, Chirac and Balladur, were wary of opening up divisions among their potential supporters, and in part because de Villiers lacked presidential stature.

The circumstances of the 1997 general elections meant that some discussion of European issues during the campaign was inevitable; in practice, however, that discussion was often confusing and sometimes confused. The election result, in consequence, was not a clear indicator of the state of French public opinion about the EU. President Chirac dissolved the National Assembly 10 months before the end of its normal five-year term, with the declared intention of obtaining a mandate for his government to pursue its policies of the economic recovery of the country. He admitted that tough decisions had to be made, notably to ensure that France would respect the convergence criteria of the TEU and thus qualify on time as a founder member of the single currency. Until the first ballot, on 25 May, the centre-right campaign was led by Juppé and many concluded that Chirac intended Juppé to remain as prime minister and to make the austere spending cuts needed to reduce the current account deficit below the 3 per cent convergence criterion. After the first ballot result Juppé resigned as candidate to replace himself as prime minister, but Chirac added to the confusion by not naming a replacement. Although the National Front campaigned vigorously against austerity measures and the entire Maastricht Treaty, other opposition parties were much more circumspect, especially when the opinion polls showed that they had very real chances of ousting the RPR–UDF coalition. In particular, the PS platform included both support for the Euro and plans for increased public expenditure to create jobs (which clearly implied that the 3 per cent deficit criterion would not be respected). Even the Communists and Ecologists focused their campaigns more on job creation than on criticisms of the EU. The victory of the centre-left coalition led to the appointment of Jospin as prime minister and a coalition government of Socialists, Greens and Communists. From the outset the European issue produced tensions not only between Chirac and Jospin but within the governing coalition, with the left-wing arguing against cutbacks in public expenditure and the centre-right emphasizing the need to meet the Maastricht criteria.

The development of party positions on Europe

The Centrists

The MRP (and its *Force Democrate* heirs) shared with its sister Christian Democratic parties a genuine enthusiasm for, and commitment to, the rebuilding of Europe after the Second World War (Burgess, 1990). This Europeanism stemmed from a philosophy founded on the ideals of integration and co-operation at all levels of society, a belief that the EEC would best serve the interests of France economically and politically and the conviction that an integrated Europe would be a barrier against Communism. Many of the politicians instrumental in setting up the ECSC and the EEC were Christian Democrats; Robert Schuman, for example, was an MRP statesman of international standing. The party was a vital coalition partner in most of the governments of the Fourth Republic and, together with the Socialists, it provided the necessary parliamentary support for setting up of the ECSC, the EEC and Euratom.

Under the Fifth Republic the centrists have continued to be enthusiastic pro-Europeans, pressing for further development of the EC through an extension of its policy competences and a strengthening of its institutions. The influence of the centrists on policy-making has, however, declined dramatically since 1958; five MRP ministers formed part of the first Gaullist government, but resigned in April 1962 over de Gaulle's negative attitude to the EEC. Thereafter, the centrists went into opposition where they remained until de Gaulle's resignation in 1969. In the December 1965 Presidential election, de Gaulle, who had assumed that his own re-election on the first ballot would be automatic, was challenged by the hitherto unknown Christian Democrat candidate, Jean Lecanuet. After a campaign which almost entirely focused on the benefits of European integration, Lecanuet scored 15.8 per cent on the first ballot and forced de Gaulle into a humbling second ballot. Lecanuet reorganized his supporters into a new party, the *Centre Democrate*, and placed the European issue at the centre of its political agenda. After a poor showing in the 1967 legislative elections the party went into opposition. However, Giscard d'Estaing's enthusiasm for Europe in the 1974 presidential election encouraged all the Christian Democrats, re-united as the CDS, to return to the government. The *Centre des Démocrates Sociaux* (CDS), created in May 1976 from the old *Centre*

Democrate and the *Centre Democrate et Progrès* has participated in the conservative UDF coalition since 1978 and has consistently tried to pull the UDF in a pro-European direction.

In 1995 the CDS renamed itself *Force Démocrate* (FD), and now forms part of the Christian Democrat European People's Party in the EP, which has always placed a strong emphasis on Community-wide social policies and more recently on European citizenship. Since the mid-1980s their leaders have argued consistently that the completion of the internal market should be accompanied by the development of social policies and the protection of workers' rights. The issue of Europe has been one of the main tensions for the FD within the UDF. This is exacerbated because the UDF is part of a wider conservative coalition with the more nationalist Gaullists.

The contradiction for the FD is demonstrated by its electoral strategies. Though the FD supported the UDF–RPR in the 1984 Euro-elections, it formed a separate list under Simone Veil in 1989, arguing strenuously for a social dimension to Europe and for a new European Union Treaty to achieve Political Union before the year 2000. After the 1988 French legislative elections the centrists separated from the UDF to form a distinct parliamentary group, the UDC. On European questions the Governments of Rocard, Cresson and Bérégovoy could all rely on the UDC for support in the National Assembly. During the Maastricht referendum debate the party was one of the most vociferous supporters for the ratification of the treaty. In the 1994 Euro-elections it once again became part of the official centre–right party list headed by Dominique Baudis.

The conservatives

The Gaullist Party, formed in 1947 to provide the necessary electoral and political support for General de Gaulle, espoused its leader's commitment to the nation state and to establishing a strong independent France on the world stage. The party shared de Gaulle's opposition to the ECSC (described by de Gaulle as a directionless 'mish-mash') and to any moves towards developing a federal Europe which would inhibit France's capacity to take independent political decisions. In 1954, Gaullist opposition in the National Assembly helped to defeat the EDC, defined by de Gaulle as 'a crafty scheme for a so-called European army which threatens to put an end to France's sovereignty'. The Gaullists also voted against the EEC and the Euratom Treaties in 1957.

However, back in power in 1958 de Gaulle realized the positive benefits which membership of the EEC could bring to France and his position of ideological opposition towards the Community changed to one of pragmatic acceptance. The Community became the focus for two important and interrelated policy objectives – strengthening France's role in the world and modernizing the French nation. In the early years of the Fifth Republic the Gaullist Party followed de Gaulle's line on Europe; it favoured French military autonomy and after 1963 an independent nuclear strike force but it also perceived the support which the Community could bring France in foreign affairs. While de Gaulle acknowledged the economic benefits of the Community for France, he was profoundly opposed to Monnet's vision of European integration and was keen to rid the Community of its supranational elements. For de Gaulle, the EC should be no more than an association of sovereign states. His views on the French nation and on the quintessential importance of national identity meant that he was deeply sceptical about any development towards a fully integrated supranational Europe. This policy was fervently supported by the Gaullist party, which gave the president unequivocal support in his handling of the Luxembourg crisis in 1965–6. The Gaullists inherited from this period a preference for an intergovernmental Europe with weak central institutions and a limited range of policies, such as external trade, agriculture and aid policy.

Although the ideas of de Gaulle came to underpin Gaullist Party policy, in the 30 years since his departure the Gaullist Party has became more pragmatic in its European policy. In fact, even during de Gaulle's leadership the political rhetoric of the president disguised a basic underlying acceptance of the benefits of European integration for France. Under the Pompidou presidency the party adopted a more outwardly conciliatory and less isolationist approach to the EC. It supported the new president's initiative to bring the UK into the Community and his vigorous pursuance of EMU. This apparent shift in support for new initiatives disguised undercurrents of divisions within the party between the nationalists, led by Debré, and the pro-Europeanists. Under the presidency of Giscard d'Estaing the influence of the Gaullist Party inevitably declined, although (re-formed as the RPR in 1976) it continued to resist any further institutional development of the Community. The Gaullist prime minister, Jacques Chirac, resigned in July 1976, giving as a public reason his opposition to Giscard d'Estaing over direct elections to the EP (in reality there were a large number of policy differences and personality clashes between the two leaders). The Gaullists were unenthusiastic about the institutional reforms proposed in the Tindemans Report (1976) and in the Genscher–Colombo proposals (1981) which were designed to give greater powers to the EP and to the Commission. The nationalistic flavour of the Gaullist approach to the Community can also be seen in the list they presented at the first direct elections to the EP in 1979 – *Défense des intérêts de la France en Europe* (DIFE). In these elections Chirac tried to gain ground from the Giscardians on the issue of French 'self-determination' in Europe. However, as Shields (1996) argues, this strategy was misplaced, with the Giscardian UDF list easily outstripping the Gaullist list. Chirac recognized that this fervent anti-Europeanism did not capture the mood of the public and proceeded to construct alliances with the UDF for the 1984 and 1989 Euro-elections. One of the consequences of this strategy was that the *Front National* was able to capitalize on the 'nationalist vote'.

Though the RPR had reservations about the institutional develop- ment of the Community, it supported various EC initiatives designed to strengthen the EC's economic and industrial bases. The conversion of some sections of the party to economic liberalism in the early 1980s meant that it was a keen supporter of the legislative programme for the completion of the internal market. Its position on other reforms and policy developments contained in the SEA was, however, more ambivalent. In particular, it expressed considerable reservations about the institutional reforms, such as the extension of majority voting in the Council of Ministers and the modest increases in power proposed for the Commission. However, by the time the ratification of the Treaty took place in 1986, the RPR was in government, and it reluctantly gave its support to the new treaty with only a few 'historic Gaullists' abstaining in the parliamentary vote.

By the end of the 1980s it had become clear that the completion of the internal market was creating pressures for the extension of the Community into new policy areas such as economic and monetary union and social policy. In addition, the moves towards the internal market produced renewed interest in Community membership from a number of EFTA countries. At the same time, the collapse of the Eastern bloc regimes raised the whole question of a wider EC to support the fledgling democracies. The Gaullists favoured the widen- ing of the Community to include countries of Eastern Europe but opposed the deepening of the Community (for a summary of this position see the Gaullist Party document '*un manifeste pour l'Union des*

Etats de l'Europe – appel au ralentissement de la construction européene, 5 December 1990). This opposition stemmed from two sources:

- the party opposed the strengthening of the Community institutions at the expense of the nation state;
- it believed that the extension of Community policies would set up insurmountable economic, political and legal obstacles for the potential new Community members.

Fears about the strengthening of the Community's powers and the growth of a 'technocratic superstate' were expressed by a significant number of nationalists on the right of the party. However, Chirac, the party leader, was reluctant to oppose publicly what appeared to be the pro-European consensus within the electorate.

The underlying divisions within the RPR over the development of the Community came to the fore in the bitter intra-party conflict which surrounded the ratification of the Maastricht Treaty in the summer of 1992. With legislative elections looming in the spring of 1993 the campaign was seen as a crucial test of the party's political standing and a test of the relative strength of key figures within the party. The Maastricht Treaty dealt with sensitive issues, such as European citizenship and the establishment of a common currency, and these caused division within the RPR–UDF coalition and within the RPR itself because they brought to the surface underlying tensions within the Gaullists about nationhood and the powers of the state. Of particular concern to many Gaullists were the constitutional changes proposed in the TEU, most especially the introduction of the right for any EC national to vote in local elections in the country of residence. This proposal took on a special significance in France because the Senate is indirectly elected by local authorities. Another worry for the anti-Maastricht lobby within the party was the extension of the powers of the Community into the fields of justice and immigration.

During the referendum on the ratification of Maastricht, two prominent Gaullists, Philippe Séguin and Charles Pasqua led the No campaign, which not only brought together nationalists but also revealed xenophobic tendencies within French politics (Criddle, 1993). The Gaullists within the No camp were at pains to stress that they were not opposed to the EC, but merely to those clauses in the TEU, such as that relating to the single currency, which limited the freedom of manoeuvre for national governments. The No group within the RPR also tried to capitalize on populist feeling by playing the anti-immigration card and by stressing the invidious centralizing tendencies of the European Commission. Jacques Chirac found himself in a difficult position: he undoubtedly had misgivings about the treaty and was sensitive to the traditional Gaullist electorate which had moved steadily to the right during the course of the campaign, but at the same time his presidential aspirations and the need to appeal beyond the party led him to support the treaty.

The impending presidential election in 1995 meant that for political and strategic reasons neither of the two main contenders wished to risk leading the right-wing list for the 1994 Euro-elections. Therefore, the RPR agreed that the UDF–RPR list should be headed by the pro-European Dominique Baudis and that the RPR should be a junior partner to the UDF. This deal was struck in return for UDF support in the forthcoming 1995 presidential elections. The significant policy differences among the mainstream right over the political development of the EU were largely hidden during the election campaign. This was also the case during the 1995 presidential election when the two Gaullist contenders, Balladur and Chirac, both took a very anodyne and low-key position on Europe and publicly agreed on major policy positions.

The non-Gaullist conservatives and liberal parties have, in general, been more pro-European in their outlook than de Gaulle's inheritors. Indeed, one of the issues which led Giscard d'Estaing in 1963 to form a distinct group, the Independent Republican Party, within the Gaullist majority was his disapproval of de Gaulle's European policy. During the 1960s and 1970s the Republicans were more favourable than the Gaullists to European co-operation and collaboration. As President, Giscard d'Estaing was very active in the European sphere, initiating the EMS in 1978 with Chancellor Helmut Schmidt and the formalization of the European Summits into the European Council in 1978. Giscard d'Estaing was keen to use the Community framework to develop a large number of industrial and economic projects, often in collaboration with the Federal Republic of Germany. When the Conservatives entered opposition in 1981 Giscard d'Estaing took up the issue of Europe more enthusiastically. The disparate nature of the Giscardian coalition, the UDF (formed in 1978 from a coalition of the Republican Party, the Radical Party and the centrists) inevitably meant that the federation has had to be more pragmatic than the more centralized RPR in its policies towards than EC. Though Giscard d'Estaing was able to present a clear vision of Europe for the UDF, he was not always able to deliver their support on all aspects of his European policy. Strands of opinion within the UDF ranged from the enthusiasm of the CDS for the rapid integration of the Community, to the selective support given by the neo-liberals within the UDF, who largely shared the Gaullists' view of the Community. Nevertheless, the official position of the UDF in the 1989 European elections was for stronger EC institutions, economic and monetary union and for further political union. In the Maastricht referendum debate the UDF initially tried to exploit the divided nature of the Gaullist Party and came out unequivocally in support of the ratification of the treaty. However, during the course of the campaign a nationalistic UDF Deputy, Philippe de Villiers, organized a No campaign from within the UDF. Like his Gaullist counterparts in the No campaign, de Villiers was against a federal Europe, but unlike them he opposed the unfettered free market principles of the EU and favoured a protectionist EU.

The more pro-European UDF was to provide the leader of the joint UDF–RPR list for the 1994 European elections. This was a tactical move on the part of the right to try to smooth over differences which had torn the right-wing apart during the Maastricht referendum debate (Gaffney, 1995). In the 1994 European elections, de Villiers headed a dissident UDF list, the *Mouvement pour la France*, and succeeded in winning 12.62 per cent of the poll. He also stood in the 1995 presidential elections, with the slogan '*Union pour la France*', campaigning again on the nationalist card, against the EU's policy of loosening immigration controls and against the Brussels bureaucracy. In June 1997, the Republican Party renamed itself as *Démocratie Libérale* and Alain Madelin, the leading neo-liberal, took over the party's presidency. The policy differences among the constituent parties within the UDF and the federal composition of the party means that without a strong leader, such as Giscard d'Estaing, it continues to be pulled in different directions over its European policy.

The Front National (FN)

The position of the FN on Europe has always been ambivalent. Paradoxically, the party's nationalism and chauvinism do not always extend to an explicit anti-Europeanism. On the one hand, the party believes that Europe as a whole suffers from the same threats as France – communism, socialism, unchecked immigration, a decline of moral and social values and the challenging of indigenous cultures –

and it argues that the EU can provide a useful framework to fight these common evils. On the other hand, the EU is seen as weakening the essential qualities of the French nation and disempowering the average French citizen.

The issue of Europe was not of central concern to the FN in the early 1980s. However, during the course of the decade the issue took on greater importance for the party leadership. A number of inter-related factors account for the party's growing preoccupation with Europe. Firstly, the policy of removing border controls between the member states (under the Schengen agreement) intensified the debate over immigration – a key element in the FN's platform. Secondly, the increasing intrusion of the Community into areas which had traditionally been the preserve of the nation state, such as monetary policy, helped to sharpen the sovereignty debate and the FN was able to capitalize on and exploit this issue. Thirdly, the FN perceived electoral advantages in playing the EU card; a considerable minority of the French public was in harmony with the party when it argued that the creeping centralization of the EC and the threatening advance of the Brussels bureaucracy disempowered the average French citizen.

Predictably, the party vehemently opposed the Maastricht Treaty and has, since the TEU referendum debate, shifted its position to one of more fervent anti-Europeanism (Fieschi *et al.*, 1996). Firstly, the party leader, Jean-Marie Le Pen opposed EMU claiming it would 'Threaten the French nation' and would lead to a 'globalist Europe' as opposed to a 'Europe of the Fatherlands'. Secondly, he argued that the principles of citizenship in the new treaty ran contrary to the 'principles of the Nation' and the 'laws of the Republic'. Finally, the party opposed the institutional reforms in the TEU, arguing that they would exacerbate the democratic deficit by widening the gap between French citizens and policy-makers. During the 1994 Euro-election, the party opposed the principle of the free movement of workers upheld by the EU, and it argued against any further enlargement of the EU. The growing powers of the EU and the worries of the French population over their loss of identity and the declining importance of the symbols of the state, such as national currency and national citizenship, under the TEU have been readily exploited by Le Pen and have helped to extend his support outside the immigration issue. During the 1995 presidential election campaign Le Pen argued vociferously for the protection of French interests within the EU, against the single currency and for the reestablishment of frontier controls on both produce and people. In the 1997 parliamentary election campaign the party tried to capitalize on the public's fears about the social and economic costs to the French nation of meeting the Maastricht convergence criteria.

The Socialist Party (PS)

The changing policy stances of the French Socialist Party towards Europe in the post-war period are, to a considerable extent, a reflection of the complex nature of internal party politics and the constraints of domestic political alliances. Until the 1980s the issue caused considerable division and dissent within the party (Featherstone, 1988). Once the PS entered office in 1981, party policy on Europe became more united around the Socialist government and the lead given by President Mitterrand. Nevertheless, ideological differences continued to surface from time to time over issues such as the institutional shape of the Community. In the early 1990s, as Mitterrand's influence and control over the party declined, the party became less committed to political integration and more critical of the social and economic costs of further integration.

Historically, the Socialists were internationalist in orientation and gave their support to organizations such as the League of Nations and the United Nations which sought to reconcile national differences. In the post-war period this internationalist outlook encouraged the party to support moves towards an integrated Europe (Cole, 1996). Nevertheless, the party always had a substantial minority of both deputies and activists who were opposed to European integration; this minority consisted of nationalists, pacifists, and left-wing socialists who took the view that the Community was a capitalist organization which would undermine the building of socialism in France.

During the Fourth Republic, the Socialist Party (the SFIO), under the leadership of Guy Mollet, was locked into a series of centrist coalitions. The centripetal pull of these coalitions and the dominance of social democrats within the party meant that it gave reserved support to Marshall Aid, NATO, the ECSC and the European Economic Community (Bell and Criddle, 1988). It was a government led by Mollet which agreed to the setting up of Euratom and the common market and was responsible for the signing of the Treaty of Rome. Mollet sought to reconcile the differences within the party by declaring that membership of the Community would help in the construction of socialism in France.

In the early years of the Fifth Republic the European policy of the Socialists vacillated in line with shifting domestic political alliances and internal party changes, and the party failed to develop any coherent strategy towards European integration. During the early 1970s, three distinct policy positions towards Europe emerged, each reflecting alternative conceptions of Socialism within the party:

- The left-wing faction CERES, led by Jean Pierre Chevènement, remained largely hostile both to the Community's further development and to its existing policies. In common with the French Communists, it argued that states needed to retain their independence in order to break with capitalism, and maintained that the free market institutions of the Community provided a haven for multinationals and thus impeded the economic road to socialism (Featherstone, 1988).
- At the other end of the party spectrum, the social democrat faction, led by Michel Rocard, believed that the European Community was an essential element of a Socialist agenda. The *Rocardians* stressed the importance of widening the French national market to the European Community, and argued that the EC provided an important arena for developing French socialism (for example, through the extension of workers' rights).
- An intermediate position, which can loosely be defined as the *Mitterrandistes*, maintained a more pragmatic stance.

Mitterrand himself had been a committed European since the mid-1950s but he was aware that he had to balance the pro-Community elements in the party with the nationalist ones in order to strengthen the middle ground and also to facilitate the Joint Programme of the Left which he had negotiated with the Communists in 1972. Therefore, though the Joint Programme stressed a commitment to Europe it also underlined the freedom of manoeuvre for the nation state to pursue its own political, economic and social programme. It was also critical of the undemocratic nature of the EC and of its capitalist tendencies. When the Joint Programme broke down in 1977, the formal position of the Socialist party towards Europe changed, and the party laid more stress on the need for the development of European social policy and common policies in key industrial sectors.

The relationship between France and Europe continued to be a source of tension with the PS during the early 1980s. The party's apparently ambiguous policy on Europe can largely be explained by the shifts in Mitterrand's positions on Europe and the complex interplay between party factions (Cole, 1996). The different positions within the party became more evident as the issues of Europe became inextricably linked with the direction of French economic policy. In 1981, Europe took a secondary place in the party's strategy for socialism. The 110 Propositions which formed the basis of Mitterrand's presidential platform contained only a fleeting mention of the PS's commitment to the democratization of the Community and to its social and industrial policy. The prevailing view in the party at this time was that the EC should be 'Socialist, or not at all'.

Initially, the Mitterrand administration elected in 1981 hoped that the rest of the Community would be persuaded to reflate their economies in line with the policies which were being pursued in France. However, it soon became clear that France would have to 'go it alone' in its socialist economic strategy, and if it chose to do so it would have to leave the EMS, devalue the franc and wage an export war with its trading partners in Europe. While the left of the party favoured this option, the majority were persuaded by Mitterrand to accept a 'U' turn in economic policy, which involved devaluing the franc, cutting back on public expenditure and introducing austerity measures to lift France out of the economic crisis which it was experiencing. These measures, which were seen as the 'European option', had the effect of pushing Europe to the core of Mitterrand's presidency.

The party, dependent on Mitterrand's own popular standing for electoral success, tended to follow his lead. Nevertheless, not all the party shared Mitterrand's vision of Europe. Both the national party organizations and Socialist MEPs were unenthusiastic about strengthening the Community's institutions. There was little support for the Draft Treaty on European Union from French Socialist MEPs when it was debated in the EP, with all except one MEP abstaining. The party's reluctance to see an increase in the powers of the EP and the Commission continued during the debate on institutional reform in the late 1980s and early 1990s. The French Socialists were out of line with their European counterparts at the special Rome conference of parliamentarians, in November 1990, when they voted against the proposed new power of co-decision between the EP and the Council of Ministers (Cole, 1996). The party maintained its reservations about strengthening the supranational institutions of the Community throughout the negotiations leading up to Maastricht Treaty.

This lack of enthusiasm for institutional reform was to some extent counter-balanced by the party's growing commitment during the 1980s to the idea of a Social Europe. The majority of the party favoured the strengthening of workers' rights at a European level in order to counter-balance the effects of the single market programme and gave support to the Social Charter, instigated by Jacques Delors, the former French socialist minister of Finance, and given political backing by President Mitterrand. Nevertheless, there were continuing strains between the party and the president in the early stages of the debate on the ratification of the Maastricht Treaty. Party leaders vigorously opposed the calling of a referendum, as they felt that it would inevitably damage the party in the run up to the legislative elections in spring 1993. However, during the referendum campaign the party was relatively united behind a 'Yes' vote, with only Chevènement's *Socialisme et République* (formerly CERES) faction opposing the ratification of the treaty, on the grounds that it threatened France's sovereignty and would lead to possible German dominance of the Community.

Party divisions continued into the 1994 Euro-election campaign. Bernard Tapie, a flamboyant and enthusiastic federalist, stood on a separate list (*Energie Radicale*) from the official Socialist Rocard and succeeded in gaining 12 per cent of the vote. Chevènement also stood separately on an anti-European ticket, *L'Autre Politique*, but his list won only 2.5 per cent of the vote. There was considerable tension and difficulties in drawing up the main Socialist list but this reflected competition among the party factions rather than any real policy differences over Europe. By 1995 divisions over Europe in the party were much less marked than within the conservative camp. Jospin, the PS candidate, capitalized on this during the 1995 presidential election campaign by attempting to project an image of himself as more pro-European than his rivals. Of those voting 'Yes' in the Maastricht Treaty referendum the largest percentage opted to support Jospin in the first round of the presidential elections. In the 1997 National Assembly election campaign Jospin played the European card to maximum advantage. On the one hand he gave support to the Euro and limited further political integration, but, on the other indicated his commitment to reducing unemployment both within France and in the EU. This emphasis on job creation was aimed at a public which was increasingly concerned about the domestic costs necessary to reach the convergence criteria for monetary union.

The Communist Party (PCF)

The PCF has maintained a consistently hostile view towards the EU. From the 1950s the party opposed the creation of any Community organization which would reinforce the division of Europe into two power blocs. In common with the Gaullists, the Communists were uncompromising and aggressive defenders of French interests across a range of policy matters – the CAP, direct elections, and enlargement – and opposed any changes which might limit French national sovereignty. Though by 1962 the majority of its voters were in favour of the EC, the party has consistently emphasized the capitalist aspects of the EC (which, it maintained, would become a haven for US multinational companies), and the damaging effect of the common market on workers' interests. In addition, the PCF has always held the view that the Community would interfere with any radical reforms which a government of the left might introduce – a view confirmed in the party's eyes by the experience of 1981–3, when pressures from Europe contributed to the reversal of the radical socialist programme.

Although the PCF has always been hostile to the EU, the intensity with which the issue has been fought has to some extent been determined by the nature of the coalition strategy with the Socialists. During the period of the Joint Programme of the Left (1972–7) the PCF made less play of its reservations about the Community. However, once the electoral pact with the Socialists had collapsed, the PCF returned to its traditional themes of nationalism and anti-capitalism. The party leaders fervently denounced the evils of the Maastricht Treaty, which it argued would exacerbate the damaging social effects of rampant economic liberalism. The PCF also made a great play in the referendum debate of the issue of national sovereignty. There were, however, dissenters from this position who argued for a more constructive criticism of European integration (Bell, 1996). Although the Maastricht Treaty debate exposed divisions within the PCF, it nevertheless gave them an opportunity to gain wider support for their nationalistic stance on the EU.

Public opinion

For most of the post-war period policies towards Europe have largely been driven by elites, with the public having little say at any stage in the policy-making process. Since the mid-1980s the French public, along with its counterparts across Western Europe, has become increasing vociferous about the integration process. There are a number of reasons for the increasing polarization of public attitudes towards the EU:

- There has been a huge increase in the volume and range of EU policies – this means that citizens are more likely to regard the EU on a 'salient issue' on their national political agendas (Anderson, 1995).
- The increasing powers granted to the EU under the SEA and TEU has provoked controversy both among parties and publics. In general there has been a trend of growing cynicism across the EU in the 1990s. As Anderson (1995, p. 112) observes,

> the 'permissive consensus' described by Lindberg and Schein-gold that seemed to characterize the interplay between European public opinion and elite action aimed at greater integration has become a more conscientious consensus and at times seems to have turned into a chorus of disharmony.

- In France the public (and parties) were able to voice this discontent because of Mitterrand's decision to ratify the Maastricht Treaty by referendum.

Since the European Union's inception the European Commission has regularly carried out surveys of European public opinion towards the EC in each member state. A number of key questions have been repeated in each of the Eurobarometer surveys: the perceived costs and benefits of membership, support for West European unification and general attitudes towards the Community. Some of the data need to be treated cautiously, since the questions may not adequately tap the complex 'attitude sets' regarding the Community. The polls are subject to fluctuations resulting from conjunctural factors – for example, the low levels of support for European integration during times of economic recession or the impact of particular policies on key sectors, such as the negative attitude of farmers towards the Community when the CAP appears to be under threat. European issues have tended to be rather remote from everyday concerns of publics, and in these circumstances the role of political elites is likely to be particularly important in shaping public attitudes.

In general terms, the original six members are consistently more *communautaire* than the later entrants. The correlation between long-evity of membership and a positive attitude from the public towards European integration is a good, though not perfect, indicator of public opinion (see Anderson, 1995). The French public shared the hopes and aspirations of the populations of the other five original members about the European Community bringing peace, security and economic prosperity to the European continent. Of the original six, however, French public opinion has historically been one of the least enthusiastic. At the same time, French attitudes towards the Community are still generally more positive than those expressed by the publics of later entrants. French public support for European unification (affective support) has vacillated over time, ranging from rather negative perceptions in the late 1950s and mid-1960s (at the time of the Luxembourg crisis and its aftermath), to a much more positive endorsement from the mid-1970s. The French public seem to favour the personalized diplomacy exercised by French politicians in the EC and consequently public opinion was shaped by the policy stances of key decision makers.

Many of the early Community policies, such as the CAP, which accounted for the largest part of Community expenditure, brought explicit economic benefits to the country, and in the 1950s and 1960s the EEC was equated with economic success in the eyes of the average citizen. This was reflected in the so-called 'utilitarian calculus' (namely an individual's perception of whether or not the Community benefits his or her country) where France consistently scored rela-tively highly. A closer analysis of French public opinion data reveals that, in line with other countries, people with higher incomes, professional occupations and higher education tend to express more favourable attitudes towards European integration. This was re-flected in the French vote on the Maastricht Treaty, where there was a strong correlation between higher income groups and those who had received higher education and positive support for further European integration; the only exception to this was the substantial number of professionals who were won over by de Villiers, the dissident UDF No campaigner.

The French public has had two opportunities to express opinion on the shape of the Community in national referenda. The first refer-endum was called by President Pompidou in April 1972, to endorse his policy of sanctioning the enlargement of the European Commu-nity to include the UK, Denmark, Ireland and Norway. In reality, the referendum was not significant in the enlargement of the Community; the Treaty of Enlargement had already been signed in January 1972 and the French parliament was certain to endorse it. Pompidou was using the referendum for political purposes:

- to demonstrate to traditional Gaullists that he was carrying out the will of the people;
- to contrast the unity of the Gaullist Party with the disunited left; and
- to bolster his own personal authority, both in France and within the European Community.

Although the referendum did show up divisions on the left between the Socialists and the Communists, who did not share a common attitude to Europe, the referendum was not really a success for Pompidou in terms of the other objectives: 40 per cent of the French electorate abstained; 36 per cent said **Yes** and 17 per cent said **No** to the enlargement; the campaign itself was lacklustre, as most people felt that the result was a foregone conclusion, and the experience did little to improve Pompidou's popularity with either the Gaullist Party or with the wider voting public.

By contrast, the second referendum, some 20 years later, on the ratification of the Maastricht Treaty provoked a much more lively debate. The ostensible purpose of the referendum in 1992 was to convince the electorate of the merits of integration in general and the TEU in particular, and to legitimate full French participation in the nascent EU. In reality, the referendum was called by Mitterrand to show up the disunity of the opposition on the European issue and to bolster his own personal authority both at home and within the EC. However, the referendum brought the European issue to the centre of political debate and provided an important test of French attitudes to the Community. The question posed in the referendum was specifically about the adoption of the TEU into the French Constitution. However, the campaign became centred around the pace and direction of European integration and about the capacity of the EC to deal with such issues as the Yugoslav crisis, the re-unification of Germany and the reform of the CAP. Domestic issues were also of significance. The unpopularity of the ageing president and his government and the lack of respect for and trust in political elites in general, after a decade marked by numerous corruption scandals, were two of these 'non-Maastricht' factors. The continuing high levels of unemployment and the risk of further job loses were clearly not consequences of the TEU, but the No campaign argued that, after ratification, governments would have no powers to take effective action to create jobs. There were also some worries in France (as in Denmark) about the possibility of further integration leading to a weaker social security system. Opinion polls have shown that for French voters social security is the policy area where joint decision is least wanted, as the national social security system has a high level of approval among ordinary citizens.

The widespread No voting of farmers expressed their hostility to the MacSharry reforms of the CAP rather than to the TEU. In a similar way, groups such as the pharmacists, who have long benefited from state-protected markets, had no desire to see the effects of free competition in the single market on their profit margins. Another No vote lobby was the movement 'Hunting, Fishing Nature and Tradition' (CPNT) which had won 4.13 per cent votes in the 1989 European elections (750 000 votes): its leaders expressed bitter hostility to the Brussels directive restricting the hunting of migrating birds (see 'Le Lobby des chasseurs contre l'Europe', *Le Monde*, 26 February 1992).

Many voters lacked party guidance in the campaign; while the PCF and the FN unequivocally opposed the TEU, the RPR, the UDF and the Ecologists were split, with large minorities supporting the No campaign. Confusingly for the public, many leaders of the No campaign (for example, the Gaullist Philippe Séguin) stressed their strong commitment to Europe alongside their rejection of the terms of the TEU. The Yes campaign centred around support from the political establishment with the Government, the bulk of the PS and the leaders of the RPR and UDF supporting the new Treaty.

The closeness of the vote, 51.01 per cent No to 48.98 per cent Yes, revealed that, to some extent, the generally favourable attitudes of the French to the EC masked some growing concerns about the nature of the EC. The No campaign successfully channelled these concerns by stressing that they were trying to preserve the interests of the average French person in an increasingly centralized and homogenized system. The referendum campaign demonstrated that French citizens were worried about the growing bureaucratization and centralization of the Community system, which appeared to many to mean the encroachment of seemingly petty Commission regulations on everyday life. For example, two vital symbols of the French way of life, unpasteurised cheese and the *Gitane* cigarette had recently come under threat from Community legislation! In addition, several well-publicized disputes such as the battle between the European Commission and Air France had heightened public awareness of the growing powers of European institutions. More substantial issues which exercised those supporting the No campaign were European citizenship, the establishment of a single currency and the fear of German domination of the Community.

Duhamel and Grunberg (*Le Monde*, 25 September 1992) identify the interplay of five cleavages:

1. They stress the importance of socio-economic cleavages with the Yes vote being predominantly urban, higher socio-economic groups and better educated. This is in line with SOFRES opinion polls, which consistently show that the higher the level of a person's education the more likely he or she is to perceive positive benefits from the EU.

2. Clear partisan differences do emerge, with the political centre (centre-left and centre-right) voting Yes and the extremes (both right and left) voting No (see Table 3.2). Not surprisingly, those parties which had remained united on the Maastricht Treaty retained the loyalty of their supporters in the vote on the Referendum. Conversely RPR voters were split with a significant majority rejecting the line of their leader and giving their support to the dissident No position of Séguin and Pasqua.

3. There was a split between authoritarians and liberals (*permissifs*). That is to say, those who took a tough line on populist issues such as the death penalty and the wearing of special head covering by Muslim school girls were much more likely to vote No.

4. There was a very significant urban/rural cleavage, with the most populated regions voting Yes and the rural regions voting No (see Table 3.3). This reflected to some extent the high level of discontent among rural communities over proposed reforms of the CAP, which was an issue entirely unrelated to the TEU but which had become associated with it. An additional regional dimension was added with frontier regions, such as Alsace, voting Yes.

5. There was an historical/religious cleavage with Catholic France voting Yes; this largely reflected the identification of former Christian Democrat strongholds with integration.

TABLE 3.2

Voting in the referendum on the Treaty on European Union according to party identification (%)

[Yes]		[No]	
Socialists	74	Front National	95
Génération Ecologie	69	Communists	92
UDF	58	RPR	67
Left-orientated	72	Extreme left	82
Left	57	Right	68
Neither right nor left	53	Extreme right	83

Source: Le Figaro, 20 September 1992.

TABLE 3.3

Regional breakdown of the results of the French referendum on the Treaty on European Union

	Yes	No	Abstentions
Alsace	65.58	34.41	29.63
Aquitaine	49.26	50.73	26.98
Auvergne	49.36	50.63	29.65
Bourgogne	48.71	51.28	29.99
Bretagne	59.85	40.14	27.76
Centre	46.10	53.89	26.40
Champagne–Ardennes	48.62	51.37	31.33
Corsica	43.27	56.72	44.69
Franche-Comté	50.26	49.73	27.32
Ile-de-France	54.44	45.55	30.03
Languedoc–Roussillon	46.40	53.59	28.75
Limousin	46.60	53.39	27.28
Lorraine	54.43	45.56	31.24
Midi–Pyrénées	57.67	48.32	27.02
Nord-Pas-De-Calais	44.28	55.71	27.49
Basse-Normandie	27.29	48.86	51.13
Haute-Normandie	44.91	55.08	27.69
Pays-de-la-Loire	53.60	46.39	27.75
Picardie	42.94	57.05	25.71
Poitou–Charentes	50.20	49.79	28.34
Provences–Alpes–Cote D'Azur	44.66	55.33	31.14
Rhône–Alpes	54.42	45.57	30.40

Source: Le Monde, 22 September 1992.

One of the main effects of the Maastricht referendum campaign was to turn the issue of Europe into a political controversy. The growing lack of confidence among certain sections of the population in the ability of the EU to solve problems (such as ethnic conflicts, racial tensions and unemployment) was reinforced by the debate. The issues aired in the referendum were rekindled during 1993 when final details of the renegotiation of the GATT deal were agreed (see Chapter 5). This did little to allay the fears of those who were worried that French interests and EU interests were increasingly diverging. Those who had organized the No campaign argued that this was an example of the European Commission overstepping its powers in the agreement which it struck for French farmers. Opinion poll data shows that the percentage of the population supporting French interests over European interests grew from 50 per cent in 1984 to 64 per cent in 1989 to 77 per cent in 1994; conversely, those who favoured Community over French interests fell from 43 per cent in 1984, to 30 per cent in 1992 and to 19 per cent in 1994 (Grunberg, 1994).

The public airing which the referendum debate gave to issues surrounding the growing power of the EU helped to make the French more sceptical about the rapid integration of the EU; In 1994 20 per cent of the French population were in favour of the integration process slowing down compared to only 7 per cent in 1984. Opinion polls seem to show a French population which is more sceptical about the EC then it was ten years ago, and which is increasingly looking to the Community for concrete policies and the protection of specific French interests.

The referendum also appeared to lead to a heightened level of interest in the EU; whereas overall voting levels in the 1994 Euroelections were slightly down on 1989, in France 55 per cent of the population voted compared with 50.4 per cent in 1989. Opinion polls also show an increasing polarization and hardening of attitudes on Europe among the mass public. An IFOP poll conducted in the autumn of 1995 shows a marked decline in the number of 'don't knows' or 'weakly affiliated' on the European issue compared to 1991 and 1993 (*L'Exprès*, 28 Septembers 1995). Nevertheless in a comparative ranking of member state opinion, the French population is still relatively positive about 'feeling European' 'wanting the EU to develop' and 'having confidence in the EU' (Eurobarometers, 1996).

The European issue did not feature very strongly in the 1995 presidential election campaign. The three major contenders spoke favourably about France's role in the future of the EU but did not enter into detailed policies. The two main leaders of the Chirac campaign, Juppé and Séguin, came from opposing sides of the Europe divide, and Chirac's own statements were remarkably balanced. This was a particularly important strategy for the centre-right, whose voters were divided. Of those who had voted Yes in the Maastricht referendum, 34 per cent voted for Jospin, 22 per cent for Balladur and 32 per cent for Chirac. Of the No voters, 8 per cent voted for Jospin, 18 per cent for Balladur and 20 per cent for Chirac (*Regards sur l'actualité*, June 1995). Only Le Pen and de Villiers tried to exploit the anti-European vote by their fiercely nationalistic campaign rhetoric.

Conclusion

As a result of France's leading position within the EC there was a happy coincidence of French and European interests for much of the post-war period. The perceived benefits which France gained from the process of European integration meant that Europe was rarely a major source of party division. Though there were differences within the centre-right about the political powers and institutional shape of the EU, this broad pro-European elite consensus was only consistently challenged by the PCF and the FN. Nevertheless, in recent years more marked divisions have emerged both between and within parties over the direction and scope of integration. These differences have come to the fore as the EU has extended from traditional policy areas such as trade and the CAP into areas which are central to notions of state autonomy, such as proposals for a single European currency, more extensive social and regional policies and a common foreign and security policy, or explicitly redistributive, such as regional policy.

In the 1980s and 1990s this extension of policy competences has produced pressure for a strengthening of the EU's decision-making structures and institutions which have further fuelled both inter-party and intra-party debate in France. As well as provoking partisan divisions, the European issue has in recent years led to breakaway factions from the parties – such as de Villiers' *Union pour la France* from the UDF. Party divisions over Europe, which have become somewhat more open in the 1990s, have provoked a growing scepticism about the direction of the EU among significant sections of the electorate as they became more aware of the impact of the EU on their daily lives. The debate in the late 1990s over the domestic costs of meeting the Maastricht convergence criteria has continued to fuel scepticism about the European project within the French population. Although there was considerable pressures on governing elites to mask party differences on the European issues, the more marginal parties have capitalized on public disquiet about the European venture. This debate about the European issue is likely to remain as a salient source partisan division in French politics.

4

Common Foreign and Security Policy

Since the early 1950s, French governments have viewed the process of European integration as an important means of promoting the country's foreign policy goals. One of the key motives behind French leaders' support for the ECSC, for example, was reconciliation with Germany. During the early years of the EC economic integration helped to achieve political stability within Western Europe. However, the development of a security policy for the Six proved to be very difficult and the experience of the failure of the EDC in 1954 (see above, p. 23) demonstrated that states were reluctant to give up their sovereignty in this area. French governments, in particular, did not want their independent, distinctive and, certainly in de Gaulle's eyes, superior foreign policy subsumed into any form of supranational policy-making body.

The leadership role which France played among the six founding members meant that its own priorities and interests inevitably shaped the development of a limited EC external relations policy. EC aid policy and the modest system of EPC, agreed in 1970, provided France with useful vehicles for some of its foreign policy objectives. Until the 1980s, it was relatively easy for French governments to further their own national interests within this limited intergovernmental framework of EPC and at the same time to exercise a independent role in world affairs. However, recent changes in the international arena and the growing role of the EU in foreign and security policy have meant that French policy has increasingly to be articulated within an EU framework which is less under French control.

There are a number of reasons for the changes in France's position. Firstly, the remarkable continuities in foreign policy, largely shared by both Gaullists and Socialists, have increasingly been challenged in recent years. Changes in the international arena and significant cutbacks in military spending have led to a growing domestic debate about the scale and feasibility of France's international commitments.

Secondly, changing power relations within the EU have affected French dominance of foreign policy issues. Enlargements of the EU have led to more varied and shifting patterns of alliances among the member states and have, to some extent diminished the significance of the Franco-German axis in shaping the policy agenda. Since the mid-1980s French governments have worked closely with their Mediterranean partners in constructing a policy for the South of the EU. The election of a more pro-European Labour government in the UK in 1997 opened up the possibility of a the UK joining France and Germany as agenda-setters in the area of security policy.

Thirdly, since the mid-1980s there has been an intensification of discussions about the decision-making procedures and institutional structures for any future EU common foreign and security policy. In the 1990s the issue of security has become more closely linked with the integration and enlargement processes .This has forced French leaders to go beyond their rhetorical posturing and to define more clearly their preferred position on the relationship between the EU and the member states in the area of security and defence policy.

Finally, and most importantly, the whole pattern of international relations became destabilized. The break up of the Soviet bloc and the unfreezing of East–West relations swept away the old uncertainties which had underpinned Europe's security and created a situation where new strategies had to be defined. This changing international context posed a significant challenge for French policy-makers. French political dominance of the Community had been largely the result of a weakened and divided Germany. Re-unification of Germany and the ending of the Cold War not only led to changes in the Western security system but also to major policy shifts within the EU and to a re-definition of France's own foreign policy priorities.

By the mid-1990s this coincidence of domestic, EU and international factors had led to a growing recognition in France that, as a medium-sized power, it had to co-operate more closely with its European partners if it wanted to play an effective role in the international arena. This chapter briefly outlines traditional French foreign policies and explores and analyses French policy towards the evolution of a European security policy. It argues that there has been a considerable amount of policy reversals in the 1990s. The changing dynamic between the USA and Europe and the warming of the relationship between France and the USA has in many ways opened up possibilities for the development of new security arrangements. French governments have become increasingly drawn into a number of collaborative projects in the defence and military spheres with its EU partners. However, many policy continuities remain. Whilst French leaders are committed in principle to a political union, which includes a security arm, they remain sceptical about the development of a fully fledged supranational security policy and continue to favour an intergovernmental approach to co-operation in this area. French governments also continue to try to exercise a leadership role over their EU partners, often if necessary 'going-it-alone' in the international arena. In short, France's rhetorical commitment to Western European co-operation on defence and security issues is still not always matched by its actions.

Traditional French foreign policy

Although France emerged from the Second World War as, in Michael Sturmer's words, only a 'half victor' and was absent from the Yalta conference (February 1945) which divided Europe, it soon asserted itself as a key actor in post-war international politics. Along with the UK, the USA and the Soviet Union it was one of the occupying powers of the defeated Germany and from 1945 held a permanent seat on the Security Council of the United Nations. Immediately after the Second World War it was the country with the second largest colonial Empire. While Fourth Republic governments were caught up with the traumas of decolonization, they were also aware of the need to shed France's image of a weak power and so began pursuing an active and independent foreign policy in every sphere of international life. A number of consistent and distinctive elements can be traced in French post-war foreign policy:

- a policy of reconciliation with West Germany
- a refusal to be subordinated to the United States
- a desire to influence 'bloc politics'
- a preoccupation with national grandeur and
- an active Third World policy.

France supported the development of a European foreign policy only in so far as it was consistent with these overriding priorities.

Though the general lines of post-war foreign policy can be traced to the Fourth Republic it was the presidency of General de Gaulle, with its political priorities of national grandeur and an independent role for France in world affairs, which marked the high point of France's international ambitions. As Gordon (1993) notes, 'The Gaullist years represented a crystallization of traditional French attitudes towards national security into a coherent, well articulated and largely implemented doctrine.'

De Gaulle's view of France's international interests and his foreign policy agenda continued to shape French governments' priorities for many years after his presidency. Both centre-right successors to the presidency, Pompidou and Giscard d'Estaing largely shared his international ambitions and even the Socialist president, Mitterrand, pursued policies consistent with Gaullist precedents (Menon, 1994). This meant that until the mid-1980s, the French foreign policy agenda was dominated by the need to preserve the special relationship with the Federal Republic of Germany, and the desire to play a global role and to maintain independence from the USA. French leaders insistence on the notion of a 'Europe of the States', and opposition to the 'Atlantic Europe', which underpinned the post-war European security system, was at odds with the preferences of their European partners and in many ways hindered the development of closer European security co-operation.

The most significant bilateral relationship for France in the post-war period has been its links with the Federal Republic of Germany. The dynamics of this relationship have shaped French foreign policy priorities and provide the key to understanding much of French European policy. Policy divergences have existed between France and Germany, but the Franco-German axis, in the form of common strategies and the recognition of mutual interests, has underpinned much of the Community's economic and political development and has become a necessary, if not a sufficient condition for any major initiative in the integration process. From the early post-war period there was a recognition in France that the Community might provide a vital framework through which peaceful and cordial relations with Germany could be developed. Initial French hostility and suspicion towards Germany gave way, by the early 1950s, to a more pragmatic policy of reconciliation and co-operation. While the primary objectives of the centrist coalitions of the Fourth Republic were to thwart

German rearmament and suppress German industrial development there was a growing recognition of the economic and political advantages of normalizing relations with its neighbour. One of the main motives behind the Schuman Plan of 1950, setting up the ECSC, was to use the benefits of economic co-operation to lock West Germany into the Western framework. The ECSC also diffused the political conflict over the Ruhr and the Saar (Simonian 1984; Milward, 1984). The idea that economic integration could lead to security in Europe (and in the case of France this meant security from a resurgent Germany) was also an important reason for the French lending their support to the idea of a customs union.

A key aim of the French proposal for setting up the EDC in October 1952 was to integrate Germany into a Western security system. For the French government it was much more acceptable for Germany to re-arm as part of a wider European force than for it to have military independence. Ironically, the failure of the EDC actually paved the way for a Franco-German reconciliation through the mechanism of the West European Union which was set up in October 1954.

For de Gaulle the German question was linked to three other areas of French foreign policy: French national independence, the construction of Europe and peaceful East–West relations. As Milward (1992, p. 334) observes:

> The whole problem was to act in such a way that these three imperatives converged – that is to say that Franco-German relations should be organised in such a way that a closer bilateral relationship would be matched by a 'greater Europe' and that a greater Europe would be matched by greater East–West security and that greater East–West security would culminate in greater independence from ideological blocs.

Consequently, de Gaulle gave a political impetus to the growing technical and industrial collaboration between the two countries by formalizing political and military links with Germany. One of the motives behind the Fouchet Plan, proposed by General de Gaulle in early 1961 was to reconcile France and Germany within a confederal framework which would have responsibility for both foreign policy and defence. The Fouchet Plan met with a cold response from the other four members of the EC, but the German Chancellor, Adenauer, was keen to salvage a Franco-German dialogue from the debris of the failed proposals. For Adenauer a formal Franco-German partnership would be the cornerstone of a secure Europe. At the same time, however, he was keen not to jeopardize Germany's close relationship with the USA. Conversely, for de Gaulle the development of a Bonn–Paris alliance would lead to greater security for Europe and hence increase its independence from the USA.

Close personal links between the two heads of state facilitated understanding and culminated in the signing of the Elysée Treaty in January 1963. This Friendship Treaty committed the two countries to regular meetings over defence and foreign policy matters. It had considerable symbolic importance, although in many ways it did not live up to its original promise and there continued to be major policy differences between the two countries. For instance, Germany supported UK membership of the Community in the 1960s and was consistently in favour of a US role in European defence and security to counter a perceived Soviet threat.

As the Community became larger and more diversified so, too, did the pattern of relations within it. The UK provided Germany with a potential new partner, and from time to time it has been more meaningful to speak of an Anglo-French axis or a Paris–Bonn–London triangle. Nevertheless, the bilateral links between France and Germany remained the most significant axis in the development of Community policy. The Friendship Treaty was re-activated in October 1984 and extended to security matters, with the two countries being committed to formal consultation with each other through a series of working parties and groups.

We can identify a large number of policies and initiatives which have stemmed from the alliance. Firstly, there have been many initiatives in the technical sphere programme including arms collaboration (used by the French to keep an independent defence force and by Germany to reap technological and economic benefits), the 1969 ALPHA JET, Tiger helicopter. More recently, there has been a growing amount of military co-operation, such as the development of a joint Franco-German brigade. Secondly, and more importantly, many political and policy initiatives have stemmed from the partnership, such as the launching of the EMS in 1979 by Giscard d'Estaing and Schmidt and joint initiatives to relaunch the Community at the Milan (1985) and Maastricht (1991) Summits. Though the axis is important to both countries, there have been increasing strains in the partnership as the integration process has deepened – with the Germans favouring both an enlarged and deeper EU and the French remaining cautious about developing defence arrangements under a political union.

In the post-war period France's historical ties and extensive colonial Empire gave it a wide range of political, economic and military interests across the world and all post-war governments have attempted to maintain a presence in the international arena. Fourth Republic governments lacked the political and economic resources which were necessary to exercise the leadership role for France, but they nevertheless shared many of the same aspirations which were to underpin de Gaulle's development of foreign policy (Costigiola, 1992; Gordon, 1993). It was under the Fifth Republic, beginning with de Gaulle's presidency, that France's extensive international ambitions were played out, with France having an active role in conflicts in Africa, the Pacific and in South East Asia. This active foreign policy was highly popular with the public for whom, as De Porte (1991) observes, 'there was an essential connection between their nationhood and the place their nation held in the world.' We now turn to a discussion of just three aspects of France's search for a global role: Third World policy, the development of an independent nuclear policy, and relations with the USA.

Third World policy

As a former colonial power, France retained a considerable number of special relationships and spheres of influence which successive governments have sought to protect and exploit. Immediately following the Second World War France incorporated its remaining colonies into the French Union which had representation in a Union Assembly. The need to preserve this special relationship was a major stumbling bloc for France in negotiating the Treaty of Rome. The other founder member states (apart from Belgium) were not particularly interested in the colonial issue, and though they were unwilling to take on extra financial burdens they were negotiated into a corner by France over the issue. Germany, in particular, was reluctant to alienate France on the issues of trade with the colonies and eventually backed down (Twitchett, 1981). France was, therefore, the prime mover behind trade and aid agreements reached between the EC and developing countries.

The rules for Community assistance to developing countries were laid down in Part IV of the Treaty of Rome. The trade and aid agreements to the 'associated states', which were agreed through the two Yaoundé and four Lomé conventions, were largely determined by France (Grilli, 1993). Community aid took the form of financial and technical contributions to development projects and the Generalized System of Preferences which abolished customs duties for industrial exports and certain agricultural exports to developing countries. While the agreements opened up the markets of these countries to the other member states, the main significance of the agreements was to spread the burden of aid provision to former colonies – but at the same time it allowed French governments to continue to exert economic and cultural dominance over them. The same system operated with the agreement reached between the EC and the Maghreb countries of Tunisia, Algeria and Morocco in 1976, which helped to channel large sums of loans and investments to former French colonies.

An independent nuclear policy

Since 1960 France has maintained an independent nuclear deterrent. The decision by de Gaulle to set up an independent nuclear strike force in 1960 was part of his strategy to re-assert France as a world actor, following the humiliations of Suez and Algeria, and mark France's independent stance from the two superpowers. From the outset, the *force de frappe* has been an important political symbol: domestically, this policy was highly popular and attracted cross-party support and it helped to sustain France's image of a leading power in the international arena. For successive Fifth Republic governments the nuclear capability has been both the active principle and the symbol of the policy of national independence. It clearly demonstrated autonomy from US dominance and gave France a certain status over its continental partners. There were also considerable economic spin-offs from the research programmes related to the development of nuclear weapons, especially in the areas of energy production.

Increasingly, however, the significance of the nuclear force even as a deterrent has became more rhetorical then real. Nevertheless, until the 1990s it was politically very difficult for governments to suggest the winding down of the nuclear programme and sustaining both strategic and tactical nuclear weapons continued to be a high priority in the defence budget.

Relations with the USA

The post-war period saw the division of Europe into two blocs, with the emerging superpowers of the USA and the USSR coming to dominate the pattern of international relations. The experience of the Korean War, in 1950, in which communist North Korea tried to take over South Korea (with massive support from the Soviet Union) increased US worries that Western Europe was potentially at threat from Soviet expansionism. The USA had an active policy of promoting integration on the European continent in order to strengthen Europe as a bulwark against communism. This took the form of economic aid to European countries through the Marshall Aid plan, which was designed to help to create economic stability and restore confidence in Europe, through support for early moves to unify Europe under the ECSC (the USA had also supported the EDC as a means of German re-armament) and through the provision of a security framework under the NATO, set up in 1949. NATO's role was to provide a system of mutual military security in Western Europe; it was organized along intergovernmental lines with each state providing forces and procuring its own weapons. From this point the whole pattern of West European security and defence policies was largely determined by the USA. Consequently there was no compelling need for the Europeans to take on responsibility for their own collective defence.

France was firmly in the Western camp but, unlike its five partners in the EEC, it refused to be subordinated to US leadership. This had important implications for the development of the EC's foreign policy. For France a key feature of any such policy should be Europe's independence from the USA. For many other states, notably Britain, a European security policy which threatened the defence and security links with the USA was politically unacceptable.

There are a number of factors which explain the cool relationship between the USA and France for most of the post-war period. Firstly, there were fundamental differences of economic ideology. France with its statist and protectionist traditions was at odds with the US preference for the liberalization of the international trading system. The establishment of mechanisms for regulating world markets, such as the IMF, the World Bank and GATT, were bitterly opposed by the French. This divergence in economic policies has manifested itself most recently in the battles over the issue of trade in agricultural foodstuffs and American film exports to Europe during the Uruguay Round of the GATT talks.

Secondly, there was considerable hostility towards the USA following the Second World War. France felt that it had been rather slow in coming to the aid of Europe, had ignored the Free French during the war, and had attempted to dictate its terms on France at the time of Liberation. This resentment came particularly to the fore under the presidency of General de Gaulle.

Thirdly, this feeling of resentment in the immediate post-war period was compounded by American involvement in the domestic politics of Western European states. One of the preconditions of the economic aid given to the Europeans under the Marshall Aid programme was that communists should be excluded from government in continental Europe.

Fourthly, there has been a general mistrust over the capacity of US leadership and a fundamental divergence of opinion over the ideological and political division imposed on Europe as a result of superpower rivalry. For France, US interests did not necessarily coincide with Europe's own interests.

Finally, from the early 1950s, there have been concerns among French political and intellectual elites about creeping 'Americanization'. There are fears that French identity and life style are being homogenized by American consumerism and that French culture is being eroded through the transatlantic media. These concerns are part and parcel of a wider anti-Americanism which is prevalent in some sections of French society.

All of these tensions existed in the Fourth Republic (Duignan and Gann, 1994), but they came to the fore under General de Gaulle's presidency. De Gaulle had a personal and deep-rooted suspicion of the USA (Kennedy, 1978, p. 6). This anti-Americanism took many forms, the most public of which was the French withdrawal from the military wing of NATO in 1966. This involved French troops leaving the integrated command structure of NATO and NATO forces being made to leave French soil. De Gaulle's decision was a protest against the dominant position of the USA in Europe's security and the result of policy differences between the Americans and the French within NATO. De Gaulle felt that NATO's nuclear strategy lacked credibility and he was keen to protect the potential role of French nuclear forces.

De Gaulle's centre-right successors did not share his hostility towards the USA but they tended to pursue a policy of political detachment from US influence. There was, however, a growing level of technological co-operation between the two countries during the 1970s, which helped to pave the way for a softening of diplomatic relations under President Giscard d'Estaing. Early in his presidency Mitterrand established much closer diplomatic contact with the USA, welcoming, in 1982, the deployment of American Cruise and Pershing missiles in Europe (though not in France). Although relations between the two countries were normalized under President Mitterrand there was still no equivalent to the special relationships which have developed between the USA and the UK and the USA and Germany. Long-standing differences have not disappeared and France has been ready to distance itself from US foreign policy; for example, in 1986 Mitterrand refused to allow US planes to fly over French air space on their way to bomb Libya. During the 1990–1 Gulf crisis, gaps opened up between Paris and Washington on the policy toward Iraq's occupation of Kuwait.

This troubled relationship between France and the USA has had implications for the development of an EU security policy. France's partners, especially Germany and the UK, but also Italy and Holland, were generally much more pro-Atlanticist than France and were unwilling to develop an EC foreign policy if this risked undermining the NATO alliance. To the extent that France wished to build up a European security system, it wanted to do so with a limited influence from the USA. As long as its European partners supported the USA's leading role in the European security system, France would not support any initiatives, whether led by the USA or not, which would lead to the development of a new security system. Thus, French insistence on a 'European Europe' as opposed to an 'Atlantic Europe', would be one problem for greater defence co-operation. Indeed the French view during de Gaulle's presidency was that European co-operation on defence offered an antidote to American and Soviet predominance. It would have to be led by France and rest on co-operation between nation states in an independent Western Europe. Eventually a wider united Europe might follow. Conversely, the softening of French policy towards the USA has been one of the factors which has facilitated the development of new policy initiatives for a European security policy since 1990.

The Franco-American relationship has also affected bilateral links between France and its European partners. It has been part of the dynamics of the Franco-German axis, with Germany sometimes acting as intermediary between France and the USA. Most importantly France's early antagonism to the USA was a significant factor in de Gaulle's rejection of Britain's application for membership of the EC in 1961 and 1967 and French suspicions of the Anglo-American special relationship have continued to affect relations between France and the UK. With some justification, France feared that the UK would act as a vehicle for USA interests within the Community.

The development of European security policy to 1989

Successive French governments have generally supported the development of a European foreign policy as long as it was consistent with their own policy objectives. This posed no real problems in the early years of the Community when political co-operation was slow to develop. There were two main constraints on the development of a European foreign and security policy:

- the USA provided a security framework against the Soviet threat; and
- the divergent patterns of international ties and historically defined spheres of influence among the member states meant that there was no real common ground for the evolution of policy.

Foreign and defence policies touched on issues of national sovereignty and, as the experience of the failure of the EDC had shown, states were reluctant to give up their sovereignty in this area. By the late 1960s, however, the EC's growing importance as a global economic player led to pressures to increase the Community's powers in the international arena.

The result of these pressures was the establishment of European Political Co-operation (EPC) at the Hague Summit in 1969. EPC was an intergovernmental framework for pooling information across foreign ministries at both the diplomatic and political levels and represented a modest form of foreign policy co-ordination. The success of EPC was mixed (Edwards and Reglesberger, 1990): while many common positions were adopted, on issues such as the Middle East, the Conference on Security and Co-operation in Europe

(CSCE), the 1973 Oil Crisis and South Africa, member states often ignored the agreed positions. Furthermore, in the early years of EPC governments could ask for certain topics to be excluded from discussion within EPC on the grounds that they fell within the *domaine réservée* of member states: France made the case for issues concerning Black Africa to be excluded from EPC. Gradually EPC achieved some successes; by the end of the 1970s the EC states increasingly spoke with one voice in international arenas such as the UN. French governments used the framework of EPC to achieve certain policy goals: Pompidou used it to develop a policy on the Middle East and to encourage a Soviet–American rapprochement. Giscard d'Estaing used it to improve the dialogue between France and the USA and to underpin Franco-German links.

By the mid-1980s there was growing support for strengthening EPC, and France was one of the member states which argued for more powers for it under the SEA. The changes which came into effect in 1987 were, however, relatively limited: EPC was given a formal treaty status and a small secretariat, although it remained firmly under the intergovernmental framework, with the European Commission playing no formal role in the formulation or implementation of policies. Under the SEA , the EPC was extended to cover some security issues but its role remained confined primarily to matters of foreign policy.

For most of the post-war period NATO provided an adequate security umbrella for the West European states. There were mechanisms for organizing common European interests within the NATO framework, such as the Eurogroup set up in 1990, which facilitated co-operation among the Europeans on research and development and military procurement policy. These arrangements were, however, relatively insignificant and NATO policy was dominated by the North Americans. By the early 1980s there was increasing pressure for the Europeans to formulate a common security policy.

One proposal under the Genscher–Colombo initiative in 1981 was to extend the EPC's sphere of competence into military and defence questions. This proposal, which was supported by the French, was unsuccessful because of the reluctance of many member states, especially Denmark, Ireland and Greece, to support the initiative. Increasing tension between the USA and Europeans particularly over the escalation of the superpowers' arms race (Cahen, 1989) and the lack of consultation by the USA with its European partners, strengthened the resolve of some member states to pursue alternative strategies for defence. This prompted France to propose the relaunching of the largely defunct West European Union in October 1984. The objective behind the revitalization of the WEU was to lay down the foundations for a greater European role in the continent's defence system, However, the Rome Declaration, which relaunched the WEU, was a highly ambiguous document reflecting the differences of opinion over the possible future role of WEU. For some member states it represented a means of strengthening the Atlantic Alliance by recognizing and accomodating the 'European Defence interest'; for other states, most notably France, it was a mechanism for developing the Community's own defence system independent of the USA (Myers, 1992).

The resolve of the Europeans to develop some independent defence arrangements was further stiffened after the October Reykjavik Summit, when the USSR and the USA negotiated the withdrawal of intermediate nuclear missiles from Europe without consulting the Europeans. France and Germany reacted by pushing for the articulation of a European Defence identity within the context of the WEU. This proposal was adopted as the 'Platform of European Security' at the Hague Conference of the WEU in October 1987. Like the Rome Declaration, the Hague Platform stressed the dual role of the WEU, both to strengthen NATO and to act as a forum for developing European security interests. The Hague Platform also gave the WEU a limited role in its own right.

By the end of the late 1980s there was a growing interest in the EC developing a common policy in the area of security. The SEA had given formal treaty status to EPC and there were the beginnings of military co-operation through the WEU. However, the key player in Europe's security remained the USA and NATO continued to provide for Europe's defence. It was not until the dramatic changes in the international arena in the late 1980s that this situation began to change.

Developments since 1989

As the moves towards EMU gathered momentum, pressure also began to build up to strengthen political union within the EC. This included giving the EC greater political powers in the area of foreign and security polices to match its growing economic power. However, it is unlikely that these internal pressures alone would have been sufficient to encourage member states to include proposals for a common foreign and security policy within the Maastricht Treaty (Forster, 1997). It was principally pressure from external events, such as the ending of the Cold War, the break up of the Soviet Union and German unification which provoked a re-thinking of strategic and defence priorities among the member states. France, inspired by the need to lock the newly unified Germany into a strengthened European framework, was at the forefront of these initiatives.

The collapse of the Berlin Wall in November 1989 and the subsequent unification of Germany sent shock waves though France. Many of the old post-war tensions re-emerged, with both leaders and public expressing fears about the re-emergence of a politically and economically dominant Germany. Despite reassurance from the German Chancellor, Helmut Kohl, the prevailing view in France was that if Germany were not contained within a strengthened EU it could once again become expansionist and aggressive. In addition, it was feared that Germany would lose interest in European integration and would turn its attention and priorities to Eastern and Central Europe.

President Mitterrand was anxious that a unified Germany would no longer need France's support on the international stage and would have less need for the international framework of the EU. The 30-year relationship with France as the dominant partner now seemed to the French government to be under threat.

These anxieties provoked a large number of policy responses from the French government, which at the time held the presidency of the EU. Firstly, Mitterrand appeared to be trying to stall the process of unification. Then he suggested the construction of a pan-European confederation. This scheme, which was partly in response to the increasing role of NATO in former Eastern Europe, consisted of two stages: the first was the deepening of the EC through EMU and the development of a common foreign and security policy; the second was moving on to enlargement. These proposals were opposed by both the British and Danish governments, which wanted to move forward on enlargement before deepening the EU, and the German government, which had economic and strategic interests in a speedy Eastern enlargement.

Mitterrand then backtracked on the idea of a confederation in the face of strong criticism from East European states (Howorth, 1990). He came to accept that the best way to contain Germany was to push for the rapid integration of the EU. Mitterrand and Kohl then entered a phase of intensive negotiations in order to harness Germany into a strengthened EU. Miterrand continued to be wary about the enlargement of the EU, which he felt would threaten the development of a stronger Europe and might lead to great German dominance. Kohl was also keen to keep up the momentum of European integration, not least in order to allay the fears of the French and other European partners about a resurgent Germany. A Franco-German trade-off was eventually forged, committing both partners to EMU and political union. France was strongly committed to EMU and recognized that the Germans could give leadership in this field. It had greater reservations about EPU, particularly the development of supranational organizations at the European level, but was prepared to support it in order to lock Germany into a strengthened EU. The German government were deeply committed to both EMU and EPU but realized that French leadership and backing was required to carry through political union. During the negotiations for the Maastricht Treaty many policy divergences emerged between the two countries' positions but the shared political will between them to carry the project through overcame these difficulties.

The Gulf crisis, which came to a head in early 1991, provided an additional external impetus to the development of a European CFSP. It had the effect of exposing the EC's weaknesses and showing the inadequacy of the EPC decision-making machinery. After the outbreak of hostilities the EC quickly agreed to the imposition of sanctions against Iraq and demanded the withdrawal of Iraqi forces from Kuwait. Disagreements emerged, however, over the issue of military conflict in the conflict. France broadly followed the US-led coalition against Iraq, but it also continued to pursue an independent policy by launching peace initiatives between the West and its former ally and by negotiating directly with the Iraqis over French hostages. Despite this independent strategy, the experience of the Gulf War did bring home to France the realization that it was difficult to pursue a policy which was at odds with that of the EC and the USA. It also demonstrated the great difficulties which France had in mounting military operations overseas.

The Gulf crisis stimulated the debate about the future of Europe's security system. For those such as France favouring the development of a European defence dimension it was a clear demonstration that the Community needed to develop a strong and coherent policy. The more sceptical states, such as the UK, viewed the crisis as a clear illustration of the inherent difficulties in reaching common positions in crisis and they continued to argue that vital national interests could not be subordinated to a common EU policy.

Events in the former Yugoslavia also highlighted in a very tragic way the weaknesses of the EC in the security field. At the early stage in the crisis there was some attempt by the Europeans to come up with a political initiative to solve the impending crisis. The Europeans were initially united on their desire to preserve the Yugoslav federation and to prevent the use of force. However, once the crisis escalated and violence broke out, historical and strategic ties soon led to this consensus breaking down. The most flagrant violation of the consensus was Germany's recognition of the states of Croatia and Slovenia. The French, fearing a divided EU, and against the background of the Maastricht negotiations, reluctantly supported the German line, even though it ran counter to its own preferences. Divisions continued to exist among the member states over the issue of military intervention. During the crisis the French government played a high profile role and was instrumental in seeking UN support to organize a military operation after the EC had failed to agree on sending peacekeeping forces to Croatia (Wood, 1993).

As the crisis intensified, the divisions between the European states, each with their own concerns, grew deeper. President Mitterrand grew increasingly dissatisfied with the inability of his European partners to agree a policy and launched his own initiative with an unannounced peacekeeping visit to Sarajevo. This gesture exposed the increasing conflicts among the Europeans about the most appropriate course of action to take. As the crisis continued the EU's role diminished although individual states, most notably France and the UK, were involved in military intervention under the UN. The Yugoslav crisis demonstrated the inability of the European states to reach common agreement in a crisis. It also demonstrated the degree of dependence on the USA and the UN to organize military operations.

CFSP and the Maastricht Treaty

A joint initiative for a new political union for the EC was launched by Germany and France in April 1990. A key aspect of their proposal was the 'definition and putting into practice of a common foreign and security policy'. This was further strengthened by a joint open letter on 7 December 1991, immediately prior to the NATO summit in

Rome, committing them to a 'real common and security policy that will lead to a common defence'. By the time of the Maastricht Treaty negotiations the French position had moved from one which supported only a stronger foreign policy role for the new EU to one which also gave it some future role in defence policy. The French negotiators wanted a European defence policy, under the auspices of the revitalized WEU, which would not tie the EU to NATO or to the USA. This change in position by the French government can be explained more by a desire to contain Germany than by an interest in empowering the Union. The proposal was strongly opposed by the UK and Holland, who favoured an Atlanticist solution, and by neutral Ireland. Germany was torn between its commitment to the French and the need to respond to the USA, which did not want to see ties with Europe loosened too quickly. Eventually there was a classic Community compromise, with the German view carrying the most weight.

It was agreed under the TEU that common and foreign security policy of the EU was to be placed under a separate inter-governmental pillar, with the Commission and the EU playing little part in the policy-making process. There were three main changes in the area of security policy under the Maastricht Treaty:

- the EU was given the authority to determine joint positions – this was to cover such matters as political or economic sanctions against states;
- the EU was able to agree joint actions, for example monitoring elections; and finally, and most radically,
- it was given the right to 'co-ordinate defence activity within the West European Union'.

This gave the EU the possibility of, for the first time, using military force to back up its policies. Since CFSP was placed under a separate intergovernmental pillar from the Community deciding policy was left in the hands of the member states. This was the preferred position of the French government. Unanimous votes were necessary to agree the framework of joint foreign policy with majority voting only being used in a very limited number of pre-arranged areas, leading Jacques Delors to predict that the only thing which would ever be decided on by majority voting would be the in-flight menu for a team of election observers! (quoted in *European Brief*, October 1995). It was agreed that the future of the European defence should be decided on the foundations of the nine-member WEU (Greece joined in 1993) with activity having at all times to be linked to NATO. This left the way open for the WEU to remain as the bridge between NATO and the EU (the preferred British position) or to become the key institution for framing European security policy (the French position). There was a commitment in the Maastricht Treaty to re-consider common foreign and security along with other political issues at the 1996 Intergovernmental Conference.

Developments after Maastricht

The CFSP has not lived up to the expectations of its champions. There have been some policy successes, such as the French-led European Stability Pact, instigated by Balladur in spring 1993, to set up procedures to help to avoid conflict in Eastern Europe. The Pact contributed to strengthening economic and political security in the region. However, the main record of CFSP has either been one of policy inertia or failure. In particular, the EU has still not succeeded in over-riding the interests of individual member states and acting in a collective fashion This has been the case in the area of Joint Actions where the EU has been unable to exploit the more proactive powers given to it under the Maastricht Treaty. As Fink-Hooijer (cited in Lofthouse and Long, 1996, p. 186) argues:

> the Joint Actions had been expected to be high profile interventions in international relations by the EU – the EU would 'react rather than react' – but have been something much more low level and certainly less well planned.

An example of the EU's lack of success in over-riding individual member states's interests was its involvement, after 1992, in the Middle East peace process. Here the EU was relatively successful in the so-called civilian aspects of foreign policy, such as aid or the running of elections, but has failed to develop a common position which will be adhered to by all the member states when crises occur. In the case of the civil war in the Lebanon in 1996, the EU was upstaged by President Chirac, who launched his own diplomatic initiative to try to stop the fighting (Lofthouse and Long, 1997). This contributed to the collapse of EU efforts in the region.

The limited strategic role of CFSP in the 1990s can also be explained by the changing role of NATO. After the end of the Cold War the future rationale for NATO seems uncertain; domestic pressure for containing cost and the disappearance of the Soviet threat seemed to point to a winding down not only of its military operations but also of its political role. During the mid-1990s NATO has undertaken a dynamic political debate about is future role and structure. The outcome of these deliberations is that NATO has emerged as a different but highly dynamic organization, as Chilton comments:

> NATO is no longer the classic military organisation it once was, based on territorial integrity and security guarantees (in which an attack on one equals an attack on all). Its centre of gravity has shifted from 'permanent collective defence organisation' to 'effective organiser of ad hoc coalitions'. (1996, p. 224).

This means that NATO is now involved in an increasing number of collaborative military projects with its European neighbours. Many of these are organized under the Combined Joint Task Forces, which allows for 'ad hoc combinations of NATO and WEU forces for specific missions under a single command' (Chilton, 1997). At the same time NATO has assumed a strategic role in assuring peace within the European continent. Of the many initiatives taken, two are of particular significance: the Partnership for Peace initiative, launched in 1994, which offered technical and military advice to countries of the former Eastern bloc; and its opening of membership to former East European countries. The first three to be offered membership in 1997 were Poland, Hungary and the Czech Republic. To some extent the steps taken by NATO have been more positive and far-reaching than those of the EU, although it can be argued that it is easier to incorporate these states into a security organization than into an economic one.

Although during the 1990s the development of CFSP at a political level remained uncertain and disputed, there have been a growing number of layers of co-operation among the European allies (Chilton, 1997). At the operational level the Yugoslav crisis provided the opportunity for considerable on-the-ground collaboration among the Europeans in joint peacekeeping operations. In particular, the French and the British worked extensively together in joint actions under the UN. Outside of Bosnia, co-operation continued to grow. The Franco-German brigade, set up in 1988, provided the model for the 35 000 strong Eurocorps which was set up in 1982. Its role was to support NATO within the NATO area, to back up the WEU in non-NATO areas of Europe and to take part in peacekeeping or peace restoration operations outside Europe (maybe, but not necessarily under UN command). The Eurocorps was more formally integrated into NATO in January 1993, which meant that it was able to be used under NATO command in the Adriatic and the Balkans. By 1995 it also included Spanish and Luxembourg troops. A plethora of multinational units were also being set up under the auspices of the WEU. These included Eurofor, a rapid reaction land force organized by France, Italy and Spain; Euromarfor, a sea force open to all WEU members; and an Anglo-French air corps (Chilton, 1997). There were also a number of units which were set up to operate jointly for NATO and the WEU. It is argued by some commentators that such types of military collaboration may pave the way to a shared approach to strategic problems and may ultimately underpin a future co-ordinated EU defence arm.

French forces participated actively in all these initiatives: the experience of this participation was mixed. The Eurocorps, while politically important, often proved to be rather inflexible in meeting France's commitments overseas – for example in Rwanda. On the ground co-operation between the British and the French was often much easier than that between the French and the Germans. At an operational level it appears that Franco-German relations may in the future be hampered by political difficulties, such as the limits imposed on military action by the German constitution. French membership of such units marked a significant change in policy – from one which until the late 1980s emphasized the vital importance of national control over military operations to one which accepted the necessity of operating collaboratively within a multinational framework. There are two major reasons for this change in policy:

- the increasing budgetary constraints placed on the military; and
- the changing relations with the United States.

In the early 1990s the French government re-evaluated its defence strategy in the light of post-Cold War developments and escalating military costs. The resulting 1994 White Paper on Defence laid down new strategic lines for France's security policy and dramatically reorganized the French military. Defence spending overall was cut by 3 per cent and there was a commitment to cut back on nuclear weapons. Conscription was to be replaced by a fully professional army and the military forces were to be reorganized. These changes had the effect of making French forces more flexible in terms of co-operating in multinational forces.

The *rapprochement* with the USA was facililated by President Clinton's endorsement of greater European independence in its own security arrangements (Menon, 1995a). Furthermore, both the Balladur premiership (1993) and the Chirac presidency (1995) emphasized the need for greater co-operation with the USA. In September 1994 France was partially reintegrated into the NATO decision-making processes and French troops were also gradually reintegrated into NATO military operations (notably thought the Combined Joint Task Force). Thus by early 1996 de Gaulle's decision in 1966 to withdraw from the military wing of NATO had all but been reversed in practice. Indeed, since 1996 the French have taken a very active role in trying to restructure NATO in a European direction. There was also a distinct softening in tone by the French government on the issue of maintaining a European defence identity separate from NATO (Bozo, 1995). This shift in the French position brought it much closer to both the German and British positions.

The 1996–7 Intergovernmental Conference

By the time of the 1996 IGC the situation surrounding the future development of CFSP was highly uncertain. Many of the old problems – institutional overlap, unclear lines of jurisdiction, competing organizations, Atlanticist versus European options – which had bedevilled any progress on the issue remained. The enlargement of 1994 to include the neutral states of Austria, Finland and Sweden further tended to slow down progress on common security policy. The international context had changed significantly and the whole security issue had become inextricably linked with Eastern enlargement of the EU. It had become clear that NATO would continue to play a key role in the security of the European continent. In contrast to the 1991 IGC, there was very little political will to carry through reform and the French and German leaders were less able to control the agenda than they had been at the previous IGC. Member states continued to be split on the issue of the institutional arrangements for the development of the CFSP, on the role of the WEU and its relationship to NATO and on the relationship between the EU and the member states in any future security arrangement.

In the IGC the French and German governments put forward a joint proposal setting out a path for the amalgamation of WEU and the EU. However, France diverged from its ally on the institutional arrangements for policy-making. Here Chirac found himself much closer to the British position by continuing to favour intergovernmental arrangements for the CFSP. The French government came up with numerous suggestions during the IGC, including a *directoire* of leading member states to decide policy (similar to the Security Council in the UN) and a proposal for the appointment of a prominent politician (former president Giscard d'Estaing was suggested) to be nominated by the European Council as a secretary general for CFSP, familiarly known as *Monsieur* or *Madame PESC*. Unlike the British, the French delegation did agree to some extension of majority voting in some areas, but also favoured the preservation of national interests through the mechanism of the constructive vote of abstention, whereby states could exempt themselves from policies decided by the other states.

The outcome of the Amsterdam IGC in June 1997 was extremely disappointing for those governments which had supported the strengthening of the CFSP. Governments failed to agree on any changes to the EU's defence capability and the UK succeeded in blocking any changes which would undermine the role of NATO. The governments did agree on a watered-down version of the French proposal for a Secretary-General for CFSP. This post, to be known as the High Representative, will be a diplomat rather than a politician and will be appointed by the ambassadors to the EU. He or she will head a policy co-ordination unit in the General Secretariat of the EU.

The main players in the EU's common and security policy will continue to be the member states. Under the new arrangements the leaders will on the basis of unanimity define the guidelines, strategy and principles of a common foreign policy and security policy; as under the Maastricht treaty, the details of the policy, once agreed in principle, can be decided on by majority voting. In addition however, the Amsterdam Treaty allows for constructive votes of abstention (under which up to one-third of member states can constructively abstain from a decision) and no majority vote will be taken if a member states claims important issues of national security are at stake (*European Voice*, 19 June–2 July 1997).

Conclusions

Up until the late 1980s French governments were able to exploit the framework of the EC to further their own national priorities. This process was facilitated by an active and close co-operation with the Federal Republic of Germany and the leadership role which France played in the Community. A key question to consider is how far France is still able to fulfil its 'penchant for leadership' and achieve its foreign policy goals in a rapidly changing European security environment. In all of the areas we have considered we see both elements of continuity and of change.

Firstly, France, like the UK, still has a large number of international commitments outside of the EU, especially in Francophone Africa and in the Mediterranean area. The changing dynamic of the EU means, however, that it is increasingly difficult for French governments to shape the political agenda to suit their interests. It has been argued, for example, that in recent years France's preference for directing aid under Lomé to particular regions has been successfully challenged by the more globalist perspective of Holland and Germany. These two states have pushed for the allocation of aid to countries other than those where the Community has historical ties: the PHARE programme of aid to Eastern Europe would be an example of this. At the Cannes Summit in June 1995 we saw the continuing preoccupation of the French with Francophone Africa and its unsuccessful attempt to keep the aid budget high and orientated towards Southern, rather than Eastern countries. While France has fought hard for the development of an EU Mediterranean policy, and has had some success with the setting up of the Euro-Med programme in 1995, its concerns have tended to be overshadowed by the EU's commitments to Eastern Europe.

Secondly, France has continued to demonstrate its capacity for independent action in line with its national priorities. Chirac's decision to break with the Comprehensive Test Ban Treaty in June 1995 (which had been accepted by his predecessor) can be explained and interpreted in different ways. However, the effects of the testing, which Chirac claimed was necessary to maintain the credibility of France as a nuclear force and keep open the possibilities of establishing an Anglo-French nuclear policy within the EU, was to alienate many smaller European states and to make them wary about French dominance of any future CFSP. Independent French action in the Middle East and in Yugoslavia demonstrated that French leaders were prepared to ignore any joint policy decided at the European level if their domestic political standing was at stake.

Thirdly, the Franco-German alliance, once the undisputed basis for Community development, exhibits both continuities and change. After the uneasiness surrounding German unification, the Franco-German alliance was revitalized. Germany may not have been such a natural ally of France as it was in the 1960s and 1970s but it was still its most important ally. France did, however, continue to be concerned with Germany's enthusiasm for the political development of the EU post-Maastricht. It gave a luke-warm response to the Schäuble–Lamers paper in 1994, which outlined Germany's supranationalist position on the future shape of the EU. Despite their misgivings, however, the French government managed to agree with the German government a large number of initiatives, especially in the security field, for the 1996 IGC. Nevertheless, certain cracks do exist in the alliance. Chirac and Kohl do not have the same close personal relationship as had Mitterrand and Kohl. Neither Chirac nor Jospin share Kohl's vision of a politically integrated Europe. Chirac's decision to break the moratorium on nuclear testing made the Germans increasingly cautious about getting too close to the French on security matters. The rhetoric of co-operation so strongly expressed at the highest political level has not always been matched by agreement on the finer details of policy nor in the area of military collaboration. Finally, domestic factors, such as *cohabitation* in France and the increasing internal pressures on the German Chancellor may fracture the relationship.

Finally, both France's priorities and the future security arrangement for the EU have become much less certain in the 1990s. Budgetary constraints and policy changes have moved France more firmly into a series of alliances with its European neighbours. Old continuities, such as antagonism to the USA and a commitment to the development of a French-led European security policy have been replaced by more pragmatic and flexible policies. The one constant which does remain is France's desire to play an active – if not the leading – role in the construction of a new European security architecture.

5

Agricultural Policy

Until the Treaty of Rome, French agricultural policy was highly nationalist and protectionist, with import quotas, prohibitive tariffs and price maintenance. Some types of production were subject to detailed regulations, and major product markets were regulated by national 'offices' which attempted to stabilise production levels and prices. In 1957, after intense lobbying by the dominant farm union, the FNSEA (*Fédération Nationale des Syndicats d'Exploitants Agricoles*) price indexation for key agricultural products was introduced. Then, in 1958, a massive process of change began. Henceforth, all aspects of agriculture concerning foreign trade, product definitions and quality controls, pricing and market regulation were to be decided jointly in the EEC. In these areas the Common Agricultural Policy (CAP) was to replace the diverse national policies, although national or local agencies were actually to implement the CAP. Furthermore, the CAP did not cover all aspects of farming. Initially, member state governments were left with responsibility for policies affecting the 'supply structures' of agriculture (education and research, transport and communications, farms sizes and investment supports), and for social security arrangements for farmers. Hence, since 1958, agricultural policy in France has become dominated by the European framework of detailed production regulations, price supports, intervention purchasing and market controls, but within that framework French governments have implemented structural and other reforms designed to ensure that French farmers – and voters – maximized the yield to France from the CAP.

Any analysis of the evolution of policy and policy-making in French agriculture since 1958 involves the exploration of a jungle of policy paradoxes, but here we focus on just four of them. Each is examined in a separate section of this chapter.

Coherence and continuity of policy objectives

The first paradox is that the original policy objectives of the CAP were confused, with the consequence that the policy package was initially extremely convoluted and doomed to change as the membership of the EEC expanded and the policy package produced perverse results. Indeed, the CAP at times appeared almost incoherent and the provision for 'complementary' national measures seemed to undermine the whole idea of a common policy. The conflict of interest between the European and national levels was a problem, since the price support system encouraged member state governments to do everything possible to convince their farmers to maximize their production. The supply side of agriculture was left to market economics and member state governments, while the demand side was reconstructed in a European, *dirigiste* and protectionist way, which created a structure of intense regulation, but left prices unaffected by the volume of production. The real significance of the CAP system of price supports was to provide income support to farmers, and to disguise a massive cross-subsidization from consumers to farmers. The 'common' price-support mechanism took a decade to become fully operational and only dealt with prices, quality controls and trade, and even for this 'common' policy, responsibility for implementation was mainly left to ministries and agencies in the member states.

Furthermore, the CAP was inherently condemned to evolve, since even before the system was fully operational it was inducing some over-production but was not sufficiently boosting the incomes of the poorest farmers. Some undermining of the original principles took place with every measure of reform adopted, culminating with the MacSharry package of May 1992 and the GATT Agreement of December 1993, which are merely the more recent of a long series of reforms which have made the CAP more complex, more expensive to administer and more subject to fraud, but have not removed its basic characteristics that farmers, and member state governments, respond to incentives which only marginally reflect demand for agricultural produce.

French agricultural policy was considerably changed by the creation of the CAP, the introduction of a group of complementary domestic reforms, and the later evolution of policies. The changes were many and varied, reflecting the enormous complexity of the CAP package itself. From 1970, the policy package changed several times, notably after each enlargement and in response to cost containment pressures, first from governments of other member states and later from GATT partners. None the less, if the price supports and protectionism at the core of the system were hugely reduced, they were not completely eliminated. The treaty provisions and original structuring of the CAP seemed to have a 'freezing' effect: essential policy modifications were postponed until imposed by major crises, and then the compromise measures adopted satisfied nobody.

For decades before the signing of the Treaty in 1957, French governments had adopted a variety of policies to isolate their farmers behind protective barriers. Established policies included not only import restrictions but also price controls, which culminated in 1957, when farm product prices were indexed to living costs. These measures, inherited from the Méline Tariff policy of the 1880s, were complemented by measures to improve agricultural methods and to increase output. Indeed, the first post-war incumbent of the agriculture ministry (the *rue de Varenne*), Tanguy-Prigent, was keen to reform land-tenure structures, while France's first Economic Planning Commissioner – Jean Monnet – was particularly concerned to modernize agriculture. The First Plan, using funds from Marshall Aid, focused spending on two projects, the 'motorization' of agriculture and the supply and use of chemical fertilizers. Hence in 1945, the decade of the 'tractor revolution' began and by 1950 the annual output of French tractors had risen to 9300 from 850 in 1945, while imports had grown from 6000 per annum in 1945 to 13 000. In 1949, the agriculture minister boasted that public spending on agricultural development had risen in three years from 16.6 billion francs to 85 billion (Boussard, 1990, p. 60).

Nor was agricultural policy merely inward-looking. In 1950, the agriculture minister, Pierre Pflimlin, a Christian Democrat and a convinced supporter of the ideas of Monnet and Schuman for European integration, proposed his own plan for a European 'Green Pool' to complement the ECSC. The government adopted the idea in March 1951, and in March 1953, a Conference on the Organization of Agricultural Markets' with representatives of the 16 OEEC states, was held to discuss Pflimlin's plan and three other proposals. The outcome was a stalemate, since there was little common ground between British plans for a loose, open trading system, the Dutch proposal for an immediate shift to a supranational authority and an open European market, and Pflimlin's idea of a gradual shift to common, but protected and regulated, product markets for Europe (Malgrain, 1965).

The Pflimlin project was not forgotten, and when the Messina Conference met in June 1955 to negotiate the creation of the EEC, one French representative, Maurice Faure, pressed the case for including agriculture, but with specific provisions for a slow adjustment to limited market competition across Europe. In 1957 the signature of the Treaty of Rome implied a distinct policy change for France – the old idea of domestic protectionism was abandoned, to be replaced by a new protectionism at the European level. While the negotiations for new policies continued, the old policies remained in place. After June 1958, both de Gaulle and Debré were determined that French agriculture should be drastically modernized, whatever French farmers thought, and that the CAP was to be made to fit French farmers.

The treaty itself was sufficiently vague to allow considerable scope for interpretation, since several mutually conflicting goals were retained for the CAP. The Articles concerned, 38 to 47, did not spell out a clear policy but merely provided a catalogue of good, but vague, objectives for the policy-makers. For agriculture, the main treaty principles of a common market with free movement of goods, services, persons and capital, were not abrogated, but Article 38 noted that special rules were to cover trade in agricultural products (meaning crops, farm animals, fish and 'first stage processed products', such as ham, sausage, cheese and flour but not subsequent 'downstream' food produce, such as bread or frozen meals). The move to this European 'agricultural common market' was to be matched by the adoption of a 'common policy' – a joint interventionist policy to check the full impact of market economics inside the Community. In practice, the term 'common agricultural policy' came to be used to describe the whole package of measures relating to agricultural production and market management.

The main policy aims, defined in Article 39, were to improve agricultural productivity 'by promoting technical progress and by ensuring the rational development of agricultural production and the optimum utilization of the factors of production, in particular labour', 'to ensure a fair standard of living for the agricultural community', 'to stabilize markets', 'to assure the availability of supplies' and 'to ensure that supplies reach consumers at reasonable prices'. The same Article, however, noted that the common policy had to be made with considerable caution, taking account of 'the particular nature of agriculture', 'the social structure', 'structural and regional disparities', and 'adjustments' should only be made 'by degrees'. Article 40 reiterated that gradualist approach: the policy was to be developed over the whole transitional period of at least 12 years.

Some defining elements of the policy package were stipulated in the treaty:

- Common agricultural market structures were to be established, either by common rules and regulations, or by co-ordination of nationally organized market structures, or by establishing European market organizations.
- The policy tools for use in a European market organization could include price and quality regulations, subsidies for production and marketing, storage arrangements and mechanisms for stabilizing imports and exports.
- The policy should involve co-ordinated efforts for research, training, the dissemination of new techniques and products, and the sales of some products.
- The Council would choose objective criteria based on national average cost by which minimum prices were to be calculated during the transition period.

Article 43, clause 3, however, allowed that the replacement of a national market structure by a common market organization would require unanimity in the Council of Ministers for the first two stages of the transition period (at least 8 years in total). Furthermore, even after that, the imposition of a common market organization on a reluctant member state could be decided by QMV in the Council only if the new organization offered safeguards for standards of living and employment equal to those already provided, and conditions for trade similar to those existing. In short, as member state governments were given an absolute veto power during the first 8 years of the Community's existence, and a qualified veto power thereafter, the possibilities for any dramatic policy change were severely limited.

If the treaty provisions were politically acceptable, they lacked any coherent economic logic in respect of agriculture. Clearly, if farmers' incomes were to depend on the prices paid by consumers, then either farmers' incomes would be low (except on big and efficient farms) if consumer prices were 'reasonable', or they would be reasonable if consumer prices were high (and imports were restricted). Alternatively, reasonable incomes for farmers and food prices could co-exist if farming became competitive on the world market, but that implied a massive restructuring and a huge reduction of agricultural population, which the gradualist approach of Articles 39 and 40 excluded.

A conference was convened by the Commission, at Stresa in July 1958, to compare existing agricultural policies of member states and prepare the 'broad lines' of the CAP. It took four years before agreement was reached on the main structures of the CAP, and a further six years before the system became fully operational. At Stresa, there was consensus among the six governments that agriculture was different from other economic sectors in two respects:

- the low productivity of many of Europe's farmers made the EC dependent on food imports, which implied risks of shortages and highly fluctuating prices; and
- most of European agriculture was completely uncompetitive in world markets, so that 'open' competition would have resulted in a rapid 'massacre of the peasants'.

It was agreed that the problem was to find the most effective policy-mix which would maintain acceptable incomes for most farmers and encourage improvements in productivity and efficiency. It was tacitly accepted that the many marginal farmers would move to industrial jobs, since severe labour shortages existed in some rapidly growing sectors of industry.

Given existing practices and strong French preferences, the policy mix would clearly involve both price supports and protectionist measures to stop imports from cheap non-European producers, as well as focused public spending to improve agricultural structures. The first practical questions were to set the levels of price supports and protectionism and to decide rules and structures for managing intra-European competition. The French government proposed high prices to encourage output increases and productivity improvements in all sections of agriculture, among large as well as small farmers, since income would depend on output. In 1958, this view reflected the shared concern of the Six about insufficient supply, not surplus production. French representatives also stressed the needs for a common financing system, for common rules and regulations on quality controls and for co-ordinating the work of the existing national market intervention agencies.

The next practical question concerned 'focused structural funding'. There was agreement that to improve agriculture across Europe, targeting public spending on structural reforms was needed – to increase farm sizes, introduce new crops and the best practices of production and marketing, and provide an infrastructure of research and advisory agencies to disseminate information on new products and techniques, agricultural colleges, advisory and veterinary services and transport facilities. Increasing farm sizes and improving labour productivity implied both increasing public spending and reducing the number of farms and farmers. French representatives argued that dealing with structural reforms required detailed local knowledge and should be left primarily to national governments, at least during the period of developing the CAP.

The goals of French politicians, were not, however, shared elsewhere in the Community. The West German government was worried that the proposal to protect agriculture might provoke retaliation against German industrial exports from food exporting countries like Argentina. However, the French position was supported by both the Dutch government and the Commission, a rather unusual coalition, since on most other issues the French and Dutch governments were in disagreement. This alliance was to be an important factor in overcoming the Germans' resistance, since on other questions the Dutch and German governments were partners. The eventual compromise between Sicco Mansholt, the first Agriculture Commissioner, and Debré was strongly marked by French concepts of gradual co-ordination of national market structures, strong protection against non-EEC imports and high product prices.

At Stresa, basic principles were agreed which were to focus subsequent discussions on the policy mix between price supports with protectionism and structural subsidies. The Community gave priority to unifying market structures around supported prices, leaving member state governments with initial responsibility for structural reforms. There were three agreed core features of the system:

- The creation of an integrated market for agricultural goods based on free movement and uniform prices throughout the Community – which implied common rules of competition, common market-management organizations and co-ordinated national market agencies, the suppression of non-tariff barriers or distortive subsidies, stable exchange rates and harmonized veterinary and public health regulations within the EEC and, finally, uniform rules and customs duties at external borders.

- 'Community preference' – which meant that the EEC gave priority to consuming its own agricultural produce, whatever the member state of origin.
- Financial solidarity – the EEC as a whole, through a common fund, should pay all costs, whatever the product concerned or the member state where the money was spent. In short, farmers' incomes were to be supported by structuring the market to force up domestic prices and keep out cheaper foreign products. Although some efficiency improvements were expected, it was recognized that costs of farming would remain higher in the EEC than in the rest of the world; hence, food prices would also be higher.

The central measures constituting the CAP commodity markets and the European Agricultural Guidance and Guarantee Fund (EAGGF) to pay the bills for the CAP were agreed only in 1962, the key decision on cereal prices was taken in 1964 and the overall financing package was agreed in 1966 (after the French-provoked crisis of 1965). With de Gaulle in power in Paris there was no question of creating a 'federal' bureaucracy based in Brussels to administer agriculture. The Six agreed to leave actual market operations in the hands of national product 'offices' or 'agencies', and to create appropriate bodies in those countries and for those commodities where they did not already exist. Management committees of the individual commodity-market organizations in Brussels were to play a role of decision-making and co-ordination of the work of these agencies in the member states.

Eventually, the cover of CAP regimes extended to 94 per cent of all agricultural produce. The large majority of products (70 per cent by final value) were covered by price support systems with both tariff protection and intervention purchasing. The markets in a further 21 per cent of products were protected simply by import tariffs; 2.5 per cent of products were given a type of deficiency payment (based on the volume of production) to make up the difference between an 'ideal' price set for the Community and the world market price (the real market price in the EEC); for 0.5 per cent of agricultural produce, special direct subsidies – on the land area devoted to the crop – were created; finally, about 6 per cent of all produce was not protected by any kind of customs barrier, price support or subsidy scheme. In short, while there was a dominant type of commodity regime, there was also considerable diversity and a few products were left completely 'unsupported'. The price levels for protected commodities were set on a yearly basis, and the annual 'farm price review' meeting of the Council of Ministers imposed a reconsideration of the costs and benefits of the whole system on the basis of a report from the Commission.

The basic system was not fully operational when its drawbacks became apparent. Even in the 1960s, surpluses of dairy produce were produced. These led to enormous costs of storage and very high levels of import levies and subsidies to exports, which in turn created major international tensions. In particular, US governments started to voice criticisms that subsidized EEC exports were both a breach of GATT agreements and a threat to US farmers. As early as 1967, a proposal from Mansholt to study changes to the CAP won support and in December 1968 the Commission published 'Agriculture 1980' (often known as the 'Mansholt Plan') with proposals to move the focus from price supports and intervention purchasing to structural funding. This was attacked by farmers' unions across Europe and the hostility of French and West German farmers was especially intense.

By 1969, however, when Mansholt put forward a revised version of his plan for reform, the exchange rate crisis had put economic and monetary union higher on the agenda than agricultural reforms. De Gaulle's departure and Pompidou's election were followed by a devaluation of the franc which heralded a period of currency instability. The ending of stable exchange rates meant that the central principle of uniform pricing across the whole EEC market was in danger. The outcome of the devaluation crisis was the agreement to create a special exchange rate for agricultural produce – the 'green franc' – and a system of monetary compensation amounts (MCAs) to prevent a massive increase in exports of food from the devaluing country and to allow the maintenance of exports from non-devaluing Member-States. The central idea of the MCA system was that a devaluing country should pay a levy on exports, so that in other states the price should not fall, while in a revaluing country exporters should receive a subsidy to keep their effective prices at the pre-revaluation level. The gradual creation of more and more 'green currencies' as the Mark revalued and other states followed France in devaluing soon led to a structure of Byzantine complexity where the whole logic of internal market efficiency was undermined. Many governments saw that a return to stable exchange-rates between member-states was a necessary pre-requisite for the abolition of MCAs and green currencies, and for an eventual major overhaul of the CAP. Thus, the 1969 crisis neither destroyed the CAP nor precipitated a move to monetary union; rather, it introduced the further complexity of green currencies and monetary compensatory amounts.

In March 1971, with negotiations on EC enlargement well advanced, the Six agriculture ministers discussed the revised Mansholt plan, but simply holding the meeting precipitated protests from the farmers. The version of the plan finally approved slightly increased spending on structural policies and left member states with full discretion for implementation. In 1973, however, Britain, Denmark and Ireland became full EC members, which meant that subsequent changes in the CAP had to be agreed by governments whose perspectives on CAP spending were very different from those of French ministers. In particular, Britain, with huge food imports, paid disproportionately for the CAP. Furthermore, the reaction to the first international 'oil crisis' by the Pompidou and Giscard d'Estaing governments in France, was to identify agriculture as a sector to protect, both to minimize increasing unemployment and to provide new exports. During the early 1980s the CAP provision for export subsidies to dispose of surplus stocks resulting from intervention purchasing was used increasingly by French cereal producers, so that French agricultural exports increased rapidly, but at a high cost in terms of subsidies.

By 1984, milk production, which had satisfied EC demand in 1974, had experienced 10 years of output growth averaging 2.6 per cent annually, while demand had only risen by 0.6 per cent each year. In short, over-production in the dairy sector had reached crisis proportions, and there was wide agreement that a means had to be found to reduce surpluses and costs. The German government at last accepted the idea of fixing production quotas for milk at guaranteed prices, and the French Government, which had long opposed any measure likely to damage the successful French dairy industry, admitted it had no alternative policy to propose. Finally, at the European Council of Fontainebleau in June 1984 the French government at last accepted a major package of reforms, including a system of quotas for dairy products, a formula to reduce the British budget contribution and a plan for phasing out MCAs.

The Fontainebleau agreement marked a move away from the principle of unlimited intervention purchasing: henceforth the guaranteed price would be paid only for a set quantity of milk. The first production target was 99 million tonnes for the whole EC, 5 million tonnes less than the actual volume produced the previous year, but still above the level of consumption of the Community. The member states agreed a distribution of the target quantity among themselves based on previous years' production. Finally, each government set production quotas either for individual farmers or for dairies. All who produced more than their quotas had to pay special levies on all excess production, and those levies were set sufficiently high to discourage overproduction. Over the next three years the quotas were twice reduced, by 3.5 per cent and 5 per cent. The introduction of quotas was accompanied by the first reduction in guaranteed prices within the CAP; on average a 0.4 per cent fall in nominal prices led to a 3.5 per cent fall in real prices.

None the less, these changes only slowed down the ever-mounting costs of intervention buying, storage and disposal, and between 1984 and 1987, the cost of the CAP increased by 40 per cent, provoking another budget crisis. In 1985, a Commission Green Paper analysed the problem and outlined some possible solutions, including setting 'thresholds' or production targets. Several changes were agreed in 1988 which again moved away from the idea of unlimited intervention purchasing. The effects, however, were inadequate.

The biggest changes, proposed by Ray MacSharry, the Agriculture Commissioner, were agreed only in May 1992 and were complemented in December 1993 by the terms of the GATT agreement. The MacSharry package included a move towards world price setting and income supports for European farmers: a 29 per cent cut in cereal prices over three years, an 18 per cent cut in beef prices, a system of obligatory set-aside of 15 per cent on cereal farms over 20 hectares in size, and a voluntary, but well-paid scheme of set-aside on other farms; the introduction of direct grants for smaller beef farmers, special grants for the use of extensive farming techniques, rural development projects and to increase forestry. Even after these measures, French ministers fought fiercely to protect their farmers (and their balance of payments) from the more drastic proposals of subsidy removal emanating from Washington in the GATT negotiations. Finally, a six-year plan of subsidy reduction was agreed, which included a 36 per cent reduction in the value of export subsidies, a conversion of import quotas into comparable tariffs and a subsequent 36 per cent reduction, and a 20 per cent reduction of structural supports.

The initial vocal hostility of French farmers to the MacSharry package was rapidly replaced by opportunistic exploitation of the new financing possibilities, including set-aside. Indeed, so great was the take-up of set-aside financing that by 1995 it seemed unlikely that the production of wheat would be sufficient to allow the 2 million extra tons of wheat exports that the brinkmanship of the GATT deal had won for France. It was ironic that there were world shortages of wheat and other cereals in 1995, that EU grain stocks reached a ten-year low and that world prices had risen so high that EU export subsidies had been stopped. The consequence was that the Commission was actually considering a proposal to reduce the amount of 'set-aside' in 1996.

In short, in 1995 the CAP was in some respects as convoluted and doomed to change as it had been 25 years earlier, when it was first fully operational. If the supply side of farming is no longer left to market economics, the demand-side is still *dirigiste*, although the protectionist aspects are now being reduced. Farmers are no longer able to increase production irresponsibly, but many can secure considerable incomes by selecting the appropriate premiums and grants from the large range now available under the CAP. The CAP system was pushed towards reform by the irritation it caused to farmers and governments in the rest of the world and by its own sheer cost which made the cross-subsidization from consumers to farmers in Europe all too apparent to the consumers. The MacSharry package of May 1992 and the GATT Agreement of December 1993 completed a long series of reforms, which have made the CAP even more complex, but not less expensive and have not removed its market-distorting nature.

French nationalism in European agricultural policy-making

The second, related, paradox is that the policy process appeared to be highly Europeanized, but it was in fact intensely national and nationalist. On the one hand, a complex mass of detailed European rules and structured commodity markets have been established; on the other, existing national ministries and agencies have done most of the implementation work, and have also carried out a lot of their own 'complementary' policies, designed to maximize the national benefits of the European policy package. By leaving implementation of the common policy and the conduct of structural reforms policies to member state governments, the CAP system institutionally induced national governments to encourage their farmers to maximize production and hence their share of the spending.

Although there are more meetings in Brussels about agriculture than about any other policy, the approach taken by French ministers, officials and trade unionists alike has remained essentially nationalist. Decisions are made in Brussels, rather than by Brussels, and EU agriculture deals are viewed as international negotiations. This approach was decided by de Gaulle and has been maintained by subsequent presidents. French ministers invoke French 'national interest', not the best policy for Europe as a whole. 'Brussels' is acknowledged as having power only when French ministers suspect a policy will be unpopular at home, and in such cases it becomes a scapegoat.

De Gaulle not only established a firm pattern of defining joint European policies as 'foreign' and French inputs as expressions of national interests, he also contributed to ensuring that this approach would outlive his own political demise by its institutionalization within the CAP system. The president and his governments were also determined to change French agriculture profoundly, building on and accelerating the reforms begun during the Fourth Republic. Hence, the first governments of the Fifth Republic were willing not only to face serious opposition from their new European partners, but also to oppose the explicit demands of French farmers and the majority of their union leaders.

From the outset, de Gaulle and his ministers wanted an agricultural policy for the Community based on established French practices, anticipating that such a system would not only provide outlets for surplus French production, but also ensure that French farmers would benefit greatly from the guaranteed prices. Hence, they argued that it was economically and socially worthwhile to pay the cost of maintaining the standard of living of small farmers throughout the Community, and constantly reminded French farmers' leaders that they were doing everything possible to ensure that the new CAP would benefit them to the full. For de Gaulle, a Community policy to provide financial support for French agricultural modernization was a political asset. The system of price-supports and protectionism which he and his ministers strove to establish in the CAP had the distinct advantage for France in that it made net importers of food, notably Germany, contribute disproportionately to paying for this support. German funds for French farmers was viewed as a positive result, and not least because it helped to legitimize both the Franco-German alliance and EEC membership with reluctant or hesitant voters at home. Paradoxically, it was by fixing product prices at German levels that the maximum gain for French farmers was attained.

From early 1959, and in parallel with the CAP discussions, Debré led the process of making domestic reforms. The objectives were twofold:

- to modernize farming rapidly
- to ensure that French farmers gained the maximum for themselves and for France from the CAP.

The many measures taken included restructuring farm land into more economically viable units, developing special banking facilities and providing soft loans, pensions and social security for farmers, subsidising co-operatives, and constructing a modern rural infrastructure of roads, telephones and schools. Some measures, however, had a distinctly nationalist flavour: public health regulations or taxes were sometimes used to discourage the consumption of specific produce from other member states.

Initially, relations between Gaullist governments and the farmers were bitterly hostile. In 1959, when the automatic indexation of agricultural product prices to the rate of inflation was abolished, the intense hostility of many farmers was often expressed at meetings of the chambers of agriculture (the official representative boards of farmers in all the *départements*). None the less, Debré pushed on with reforms. First, in April 1959, the government attempted to encourage the use of new techniques and to improve the education of farmers. The idea was not only to propagate new ideas to improve the efficiency of farming, but also to ensure that farmers themselves and their unions and professional associations played a very active role in spreading the message. A special Treasury fund and a national committee on 'vulgarization' were created, with committee membership dominated by representatives of farming associations and unions. In every *département*, a local committee was established under the leadership of the prefect. In short, the government was inviting the farmers' unions to share in implementing the new policy.

Debré's framework law on agriculture followed in 1960, but that law had not yet been applied when a wave of farmers' protests broke out, culminating in the storming of the subprefecture of Morlaix, in

Brittany. The response to these protests came from the president himself, who chose a new minister of agriculture, Edgard Pisani. Pisani at once set out to draft a complementary framework law which was intended to 'positivise' Debré's package of measures, and to undermine some of the fundamental hostility of the farmers. Pisani and his package of reforms were never to win great popularity in the farming population, but many of the measures adopted did become permanent fixtures.

One element of the Pisani reforms was the admission that the excess of farmers with small plots was partly a consequence of the absence of retirement pensions for old farmers and partly a reflection of the difficulties involved in leaving farming and moving to another job. To deal with these problems, the Pisani law provided for a system of 'departure premiums' (*indemnités viagères de départ*, or IVD), which could either take the form of retraining grants for farmers in mid-career or that of early retirement grants for older farmers.

A second element was the creation of local agencies to increase farm sizes and thus build more efficient units of production; these land agencies (known as SAFERs or *Sociétés d'aménagement foncier et d'établissement rural*) were given funds and limited pre-emptive powers to purchase whole farms or individual plots and to sell to local farmers to increase the size of their farms. Altogether 32 SAFERs were set up to cover all farm land in France. In many areas where strip-farming had led to completely fragmented farms, the SAFERs had the task of 'piecing together', or *remembrement*. Often a SAFER had to work out a plan for the *remembrement* of the entire territory of a commune, buying out some older farmers with IVDs, and redistributing the entire land as a smaller number of economically viable farms.

A third element of the reform package was the establishment of set-up grants for young farmers (DJAs or *dotation aux jeunes agriculteurs*) to help young people with education and experience to become independent farmers; but one conditional for getting such a grant was to acquire a farm of a viable size. In 1967, a National Centre for Improving Farm Structures (CNASEA) was established to administer these grants.

These measures were complemented by reforms intended to encourage joint ventures between farmers, both for production and marketing. Farmers could create a simple association, a co-operative or a special 'joint agricultural company' (SICA or *société d'intérêt collectif agricole*), but if their organization respected the qualifying norms for official recognition as a 'producer's group' they received set-up funding, technical advice and administrative support from the local agriculture ministry offices. In turn, several producers' groups in one area with the same crop could create an 'economic committee' to share marketing arrangements and thus gain further support. Another important reform was the extension of the social security system to cover the farming population and provide benefits and retirement pensions.

Although Pisani attempted to rebuild links between the government and the farmers, the policies with which he was associated were resented, and the positive effects on farm incomes took a long time to become visible. Furthermore, the government's 'empty chair' strategy during the crisis of 1965 convinced many farmers that de Gaulle's hostility to European integration would wreck the CAP. In 1966, Edgar Faure replaced Pisani at the *rue de Varenne* and at once set out to convince the farmers that the entire policy was in their interests. The government claimed that by accelerating the modernization of French agriculture, it was helping French farmers to maximize their incomes, defending the national interest of France. That remained the message of all French leaders until the 1980s. There were occasional problems, as in 1967, when an official report (the Vedel Report) forecast a continued exodus from agriculture of 100 000 farmers per year for five years. In 1972, Jacques Chirac became agriculture minister, and he stressed that the government never stopped pushing in Brussels for the best possible deal for French farmers against the demands of other member state governments. As prime minister from 1974 to 1976, he maintained this line. After Chirac's resignation, President Giscard d'Estaing went even further and extolled the merits of agriculture as France's 'Green Oil' to export to the rest of the world.

The election of President Mitterrand in 1981 heralded a change of approach, and relations between the FNSEA and Frances's first female agriculture minister, Edith Cresson, rapidly deteriorated, as the need to reduce spending, especially on dairy products, became clear. Both Cresson and Rocard, who replaced her, strove to defend French farming interests, and Rocard presented the outcome of the 1984 Fontainebleau summit as the best possible deal for the farmers. As prime minister in 1986, Chirac showed his sympathy for farming by appointing Guillaume, leader of the FNSEA, as agriculture minister, but that did not mean that he would stop the reform of the CAP.

The long negotiations for the MacSharry reforms and the GATT deal were not greatly affected by the changes of government between 1988 and 1993. Neither Mitterrand, nor any of his prime ministers, including Balladur, wished the GATT deal to collapse over agriculture, but they were not willing to agree to a GATT agreement that would have destroyed all the exporting advantages of French farmers. They all shared a reluctance to allow overbidding on the defence of French farming interests from either friends or rivals at home. The result was a carefully staged spectacle, in Paris, Brussels and Washington. When a French veto was threatened, the National Assembly was allowed to debate, and even vote on, this foreign policy issue, and Jacques Delors and Leon Brittan were asked to play their roles. This *son-et-lumière* not only impressed many farm leaders that there was little point in organizing protests or boycotts, but also contributed to winning some concessions from the US negotiators (which slowed down the reduction of subsidies to exports). Talk in Paris of resuscitating the national interest veto of the Luxembourg Compromise was intended to be taken seriously by EU partners, US negotiators, and, above all, French farmers. In short, if the approach to agricultural policy-making remained essentially nationalist, the GATT deal concessions showed that agriculture was no longer the top priority.

Stability and change in the French agricultural policy community

The third paradox is that the existence of a closed 'policy community' within France, including agriculture ministers, ministry officials and farm union leaders from the FNSEA, has not prevented other actors impinging on agricultural policy-making at the most crucial moments.

Observers of agricultural policy-making, both inside and outside France, have noted these close, almost cosy, links, which Keeler (1987) described as the 'politics of neo-corporatism', while Muller (1992) referred to 'co-gestion' in agriculture. As noted above, such close ties have not always existed during the Fifth Republic. Although a closed 'policy community' appears to have formed, the actors in that community have not always been able to solve the problems they faced 'within the family'. The divisions between different product groups or between big modernized farms and old small farms have deepened as CAP funds have decreased and the FNSEA and *rue de Varenne* has been unable to draw everyone into agreements. None the less, dissident groups have usually adopted nationalist slogans, and there have been few serious attempts to develop strong Europe-wide lobbies for particular crops or types of production. Governmental nationalism in agricultural policy-making has been matched by interest group nationalism.

The FNSEA, the peak organization of French farm unions, was initially keen to create a European umbrella organization, COPA (*Comité des Organisations Professionnelles Agricoles des Pays de la Communauté Européene*), but remained determined to focus its efforts on building and maintaining an intimate, self-interested relationship with the French agriculture ministry. French farmers expected *their* minister to fight for *their* interests in both Paris and Brussels, while many outside agriculture complained that governments were too subservient to the farmers' demands. Modifying the CAP and national structural policies has often led to crises when the farmers have bitterly criticized the government for betraying their interests. At such times, many farmers have resorted to violent demonstrations which the police have done little to contain.

Equally, at the EU level the usual appearance of French domination of agricultural policy-making is sometimes replaced by demonstrations of weakness. Since the French walkout from the Council of Ministers in 1965, French ministers have been repeatedly pushed by other member states' governments into agreeing to reforms which French farmers disliked. One particular result was to make French governments the object of bitter criticisms from governments of other member states and GATT trading partners, but also extremely unpopular with their own farming community. Inside France, many farmers' union leaders have argued that successive governments have sacrificed French farming interests on the altar of European integration. Outside France, however, the same governments have been accused of hijacking the EU to pay for modernizing French farming and for providing income support to inefficient peasants, and of failing to make French farmers respect the rule of law.

During the Fourth Republic, the political and economic weight of farming was such that no government could ignore it. The centre-right parties faced constant electoral pressure from small, inefficient producers who were determined to retain their independence. After the collapse of the Socialist-inspired *Confédération de l'Agriculture*, the FNSEA became the dominant pressure group of French farming.

Although many of its leaders had big farms, the mass membership came from small farms. In the 1950s, the 'peasant' way of life seemed under threat as the take-off of industry and the rising wages of industrial workers enticed many to give up farming and move to the towns. Many small farmers were resentful that their own incomes stagnated while urban, industrial France was getting ever richer. The threat of cheap food imports from Canada, Australia and the USA, where large-scale production and modern technology allowed much lower production costs, was unacceptable. Though in 1952, the FNSEA supported the Pflimlin plan for a 'European Community of Agriculture', it remained opposed to free competition in world markets (Muth, 1970).

The pressure for protection did not come only from inefficient small farmers. Already in the 1950s, parts of French farming were efficient and profitable, but the more efficient farmers favoured protectionism and price supports as much as the small farmers did, since that policy had the double advantage of increasing their own profits and cementing the political unity of the FNSEA. They anticipated that Europeanizing protection would not only provide purchasers for surplus French products, but also increase French farmers' incomes greatly. Hence, they argued the case for maintaining the living standards of small farmers throughout the Community by protecting markets. As the ruling parties faced competition from the Gaullists in 1951 and the Poujadists in 1956, groups which had no qualms about promising farmers the tariff protection they desired, agriculture ministers, with close links to FNSEA leaders, never really contemplated opening competition to world markets.

In 1958, however, the Gaullists realized that without shock treatment to impose modernization farming would slow down the growth of the whole economy. Debré believed that to change the behaviour of farmers there should be both a threat of competition within the CAP and a package of domestic reforms. He knew that these measures would be unpopular with farmers, and he distrusted officials at the *rue de Varenne*, whom he suspected of having too close ties with the FNSEA. He hoped to form a tactical alliance with dynamic elements in the farming unions, notably the CNJA (*Centre National des Jeunes Agriculteurs*), a young farmers' organization (formally part of the FNSEA). Several CNJA leaders had previously been active in the young Catholic farmers (*Jeunesse Agricole Chrétienne*) which, in the 1950s, had argued for modernizing farming. Indeed, Debré's first measures were prepared in consultation with CNJA leaders, but with little input from the agriculture ministry. Although Debré's strategy proved successful in the long term, the immediate reactions to the abrogation of price indexation in 1959 and the Framework Law in 1960 were massively hostile. The huge demonstrations, culminating in the storming of the Morlaix Subprefecture, led to a minor constitutional crisis after de Gaulle refused a deputies' petition for a special session of parliament to discuss agriculture. They also inspired the appointment of Pisani as agriculture minister. His Complementary Law not only included many measures advocated by the CNJA, but also provided means for co-opting farmers' leaders into the new institutions for improving farming.

Replacing Debré in 1962, Pompidou set out to win the agricultural vote away from the traditional centre-right parties (especially the Radicals, MRP and CNI), which implied improving relations with the FNSEA. As CNJA leaders were gradually winning key posts in the FNSEA, he started with some advantages. None the less, FNSEA hostility was provoked by the low price set for milk (in the 1963 austerity programme). Then, tough handling of a milk delivery strike in 1964 led to a break-down in contacts with the FNSEA. In 1965, the FNSEA again attacked the government, this time over the crisis in the EEC and the financing of CAP. Indeed, FNSEA leaders urged farmers to vote against de Gaulle in the presidential election. When Lecanuet, standing on an intensely pro-EEC platform, scored 16 per cent at the first ballot, and forced de Gaulle to fight a second ballot, FNSEA leaders expected concessions. The choice in 1966 of the highly diplomatic Edgar Faure as agriculture minister seemed to signal the end of a period of tension.

1966 to 1981 was the period Keeler (1987) described as 'neo-corporatist', when close harmony reigned between the ministry and FNSEA. The FNSEA was the only official interest group recognized by the ministry, which gave it seats on advisory councils at all levels. In the *départements*, FNSEA leaders won elections to preside over the Chambers of Agriculture and appointed themselves and their friends to run the *Crédit Agricole* bank and GROUPAMA mutual insurance society. FNSEA leaders encouraged officials to exclude rival organizations which contested elections to the chambers of agriculture (notably the Communist-led MODEF). In the monthly consultative meetings held by agriculture ministers from 1969 to 1981, FNSEA leaders occupied all the seats, whether formally as union leaders or under other guises such as representing chambers of agriculture or mutual or co-operative bodies. From 1971 to 1982 the FNSEA had a similar monopoly in the annual conferences chaired by the prime minister.

As in all neo-corporatist arrangements, the problem of maintaining this cosy collaboration was that both sides had to keep gaining from it. Governments hoped to convince the farmers that whatever deal had been struck was the best possible one, and in return, governments expected the FNSEA to deliver rural peace. The FNSEA expected the government to make policies which the farmers would see as positive achievements on their behalf. However, the continuing modernization and land restructuring policies created losers as well as winners. Vedel's predictions in 1967 of continuing rural exodus proved exact. Hence, agricultural protests did not die out, and many on small farms became increasingly disillusioned with the FNSEA. By the late 1970s, the right-wing FFA and the leftist MODEF were gaining significant votes and even seats in elections to the chambers of agriculture.

The growing tensions between the *rue de Varenne* and the FNSEA became a crisis with the election of Mitterrand as president and the appointment of Cresson in 1981; in her first speech as minister, she attacked the privileged position of the FNSEA. Her ministry subsequently gave official recognition to the rival unions of MODEF, FFA and the newly-formed, pro-Socialist CNSTP. The effect of Cresson's attacks, however, was to free the FNSEA of all inhibitions. Its leaders set out to lead attacks on government policies, to organize demonstrations and to show farmers that the FNSEA, rather than the Socialists or their client groups, was the best defender of farming interests, big or small.

With the need for a deal on CAP reform looming, Mitterrand called Rocard to replace Cresson and to make peace with the FNSEA. Culpepper (1993), however, has shown that Rocard did not simply reconstitute the old arrangements. Instead, a more competitive collaborative policy network developed, with the FNSEA as the dominant – but not the sole – interest group actor. One reason for this change was that the continuing process of CAP reform required detailed inputs from experts in the various product groups. Rocard's first big dossier concerned dairy produce reform, and for this input from the producers' association, the FNPL, was essential. The minister appreciated that this association would also be the main channel of information to milk producers about the reform, so he sought its leaders active co-operation. As the focus turned to cereals in the late 1980s: so the ministry increased its links with the AGPB, the wheat growers' association.

During the late 1980s, however, the pressure from European partners and from other GATT members was for a move away from both export and production subsidies within the CAP. French governments were torn between a realization that most of the French economy would benefit considerably from the increased trade which a GATT deal was expected to encourage, and the appreciation of the substantial pockets of poverty which remained in agriculture despite the massive expenditure. Under both Bérégovoy and Balladur the resolution of the problems of CAP reform (the Mac-Sharry package) and of the agricultural branch of the GATT deal were seen as too important to be left to the collaboration of the *rue de Varenne* and its normal clients. Both Mermaz and Puech as agriculture ministers had a special role to play – as mobilizors rather than as co-ordinators. It fell to them constantly to remind farmers' leaders in all kinds of interest organizations that the president, prime minister and government were doing everything possible to obtain the best deal for them – and that whatever agreement was made could not be improved, so that protest of any kind would be a complete waste of time and energy. Although the levels of protest after the MacSharry and GATT agreements were low, the considerable hostility of farmers to further integration, in the Maastricht Treaty referendum in 1992, and to Balladur, in the 1995 presidential election, suggest that mass opinion in farming is barely resigned to these changes in the CAP.

After an initial period of hostility between Debré and Pisani and the FNSEA, close relations developed between ministers, ministry officials and the union. French farmers' lobbying has continued to focus on national governments, rather than on the European Commission or EP. Action with other European farmers groups within COPA has been limited – a last resort rather than a usual pressuring technique. Periodic violent protests have been made by groups of farmers as a sign of despair, or an attempt to strengthen the hand and the will of French ministers in Brussels negotiations, or an expression of discontent with the FNSEA leadership. Increasingly, however, the FNSEA has seen its claim to be the sole voice of French farming to be challenged. Increasingly too, the hostility of French farmers to the reform of the CAP and, hence, to European integration in general, has grown. The sentiment strongly felt among small farmers is that the CAP has failed.

Appraising policy effects

The fourth paradox concerns the policy effects of the CAP and the national policies in France: the data is used by some to demonstrate that the policy package has been a great success, and by others to prove that it has been a huge failure. The conclusions drawn depend on the standards used for comparison. Successes may be measured in terms of increased output, productivity, exports, greater self-sufficiency and more stable supply. Failures, however, include the huge commodity stocks, high costs, welfare losses to EU consumers and foreign producers, frauds, and the large reduction of the EC farming population. Protectionism has operated to the detriment of world trade and the export markets of less-developed economies, in both Eastern Europe and beyond. Though the justification of higher prices was to allow marginal farmers to survive and remain in farming, the impact of those prices was to give unnecessarily high incomes to intra-marginal farmers, while the rural exodus continued apace. Much marginal land has been abandoned and considerable environmental damage has resulted from the over-use of intensive techniques.

The only undisputed consequence of the CAP since its inception has been its enormous cost. The CAP has been by far the most expensive of all EU policies, consuming over 75 per cent of the budget during the early years and even in 1996 taking over 46 per cent. Furthermore, spending from the French national budget on structural measures has also been considerable. Almost every other outcome of agricultural policy has been an unending source of controversy inside and outside France, with the economic and social consequences hotly debated. The difficulty of attempting to measure accurately the impact of the CAP on French farming is enormous, partly because of the absence of a standard for comparison and partly because of the difficulty of constructing a 'counterfactual' of what French farming would have been like without the CAP.

A vast array of quantitative data is available about agricultural production, output, employment, exports and policy costs, but these data reflect not only the impact of the CAP, but also other policies and many other factors. Those factors include the transformation of farming by technological innovations, both in 'upstream' industries, including fertilizers, bio-engineering and machinery, and in 'downstream' sectors, such as distribution and food production. The CAP and the complementary policies have encouraged the more rapid exploitation of such innovations, and have financed some of the research, but these supply-side changes cannot be simply counted as results of the agricultural policy package. In a similar way, the price levels of the CAP do impact on the demand side, but major changes in demand also reflect both the addition of new groups of consumers with distinct national taste patterns with each enlargement, and international changes in consumption patterns, related to growing prosperity and new life-styles.

The most striking comparison between French farming in 1995 and 1958 is in terms of the massive increase in output. During that period, the output of European farming doubled, while the volume of production in France tripled. In 1958, France was already the biggest agricultural power in the Six, producing 40 per cent of the EC's cereals, meat and milk. In 1988, however, the value of French farm output reached 280 billion francs, and the volume was 25 per cent of the total agricultural production of the Twelve. In 1996, the value of agricultural output was 22 per cent of the total output of the Fifteen. The effect of this increased output has been felt on the balance of trade. During the early 1960s, the French trade balance in agriculture remained in deficit, despite the considerable rise in production. By 1987, however, French agriculture was producing far more than was necessary to satisfy domestic consumption; the rates of self-sufficiency were 190 per cent for wheat, 137 per cent for poultry, and 120 per cent for corn, sugar and oilseeds. In 1989, France, with an agricultural trade surplus of over 50 billion francs, became the world's second largest exporter of agricultural products, behind the USA, and Rouen was the world's largest grain port. In 1993, agricultural products constituted 3.6 per cent of GNP and 15 per cent of exports.

The expansion of production was largely achieved by improvements in efficiency, notably in labour productivity. Cereal farming clearly illustrates this increased labour efficiency: in 1958, an average of 10 hours of labour was needed to produce 20 quintals of wheat, but by 1988 the same labour input produced 90 quintals. A huge decrease in the size of the farm labour force both encouraged and reflected this trend. In 1958, agriculture was one of the major employers, since the farming population of almost 5 million constituted 24 per cent of the workforce in France. By 1996, in contrast, farming employed only 2 million people, and the majority of these on a part-time basis. Although agriculture accounted for only 5 per cent of full-time employment in 1996, that proportion also reflects the increase of the total labour force, with population growth and a higher percentage of women in full-time paid employment than in 1958.

Farming, traditionally a full-time family business in France, has become a part-time business for many. In 1963, the total farm labour force of 4 891 900 was composed of 1 899 200 farmers and 2,521,500 working members of their families, but only 471 200 farm labourers (not including seasonal workers). Twenty years later, the total labour-force had fallen to 2 400 400, including 1 129 600 farmers, 1 093 700 working family members and only 177 100 labourers. In 1983, however, only 637 800 of the 1,129,600 farmers actually worked full-time in agriculture, and of the remainder only 349 520 declared farming as their main job, leaving 131 281 farmers for whom farming was a second, part-time job. In the same year, of the 1 093 700 working family members, only 201 100 were full-time in agriculture. Even among the farm labourers, 49 500 were part-timers in 1983. In short, labour force total figure of 2 400 400 was misleading; the full-time farming population of France was less than 1 000 000. By 1996, it was fewer than 950 000.

These statistics, however, in some ways overestimate the decline in importance of farming as a way of life. Farming may be a part-time occupation for many, but a large number of families continue to live on farms. In 1983, the total population living on farms included 591 505 children of school age (under 16), as well as the wives, children, parents, cousins – in all some 1590 564 – who lived on farms but did not work there. In 1983, the farm-based population – all those working or living on farms – totalled almost 4 million, and there has been little change since then. Furthermore, there is a large annual summer school-holiday return to family farms by urban immigrants of earlier decades. Hence, despite the massive decline in full-time farm employment, the section of the population which has close direct contacts with – and nostalgic sympathies for – agriculture, remains very large.

Efficiency improvements have been achieved by mechanization, irrigation and drainage schemes, increases in the sizes of units of production, and by widespread use of such results of scientific research as new fertilizers and pest-control products, and improvements in crops and animal husbandry. Mechanization has been a key element in the efficiency increases, by both speeding up production and encouraging the creation of larger farms. The ownership of tractors grew dramatically from 623 000 in 1958 to 1 485 000 in 1986, while the number of combine-harvesters rose from 42 000 to 148 000 in the same period. Such capital investments were most profitable for bigger farms, where they could be used very efficiently.

Hence, mechanization encouraged farmers to increase their land holdings.

The major encouragement, however, came from the government-financed SAFERs, created in the 1960s to make farms economically viable in size. This policy of *remembrement* had led to consolidation of land-holdings on 8.7 million hectares by 1973 and 12.2 million hectares by 1983. In 1955, there were 2 307 000 farms in France and over 35 per cent of farms were smaller than 5 hectares. Between 1955 and 1983 the total number of farms halved, and two-thirds of farms under 10 hectares had disappeared, leaving 62 per cent of farms over 10 hectares in size. By 1993 the average farm size was 34 hectares, the third largest in the EU after the UK and Denmark, and there were only 130 000 farms of less than 5 hectares. Furthermore, many of the small farms in 1993 were either intensive factory farms (notably for chickens, pigs and calves) or luxury crop producers (especially vineyards, flowergrowers or *primeurs*). These figures also underestimate the real size of many units of production, since frequently those who retire prefer to rent land to neighbours, rather than sell it.

Farms in the Rhône valley and in most of Languedoc have benefited substantially from the provision of irrigation water from barrages constructed on the Rhône and its subsidiaries. Improved efficiency has also resulted from the use of more and better fertilizers and scientifically improved strains of crops or animals. Ouputs per hectare have increased for most agricultural products in France. The average yield in cereals has increased from 3380 kilograms per hectare in 1970 to 6070 in 1990, whereas in rape-seed the increase was from 1750 to 2780 kilograms per hectare over the same period. Between 1960 and 1985 the potato yield per hectare doubled, from 14 to 29 tonnes. At the same time, the product range has changed. Between 1974 and 1985 alone, the area devoted to the cultivation of oilseeds rose from 352 000 hectares to 952 000 hectares.

Average living standards in farming have increased, but not at a constant rate. Farms' incomes increased less than industrial salaries until the late 1960s. Between 1968 and 1978 farmers incomes grew in step with other incomes, at about 3 per cent per year. Since then average incomes declined and the gap between the rich, big farmers and the small, marginal farmers has increased. The inevitable effect of supporting farm incomes primarily by means of product price supports was that those farmers who produced the most in the most efficient way received the highest incomes. By 1988, the owners of the largest farms in rich regions were the main beneficiaries of the CAP.

The characteristics of demand have undergone changes equally dramatic as those on the supply side. France is moving towards post-industrial society, and the rapid growth of the service sector and mechanization or robotization in industrial production have led to a substantial decline in the number of jobs involving hard physical labour. The average working week has grown shorter. In 1997, most work takes place in heated or air conditioned buildings. In consequence, average daily calorific needs fell between 1960 and 1990 – from 3000 calories to 2200 for men and from 2400 to 1800 for women. The demographic shift towards an ageing population, as a consequence of falling birthrates and health improvements among the elderly, also contributed towards this trend. Inevitably, the nature of demand for foods has changed.

Increasing prosperity, better education and changing tastes have also transformed demand patterns. Growing health consciousness during recent decades has had an impact on both the quantity and the quality demanded. Public health campaigns against alcoholism have had important effects; in 1965, the average French consumer drank 90 litres of wine and 21 litres of beer per year, but by 1985 these figures had dropped to 40 litres of wine and 11 litres of beer. In 1988, new campaigns were launched to discourage smoking and drunken driving. Green concerns have become widespread and dieting has become a common middle-class hobby. Almost every supermarket sells skimmed milk, fat-reduced cheeses and low-sugar jams as standard items. A survey in 1990 showed that 25 per cent of French adults were following some kind of diet.

The feminization of the work force has also had its impact. In 1960, at a time when there was a national labour shortage, 36 per cent of women were in full-time employment. In 1993, 60 per cent of women of working age were in full-time employment, despite the economic recession and the subsequent rise in female unemployment rates (twice as high as for men). There have been three effects for agriculture, one on farm incomes, one concerning the distribution system, the other, the processing of food products. Dual income families have become increasingly common and most households' real disposable incomes have risen sharply since 1960. Female employment outside the farm has meant that some small, inefficient farmers have been able to remain in production thanks to the wife's income.

The daily purchasing of food from local markets or small shops by housewives has given way to weekly family shopping in out-of-town *centres commerciaux*. The disappearance of the *femme au foyer* has brought a rising demand for prepared foods and a consequent fall in demand for raw foods. The growth of canned foods has been considerable, but less than that of frozen foods. Freezers and microwave ovens have become standard features of middle-class homes. The prepared meal (even the TV dinner, *le plateau-repas télé*, once reviled as a symptom of encroaching American decadence) is widely sold. Meat, cheese and vegetable products are increasingly sold in pre-packed forms. Whereas in 1960 over half of all foodstuffs were sold unprocessed, by 1990 almost 80 per cent of foods sold had been processed. Food packaging and processing have became major industries: *les industries agro-alimentaires*, employing some 350 000 workers by 1996.

In short, since 1958, the technical, economic and social context of French farming has been transformed. There is still a large variety of products, techniques and types of farming but major changes have taken place almost everywhere. The importance of farming in relation to its upstream and downstream industries has been modified. So too have the number of farmers, farm sizes, production totals (in both volume and value), levels of productivity and efficiency. EU membership was only one of the causal factors. The process of change began long before 1958, and the CAP market structures were not fully operational until 1968. In short, the considerable gains in productivity, total output and quality control in France cannot be attributed solely to the CAP.

Nor does the CAP alone explain the French contribution to the waste of food 'mountains' and wine 'lakes', the scandals of frauds, the environmental problems arising from over-use of intensive production methods and the welfare losses both to consumers within the EU and to producers elsewhere in the world (from customs levies and exports subsidies). The CAP, however, did provide a responsive financing system which many French farmers, with substantial aid and encouragement from governments and agriculture ministry officials, massively exploited, for their individual benefit and for the balance of trade advantage of the French economy.

Conclusions

Many cases have been argued for the price support and protection side of the CAP. One is that Europe should be self-sufficient in food supply, because there are periodic shortages caused by climate or war which mean that imports are not reliable. Another is that French and other EU farmers grow higher quality produce than those mass-produced in Australia, Canada, the USA and New Zealand, so these produce should command higher prices. A third is that farming maintains a traditional way of life with rich village life and a population spread across the territory: the whole of society gains from preserving its rural roots, and without the CAP the French countryside would be a 'desert' with rare, massive, industrial farms and thousands of 'ghost villages'. Yet another argument is that agriculture is France's 'Green Oil' – a massive export resource, thanks to CAP subsidies. A related point is that agriculture keeps many people in work who would otherwise join the 'army of the unemployed'. A Green variant is that farming is becoming more ecologically balanced, as the CAP is now paying farmers to return to more ecologically sound practices. At the same time, keeping a large number of small farmers in farming, occupying the territory and making rural France a place where urban dwellers can retreat to recover from the stress and pollution of towns is a valuable contribution to the health of society.

Though French agriculture has changed dramatically since the inception of the CAP, it is unclear whether the changes have been generally positive, and for whom, and the extent to which the CAP is responsible for that transformation. In their claims for higher incomes and export subsidies small farmers have the backing of a population which has a strong farming 'sympathy' and a rural nostalgia. In 1997, many small French farmers remain dissatisfied with the re-formed CAP. In 1992, they fought hard against the MacSharry package and voted massively against the TEU. They campaigned actively against the GATT deal in 1993. None the less, the take-up rates for set-aside grants, reforestation and extensive farming methods have been very high. Although in interest group terms the farming community has become more diversified, the protests bring together those who farm the large efficient farms whose expectations of continuing wealth from export subsidies are challenged, and those who remain from the old traditions of peasant agriculture, where CAP price supports are insufficient to provide a decent income. Perhaps the ultimate paradox of French agricultural policy is that, despite the vast expenditure and the many reforms, it has frequently dissatisfied those for whom it has been designed.

6

Economic and Industrial Policy

When the Treaty of Rome was signed, a primary objective of the EEC was to create a customs union between six national economies. Agreeing a common external tariff and trade policy and phasing out internal tariffs and quotas took a decade. Enlargement and the collapse of fixed exchange rates in the IMF system followed. By the late 1970s, with most internal tariff barriers abolished, EEC policy-makers turned their attention to two different, but related problems: non-tariff barriers and money. The SEA and its internal market programme were primarily concerned with eliminating non-tariff barriers and transforming international trade between member states into competition within a unified market. The 'Snake', the EMS and the EMU section of the TEU addressed the problem of exchange rate instability and the introduction of a single currency. EMU was designed to underpin the internal market.

Within the trade, competition, industry and monetary policy areas, governments of member states have gradually accepted, often with ill grace, shared policy-making with the EU instead of autonomous national policy-making. Implementation remains primarily the re-sponsibility of national administrations in the member states. In France, as elsewhere, this 'pooling of economic sovereignty' appeared to involve significant policy changes. Europeanization has been blamed, or praised, for several transfers of power; from political authorities to expert and quasi-judicial agencies; the move from state to market; the shifts in industrial investment from loans to equity, the reduction of state industrial strategies; the reduction of taxes and public spending; and competitive deflation in monetary policy. However, for France and other member states, Europeanization has coincided with globalization, and it is difficult to distinguish between the effects of Europeanization and globalization. Many aspects of French economic policy-making are not decided jointly in Brussels. Public spending, welfare and taxation policies continue to be determined primarily at the national level. As in agriculture, one aspect of the EU 'political game' is that there is considerable scope for member state governments to use domestic policy tools to maximize the yield to their states from joint EU policies.

In the 1990s, French governments have had to deal with the immediate political costs of unemployment, public spending cuts, market liberalization and deregulation, but have had little evidence to show their voters that the promised benefits of EU membership were appearing. Hence, distinguishing effects of EU membership from the consequences of globalization has mattered relatively little to French politicians. Rather they tend to focus on whether the EU is catalysing a global trend towards unfettered free trade and unchecked market economics (with high social costs) or facilitating the eventual emergence of a specifically European model of welfare capitalism.

The former view is gloomily exemplified by the economist Alain Minc, who has argued that the internal market programme is transforming the European economy into a mere sub-section of the global economy, with free competition between firms, irrespective of national roots, and free movement of factors of production. As such, the global liberal market represents a victory of 'American philosophy', and is nothing less than 'a Darwinian nightmare'. It implies not only the death of French economic sovereignty, but also, for the entire EU, a significant transfer 'from the State to society, from the law-maker to free agents in the economy and from the principle of order to the principle of disorder' (Minc, 1989).

The alternative view is that, if some features of traditional French capitalism have been modified, others have been incorporated into a new model of capitalism emerging at the EU level, captured most evocatively by Albert's (1991) term 'Rhine–Alpine capitalism'. The development of the EU structural funds, research policy and the social chapter are cited as evidence here. The relatively free hand left by the Commission to French governments to provide state aid to firms in difficulties (notably *Air France* and *Crédit Lyonnais* in 1995) or to privatize public sector corporations in a way which ensures that control is retained, through a hard core of institutional investors, by trusted French business leaders, have been seen as signs that some traditional approaches of economic nationalism are still being practised, either with the consent of EU partners, or within a new pattern of EU-agreed constraints.

Whether or not both views are exaggerated, or both contain elements of a more complex and still evolving picture, they do reflect a widespread recognition of the fact that French economic policy-making has changed in the context of EU membership. This chapter analyses the nature and extent of the changes. Such an analysis, must, however, tackle major obstacles. Was there historically a consistent pattern of French economic policy-making and if so what were its defining characteristics? Certainly the *dirigiste* and protectionist traits of French policy were never absolute, and the process of internationalizing the economy began long before the Treaties of Paris and Rome were signed. The defining features of post-war macroeconomic strategy were laid down by participation in Bretton Woods, GATT and Marshall Aid, all of which implied a commitment to international trade and competition. On the other hand, if the creation of the customs union, the Snake, EMS and EMU, and the internal market have influenced the ways in which decision makers approach macroeconomic policy and micro-economic strategies, then thinking about the economy has also been influenced by other changes – ideological, technological and hegemonic – which were global in nature and globalizing in impact. The impact of EMS and EMU clearly meant a shift from tolerating inflation (and hence devaluations) to price stability in France, but 'the German model' was also imitated in many places outside the EU.

In the first section of this chapter, we examine both the traditional approaches to economic policy-making in France and the new globalizing pressures. We also address the problem of how to assess change in economic policy-making, the absence of suitable cases to allow a comparative approach and the difficulties of assessing what French economic policy-making would resemble if Europeanization had not taken place. In the second section, we examine the development of EU economic policies and policy-making, considering the extent of policy changes, the coherence of the policy packages and the continuity of the main lines of policy. This leads to a third section which addresses the question of the restructuring of the policy communities. Here we identify significant changes in actors, institutions and processes. In conclusion, we assess whether Minc's 'American nightmare' sheds more light on the evolution of negative economic integration in France than Michel Albert's concept of an emerging French variant of 'Rhine–Alpine capitalism'.

France and the world: dirigisme and globalization

To assess the impact of EU membership we try to identify how policy-making was characterized before the EC was created, to consider influences other than the EC and to compare with what might have changed if the EC had not been created. All are fraught with difficulties. Was there a French model of economic policy-making? What aspects of traditional patterns of formulating and implementing economic policy in France were distinctive? Our attempt to answer these questions leads on to a brief account of the major globalizing trends which have influenced recent evolution in economic policy-making in France as Europeanization has taken place. Finally we consider some problems of distinguishing EU and global impacts on policy patterns.

In the mid-1980s, Hayward (1986) identified a 'French economic policy community' which was characterized by two distinctive traits:

- the search for national economic policy coherence
- the essential inequality of the various actors.

The outcome was a process of state-led, limited pluralism, but containing considerable variations between sectors and overtime, from neo-corporatist practices to conflictual pluralism. It was summed up by Bloch-Laîné, the great defender of the concerted economy, as a system

> where representatives of the State or its subordinate bodies and those of business . . . meet to exchange information, compare their forecasts and together take decisions or present advice . . . Major decisions are based upon continuous collaboration so that the public and private sectors do not correspond to two sets of separate unconnected acts. (Hayward, 1986, pp. 27–8)

While Hayward acknowledges that the macroeconomic co-ordination in French planning was less than perfect, there was a general aspiration for coherent policy-making, and sometimes it was practised.

The protectionist and anti-market aspects of this traditional search for statist coherence in economic policy-making were underlined by Zysman:

> In France, the market place was never really allowed to impose its
> will on the community . . . closed borders, active entrepreneurial
> intervention by the State, and negotiation rather than competition
> between business within France have all served to insulate the
> economy from the market. The post-war variant, indicative
> planning for the 'concerted economy' allowed for some opening
> of the borders but still involved negotiation rather than
> competition. (Zysman, 1977, p. 57)

None the less, neither French industry nor the government was
willing to accept very strong competitive pressures from abroad. This
was clearly shown in the 1982 video-recorder war. The French
government, alarmed at massive imports of cheap Japanese video-
recorders, adopted delaying tactics, by enforcing the use of one small
customs post – Poitiers – for all video-recorders. In turn, the EC
adopted a Community-wide policy on such imports, and persuaded
the Japanese government to set minimum export prices to stop
dumping. The Japanese industrial response was for firms to create
joint ventures with European companies, or set up their own assembly plants in Europe. As they then imported most of the components
from low-cost Asian suppliers, the result was that lost-cost import
competition could continue, but in components rather than video-
recorders. A further case was that of the imports of Japanese cars.
Although France had import quotas pre-dating the SEA, other EC
states had no such restrictions, and so their car industries – whose
products could freely enter the French market – did respond to
Japanese competition, in terms of quality, product innovations and
price. In this way, despite national import quotas, French firms have
faced *indirect* competition from Japanese cars. Productivity in the
French industry rose greatly during the 1980s, although Jacques
Calvet, chairman of Peugeot–Citroën, continued to call for EC-wide
restrictions on imports of Japanese and Korean cars on the grounds of
unfair competition.

For Hayward, most economic policy choices were determined by
the convergent assumptions and purposes of two types of partners –
selected leaders of major enterprises and elected or appointed state
officials. This elitist system ensured that

> most of those who are essential to liberal, social and economic
> democracy are effectively excluded from the economic policy
> community, whereas most of those included, notably the elite

economic bureaucrats and the selected business leaders, have no democratic legitimacy. (Hayward, 1986, p. 18)

Among those who were usually kept out of major policy decisions were the consumers, the shareholders, the trade unions, the local authorities, parliament, the parties and the voters.

Schmidt nuanced Hayward's position by stressing the distinction between the formulation and implementation stages of policy-making. In France's 'statist polity' a close relationship developed between some (notably business) interest groups and government, based on government dominating the formulation stage of policy-making, but business having a major role in policy implementation. Schmidt stressed the wide discretionary power of civil servants to interpret and grant derogations to the rules formulated by the state (often known in France as *le système D*) (Schmidt, 1995). As Hall (1986) has shown, institutional arrangements allowed government discretionary favours in the form of allocations of credit from state-owned banks, public subsidies or cheap loans, lucrative public procurement contracts and the selective application of price controls and tax rules – all tradeable assets of great interest to most businesses.

Other scholars have stressed the elitist sociology of this exclusionary policy-making system. Following Bourdieu and Birnbaum, Bauer (1987) showed both the national insularity of business elites and the importance of the highest *grandes écoles* in recruiting and training both the top civil servants and many senior leaders of business in the public and private sectors alike. Those who led major French companies, like those who led the state, were always French, usually male, and very often former senior civil servants and graduates of ENA or *Polytechnique*. In short, there was an elite economic caste, educated at the same schools, sharing the same values and objectives.

Was this model of industrial policy-making ever operational? Politicians proclaimed it was: Giscard d'Estaing launched his strategy of 'niche sectors' (*la politique des créaux*), focusing investment into narrowly defined activities where France could – it was hoped – lead the markets. Under Mauroy, a strategy of 'streams' (*la politique des filières*) had been substituted, with a wider investment focus on vertically integrated streams of production. Fabius instead adopted a 'technology clusters' (*grappes technologiques*) approach, with the objective of developing 'economically inter-active technologies'. The tools of all of these industrial policies were mergers, subsidies and soft loans, selective enforcement of regulations, and public purchasing; the objects of these policies were key industrial sectors, rather than industry as a whole.

In practice, since the 1960s, industrial policy has never really been very effective or coherent. Even during the early 1980s the draining of investment to keep Renault, Usinor and Sacilor afloat greatly limited the extent of action elsewhere. Hayward (1986, pp. 2–3) admits that in practice there was less an 'economic policy community' than a 'series of competing sectoral sub-groups':

> Each economic policy – trade, industrial, energy, monetary, prices and incomes, employment, regional and so forth – has its own particular state-society sub-system, so that attempts to co-ordinate them, by the Finance Ministry, or either its budgetary or treasury division, by the Planning Commissariat, by the interministerial economic committee, or by the Prime Minister or President of the Republic, are illusory.

Furthermore, as the economy grew and diversified, attempts to impose inter-sectoral coherency became increasingly doomed. In short, economic policy-making was never very coherent, while industrial policy was incoherent and sector-specific.

A second caveat is that policy-making was often not effective. Hayward (1986, p. 2) noted:

> It is flattering to politicians and bureaucrats to believe that decisional voluntarism – such a feature of French public policy rhetoric – is relatively free from constraint. The notion that the government has sovereign command over the complex domestic and international forces that will decide the fate of its economic policy initiatives flies in the face of reality.

Market pressures might be postponed but could rarely be totally ignored, especially as international trade became increasingly important. Furthermore, the supposed autonomy of the state at the formulation stage was very often illusory. Hayward notes the irony that what was heralded as industrial policy 'frequently amounts to an industrialists' policy'. A detailed study of the allocation of public loans and subsidies to industry has shown that there was very little correlation between what national economic plans laid down as sectoral priorities and how funds were actually used (Pencurd and

Gaudichet, 1985). Indeed, whatever the rhetoric of politicians and civil servants, public investment in industry generally had a lower priority for governments than housing, public service infrastructure and agriculture. If trade unions were often neglected, then sometimes they hit back dramatically. De Gaulle might boast of the importance of the plan and the insignificance of 'intermediaries', but throughout his period in office the lesson of the 1963 miners' strike was never forgotten and a huge proportion of the budget of the ministry of industry was spent in subsidizing the closing down of the coal industry. Union views of social security reforms were ignored in 1967, but the government conceded the Grenelle wage rises after the 'Events' of May 1968.

Above all, the objectives and methods of economic policy evolved considerably in the post-war decades. The consensus which held through the 'Thirty Golden Years' (1945–75) of 5 per cent per annum (Fourastié, 1979) economic growth, reconstruction, industrialization and internationalization, has been characterized by Cohen (1995) as an 'inflationist social compromise' based on the political economy of administered finance to a 'capitalism without capital'. There was an implicit agreement between governments, business leaders and trade unions to make only nominal attempts at controlling rising prices and wages and to accept the inevitable periodic devaluations of the franc that were required. Corporate managers were left to develop and prosper in a opening market environment, and unions gained a statutory minimum wage, a welfare state in which they played a management role and considerable legislation protecting workers' rights in the labour market. Governments decreed overall regulation, took occasional initiatives in areas neglected by the private sector, developed the public infrastructure for a rapidly urbanizing consumer society, and expected the electoral credit for the general increase in prosperity. Private industry was financed by borrowing rather than issuing shares, and the banks, public and private alike, often specialized in financing particular sectors. State weapons for influencing market outcomes were focused on six kinds of objectives:

- building essential economic infrastructures
- encouraging more and better research
- promoting growth in under-developed regions
- inducing the remodelling of corporate structures to strengthen competitiveness

- caring for industrial lame ducks ('the stretcher-bearer state' in Cohen's [1995] terms) and pursuing grand projects.
- Many of these objectives were shared by most governments of other EU member-states, and France was certainly not exceptional in its supply of lame ducks or outdated corporate structures.

Cohen (1995) argues that an enduring characteristic of French economic policy-making before the Single European Market was the *dirigiste* approach of 'high-tech Colbertism' to develop large-scale 'industries of the future' (in chemicals and oil – Elf; telecommunications – France Telecom; electricity – EDF; railways – TGV; aircraft construction – Aerospatiale). Governments provided protection from foreign competition, subsidies and soft loans, and guaranteed markets by lucrative public procurement projects. The success of these *grands projets* could not be guaranteed, as costly failures in computing and cabling demonstrated. Furthermore, if the test of success – selling the product profitably in the international market – was achieved, it was often by means of the firm finding a European partner. Such success almost always led to the firm wanting to cut the cord to the state and henceforth to be judged by the market alone. Each case, however, exhibited the 'elitist conspiracy' and 'protectionist' traits of the generalizations of Hayward and Zysman. Whether such practices can continue within the internal market will show how viable is the French model of industrial policy.

A second major difficulty in ascertaining how traditional French patterns have changed in response to EU membership, however, is that the shift from national to joint domestic-European policy-making has taken place in the context of globalization, and globalization has been a multi-faceted, multi-speed phenomenon. One aspect of globalization concerns trade. Since Bretton Woods, there has been increasing international co-operation between governments to develop freer trade within the GATT/WTO framework, notably in the Kennedy and Uruguay 'rounds' of negotiations. The decline of empires, the disintegration of the Soviet bloc and the opening of previously closed economies in remaining authoritarian states have facilitated the growth of international trade in all types of goods and services. One early development of an international market was that of oil and natural gas; old strategies of national energy self-sufficiency were quickly dumped when these new energy sources were so cheap and plentiful. The French dependency which resulted, and the subsequent impact of the OPEC oil price rises of 1973 and 1979, revealed that globalization did have some dangers.

Another type of globalization concerns firms and financial markets. Specialists identify three steps in the transformation of firms:

1. First came multi-national enterprises, in which national firms acquire production and marketing subsidiaries abroad to form relatively loose conglomerates, with considerable autonomy for national subsidiaries to adapt to local market conditions.
2. Next to appear were the international firms, characterized by integrated products and technologies and a plurality of national roots.
3. Finally, many now see the emergence of a new species, the transnational corporation, with a single, global range of products and marketing approaches, an integrated world-wide production system and without any dominant nationality group in management. Here, the international mobility of management and the international recruitment by international and transnational firms develop in parallel. This does not imply that there has been global agreement about forms and rules of corporate governance; indeed there is very little EU, let alone WTO, consensus on how power in firms should be distributed or how rates of profitability should be calculated. There is evidence of 'competition among rules' allowing corporate managers to choose the state (or regulatory region) of the world in which to base their headquarters according to the costs and benefits of the regulatory regime. Furthermore, in financial markets, a 24-hour, three-zone world market has evolved, dominated by New York, Tokyo and London, and characterized by shared information and competitive creativeness in new financial products.

A third type of globalization is that of information and economic ideas. This is partly a consequence of new technologies in television, telecommunications and computing (with the Internet symbolizing the advent of a global 'information society') but partly too the political outcome of the failure of Stalinist economics. Governments, firms and investors around the world very rapidly learn of all market and public policy innovations, successes and failures. Imitation of what succeeds quickly follows information.

French attitudes and behaviour have been affected by all these types of globalization, but it is far from easy to distinguish between global and EU membership effects. Unfortunately there is no European state and economy really comparable to France which has not joined the EU, so that a comparative standard to identify globalization effects is lacking. Nor is the construction of an abstract counterfactual a serious possibility. To hypothesize an assessment of how French economic policy-making would be conducted if the Treaty of Rome and SEA had not taken place would require adopting so many debatable premises as to lose any value. We can, however, examine how policy-making has evolved within the EU and make some modest identification of changes when clear linkages can be established.

Patterns of policy evolution

The Treaty of Paris in 1951, marked the first major Europeanization of French economic policies and the institutions of policy-making. It involved three core ideas:

- the customs union
- the integrated market with common rules and regulations, and
- the supranational administrative and judicial authority to police implementation of the common policy by the administrations in the member states.

The customs union covered only coal, steel and associated products, but these were seen to be at the core of economic activity at that time, and the idea of removing all internal tariffs and quotas and creating a common external tariff was a radical innovation. The Treaty of Rome set down the goals of creating a much broader customs union and common market, covering most sectors of the economy. It was not, however, all-embracing, since the production and trade of 'arms, munitions or war materials' was excluded (Article 223), and governments were allowed to limit free trade (Article 36) or free movement of workers (Article 48) for reasons of public health, public security, or public morality. There was provision for a transitional period, 12 to 15 years, and for the first eight years all decisions of the Council of Ministers required unanimity.

The main policy shifts between 1 January 1958 and 1 July 1968 were a reform of the structures of customs controls and tariff levels to establish a common external tariff, and a tax reform, including the introduction of valued added tax. These changes were made slowly. Initially, there was no attempt to abolish customs controls between member states, but merely to simplify procedures. In addition, while the existence of such non-tariff barriers as preferential public procurement was recognized, little was done to check their distortive effects. Furthermore, the limits to free market competition imposed by national health and safety standards were dealt with by attempts at only minimal 'harmonization'. The period of transition to a full customs union in 1968 coincided with de Gaulle's presidency and, given his view of the EC as merely a community of national economies, his ministers encouraged French firms to improve efficiency so as to be able to compete effectively in the common market. However, ministers continued to treat the EC itself as an international organization.

With the resignation of de Gaulle and the election of President Pompidou in 1969, new policy changes began, including the enlargement of the Community and the definition of common policies to deal with the new problem of exchange rate instability. With the admission of the UK, Denmark and Ireland, all with governments of free trade preferences, there was pressure for more 'negative integration' to increase competition. Yet, the need for unanimity in the Council of Ministers (after the 1966 Luxembourg Compromise) prevented any major change.

The ending of the Bretton Woods system and the floating of currencies threatened to disrupt trading relations between member-states, and created particularly acute problems for the CAP, which necessitated the creation of the convoluted system of special exchange rates for agricultural trade ('green currencies') and monetary compensation amounts (MCAs). After the 1969 French devaluation, the Barre Report, from the Commission, envisaged a series of steps to create a single currency. In 1970, the Werner group, set up by the Council, analysed the effects on trade of the new exchange rate instability and the possible steps towards a single currency by 1980. The first attempt to move towards greater exchange rate stability – to create a 'regional pool of stability in a storm of floating exchange rates' was the 'Snake' system, established in 1972. As explained by Delors, the Snake was a policy of keeping intra-EC exchange rates within a limited band, so that all would rise or fall together in relation to other exchange rates (Delors, 1992). The European partners subsequently made an agreement with the US government to keep their band of exchange rates within a limited range of exchange rates against the dollar, and this EC–USA range became known as the 'tunnel'. For many observers in France and elsewhere, the image of a snake wriggling blindly in a tunnel was not a reassuring vision of a European monetary system.

Whatever the government's intentions, the 'Snake' proved extremely difficult for the franc and embarrassing for French political leaders. Indeed, large speculative pressures led to the Government's withdrawal of the franc from the 'Snake' in 1974. The major problem, which financial markets recognized and speculators sought to exploit, was the lack of co-ordination between the wider economic policies of the EC member states. Although the franc was later able to re-enter the Snake, renewed speculation led to a second withdrawal. It was soon recognized that without a close linking, or 'convergence', of economic policies, the Snake was simply unstable.

In 1979, a further stage of policy development to deal with currency instability was inaugurated by the creation of the EMS and its Exchange Rate Mechanism (ERM), initiated by Helmut Schmidt, Valéry Giscard d'Estaing and Roy Jenkins. The EMS represented an attempt to tackle the problems revealed by the Snake by creating a European unit of account, the European currency unit, or ECU, based on a 'basket of currencies' and by establishing the ERM with a limited band of exchange rate fluctuations between all the currencies and the ECU. Although, in theory, the EMS and ERM shared power between member states, the practice soon came to mean that French interest-rate policies had to be kept slightly higher than those of the Bundesbank – the semi-autonomous custodian of the EC's strongest currency. The policy of the *franc fort* was thus initiated, and with it came the strategy of competitive deflation.

The existence of the EMS had serious implications for Mitterrand and the Socialist government elected in 1981, since their policy of reflation required lowering interest rates, and that involved a substantial devaluation against the Deutschmark. The EMS rules, designed to stop competitive devaluations, required that realignments within the ERM be agreed by all members, and initially the European partners would agree to only limited devaluations. In 1983, however, the March devaluation crisis revealed that for the franc to stay in the EMS the French government had not only to negotiate a further devaluation, but also to change policy and follow the anti-inflationary strategy of the Bundesbank. However, Mitterrand and most of his ministers calculated that the cost of leaving the EMS was higher than that of staying in. In short, the crisis revealed that European monetary interdependence without a single currency actually implied some degree of economic dependence, at least for France.

At the 1988 Hanover European Council, it was a logical step for Mitterrand to support the establishment of the Delors Committee to study the way to achieve EMU. The amendment of the EEC Treaty by the TEU (1991), to prepare for EMU, heralded the start of a new phase of harmonized economic policy-making. The practical problems of the transition are enormous, as the speculation crisis of July 1993 showed. Although the French government was better prepared than the British Treasury had been the previous September to resist speculation against the franc, it could not resist the downward pressure on the exchange rate. Even the currency resources of the Bundesbank were insufficient to check the speculation, and the limits of the ERM bands were enlarged so that the franc could officially remain within the system.

The institutional arrangements and convergence criteria laid down in the TEU were also to have profound implications for the conduct of French economic policy. By ratifying the TEU in the 1992 referendum, French voters effectively committed subsequent governments to respecting the convergence criteria (of Article 109j(1)) and to making the Bank of France autonomous. During the second of the three stages leading to EMU, which began on 1 January 1994, the establishment of the European Monetary Institute (EMI) at Frankfurt was agreed, and the Balladur government used its massive parliamentary majority to enact the independence of the Bank of France in 1994. This reduction of the government's leverage over an instrument of economic management was not without its critics, on the left and on the right. Furthermore, in early 1995, the extent of the bank's real autonomy was called into question when Chirac, in an election speech, criticized Trichet, the Governor of the Bank of France, for making remarks about the possible inflationary consequences of the policies he was proposing. Once elected, however, Chirac was quick to demonstrate his respect for the newly independent bank.

Respecting the 'Maastricht criteria' for EMU was not politically easy for French ministers. To be eligible to join the single currency, a member state must have a rate of inflation not more than 1.5 per cent above that of the three lowest rates in the EU, a budgetary deficit of less than 3 per cent of its GDP, an overall public debt of less than 60 per cent of its GDP, average long-term interest rates of not more than

2 per cent above the three lowest rates in the EU, and its currency within the narrow band of the ERM without devaluation for the previous two years. Although as prime minister Balladur was as tough in his speeches as the previous Socialist prime minister, Bérégovoy, had been in his policies, it was very difficult – with over 3 million unemployed and a presidential election looming in April 1995 – for any government to maintain absolutely tight discipline in monetary policy. None the less, Balladur continued to press for an early start (1997) to the final fixing of exchange rates, and the Bank of France and the finance ministry undertook detailed practical studies of the changes necessary to introduce a single currency. In 1995, following the publication of the Commission's Green Paper which set practical steps to achieve EMU, President Chirac accepted the German position, at the European Council in Essen, that the start of the third stage of EMU be postponed until the residual treaty date, 1 January 1999. At the beginning of the Chirac presidency, the policy was unchanged but the debate about costs and benefits was re-opened.

In 1997, the election of the centre-left majority and the appointment of Jospin as prime minister heralded new domestic debates (notably with President Chirac), but also some tensions with governments in other member states. At the Amsterdam summit in June 1997, Jospin made clear his determination that the Maastricht criteria should be interpreted in a broad way, despite the open dispute with Chancellor Kohl which inevitably ensued. The Socialist government also made clear its intention not to compromise its job-creation programme simply to respect the 3 per cent current-account-deficit rule.

Competition policy

In the area of competition, 1979 was a key date for policy development, as a consequence of the ECJ decisions on the '*Cassis de Dijon*' and '*Dassonville*' cases, which changed the approach to competition policy-making. When the Court ruled that *Cassis de Dijon* (a delicious alcoholic blackcurrant drink) made under French specifications could be sold in Germany, despite the fact that it did not meet German rules (and a health question was involved), it signalled that harmonizing national regulations was not the only way to remove tariff barriers. Henceforth, the almost impossible task of persuading all member state governments to agree on common rules could be replaced by the process of 'mutual recognition' of different norms, within reasonable limits. Although attempts at harmonization were to continue within the CAP, the approach of mutual recognition offered the possibility of really opening up market competition in all other areas.

The 1984 Fontainebleau Summit prepared the way for a period of massive policy evaluation under the Delors Commission by sorting out the thorny problems of the British budget rebate, some measures of CAP reform and the common objective of moving from a customs union to an integrated single market by removing non-tariff barriers. The adoption of the Cockfield White Paper in 1985 and the passage of the Single European Act not only clearly reasserted the treaty goals of free movement of goods, persons, services and capital by the removal of non-tariff barriers, but also set a deadline and the means of achieving it – qualified majority voting in the Council. One immediate effect of the programme to enhance competition through-out the EC was the abolition of resale price maintenance and price controls in France. The Ordinance of 1 December 1986, enacted by the Chirac government, not only abolished state price fixing, but also created a competition council to act as a watchdog to prevent abuse of competitive practices. Furthermore, the civil courts were given new powers to deal with illegal uncompetitive behaviour and to award damages to those who suffered thereby.

A second aspect of that programme was the restriction of prefer-ential public procurement and employment. The French govern-ment, like all others, accepted that its public purchasing and employment policies would henceforth be open to firms and indivi-duals from all member-states. In the decree of 17 April 1989, it applied the directive of 22 March 1988; henceforth, in theory, the use of state contracts to support French firms was to cease, and bids from companies based in any member-states were to be treated equally. Another aspect of the internal market programme was the move to liberalize capital markets. After the directive, the Rocard government responded by abolishing exchange controls in 1989 so that for the first time since the Second World War French citizens and firms could move their savings and investments when and wherever they liked.

At the same time, the French government agreed to increasing the Commission's power of scrutiny of state aids to industry. Article 92 of the Treaty of Rome had prohibited state-aid in any form which distorts competition and created a system of notifying the Commission of all state-aid schemes and allowing the Commission (under Article 93) to grant specific derogations from Article 92. In practice, however, very few schemes were refused derogations. In many cases, the problems were too politically sensitive. In France, the reduction of aids to industry began in 1983 for domestic budgetary reasons, and continued under Chirac after 1986. In 1986, the Commission issued guidelines on acceptable practices of state funding for research and development, and in 1988, in line with the reform of the structural funds, Commission guidelines for regional development aid in member-states were also laid down.

However, problems arose over the rules on loans and grants to public corporations. The French government discovered that these rules were serious in the case of its financial assistance package to Renault: in 1990, after four years of dispute with the Commission, the government accepted that Renault should pay back 4 million francs of the state aid. The French government opposed the Commission's directive on the transparency of public sector financing. Indeed, it joined the British government in an appeal to the ECJ to over-rule the Commission, but to no avail. In 1990, the Commission issued guidelines on 'market economy investor principles' by which hidden subsidies to public corporations could be revealed and measured against what normal financial markets would charge for what a member state government might call a 'shareholder stake' investment.

There were three related areas of policy change. The first was that of competition in the provision of public utilities. For years the Commission had tried to avoid conflict with member state governments in its attempt to impose common standards and a degree of market competition in sectors such as telecommunications and transport (which in France were defined as 'public services' even when part-privatized). Even in telecommunications, where new technologies and new services were provoking demands for privatization and for trans-European compatibility of systems and standards, the Commission had to move slowly and carefully. When it finally issued a liberalization directive, based on Article 90 of the Treaty of Rome (dealing with competition), the French, German and Italian governments together challenged its legal right to do so at the ECJ. The Commission won its case, and may now use Article 190 powers in respect of other public utilities. *France Telecom* is now preparing for 1998, when international competition will be introduced into a previously protected market.

The second linked reform was creation of a system of Commission supervision of mergers and take-overs. Until the internal market programme, the Commission's initiatives had been blocked by disagreements in the Council, and in 1987 the Commission had had to make imaginative use of Article 85 of the Treaty of Rome to block a merger (the Philip Morris case). Many major business groups lobbied the Council to create a single EC-wide merger control system. The Council decided that the Commission should be empowered to review only mergers and take-over bids worth more than 5 billion ECU worldwide, or over 250 million ECU in the EC (by Council Regulation 4064/89 of 21 December 1989). That left smaller mergers and acquisitions (and those which involved over 66 per cent of world turn-over in one member-state) to the member state governments. None the less, it was soon clear that French 'high tech Colbertist' preferences for building up 'national champions' or 'Eurochampions' might be considerably hindered by this. The decision by the Commission to veto the proposed De Havilland–Aérospatiale merger was accepted by the French government, but only after considerable criticism by politicians and in the press. That decision seemed to confirm that the Commission approach was more concerned with promoting market competition than building up particular European industries or firms.

The other policy change concerned public procurement, one of the traditional weapons of French government for developing '*grands projets*'. The public procurement directives means that for all substantial public purchases of goods and services there must be open and fair calls for tender, and the Commission is empowered to investigate any disputed cases. In theory, the Treaty of Rome had outlawed exclusive national practices in public procurement, but with the notable exception of armaments. In 1985, however, less than 4 per cent of all public purchase contracts in member states went to firms based in other member states, and there was a surprising absence of litigation at the ECJ in this area. The internal market directives pushed for transparency in tender procedures. French governmental reactions have not been hostile; one part of an education ministry bulk purchase of personal computers went to Olivetti (although Bull, a French group, won the lion's share). In practice, in 1996 over 90 per cent of French public procurement contracts were won by French firms. Despite Article 225, French governments now participate in limited open tendering for armaments within the European group of NATO. French ministers, however, along with their British counterparts, strongly resisted the initiative of Sir Leon Brittan to include military purchasing within the treaty terms on competition. In short, theory has changed more than practice.

The changing actors and relations of economic policy-making

A major modification in the dynamics of economic policy-making is that the French political executive no longer takes many decisions completely outside the European policy processes. What was clear in agricultural policy-making by the late 1960s was that French and European political executives are inextricably intertwined. That has become increasingly true for the economic 'policy community' in general, especially since the internal market programme. During the transition period towards the customs union, the locus of a highly symbolic power, that of imposing tariffs and quotas and negotiating trading agreements, shifted from Paris to Brussels. Obviously, the French minister in the Council of Ministers was still a co-determinant of the political choices taken by that Council which have force of law throughout the Community. For the first two phases of the transition period, he could block any proposal by insisting on unanimity. Subsequently, the Luxembourg Compromise prolonged this notion of national interest veto'. None the less, even under de Gaulle, the dynamics of economic policy-making more frequently involved compromise than crises and blockages between the Six. In part this reflected the treaty terms which imposed Commission–Council dialogue, and gave the right of initiative to the Commission. In part, it resulted from the desire of French governments to achieve certain policy aims and from their willingness to make package deals to reach these goals.

As de Gaulle himself admitted in the Fouchet Plan, it was clearly easier to negotiate major package agreements if the heads of government – in the French case, the president – themselves led the crucial discussions. Pompidou organized the first of such summits, and under Giscard d'Estaing they were formalized as the European Council. The existence of the European Council was recognized in the SEA, and the President of the Commission was recognized as a full member of that body. In taking part in these meetings successive presidents of France implicitly acknowledged the central role of the EC in economic policy. Major decisions, including the multi-annual expenditure limits for the EU, were henceforth taken by the European Council.

The dynamics of EU economic policy-making at the governmental level have also been complicated by the three waves of enlargements (from 6 to 15 member states) as well as the provisions of the SEA and the TEU. Enlargements have complicated 'package deals' and have halved the frequency of French presidencies of the Council (from 6 months every 3 years to 6 months every 7.5 years). Knowing their normal difficulties in reaching unanimous agreements, the member state governments acknowledged that qualified majority voting in the Council had to be used if the 300 directives needed to abolish the non-tariff barriers of the internal market programme were to be adopted before the chosen deadline of 31 December 1992. The consequence was that the nature of decision making in the Council changed. If the Commission and the Presidency still sought consensus, coalition building and voting became standard practices. For the internal market programme, French ministers had effectively wiped out the Luxembourg Compromise; they could be outvoted, and sometimes they were. In short, French governments had henceforth to implement some policies formulated and voted into EC law in Brussels against their expressed wishes. The TEU further developed this centralized aspect of economic policy-making by introducing the codecision process, which gives the EP a limited a limited power of veto. French ministers now faced the prospect of having to negotiate not only with ministers from other member states but also with MEPs, and of having to modify compromises agreed with the Commission and member state governments to defuse parliamentary opposition.

A second modification was also important in this context – the growing role of the ECJ. Over the years, all actors in French economic policy-making have come to realize that the rule of European law has to be respected and that ECJ decisions have to be obeyed. In his analysis of the traditional French system, Hayward minimized the role of law and the courts, emphasizing the accepted right of the political executive to make exceptions to regulations and the restraint of firms and groups in using courts against the government. Europeanization, however, has brought real changes here. In leaving responsibility with national governments for transposing European directives into national law and then implementing them, the Treaty of Rome foresaw the possibility that member state governments might make interpretations of particular generosity to their domestic firms or markets. Not only was the Commission empowered to investigate accusations and prosecute suspected miscreants, but the ECJ was given absolute discretion to rule on conflicts of interpretation and responsibility. Furthermore, the treaty also provided for private prosecutions so that firms or groups in other member states could challenge the actions of the French government, as indeed could French companies.

In this context, two ECJ decisions were of great significance; those in the *Cassis de Dijon* and the *Nouvelles Frontières* cases. The first (discussed above, p. 172) allowed European integration to develop by moving away from the almost obsessive attempts to agree on common standards. In contrast, the *Nouvelles Frontières* case demonstrated that a small French travel agency could take on not only the French government but also the Council of Ministers and the Commission, and that the ECJ could instruct all these parties to respect the terms of the treaties. Sceptics might point out that French governments had a poor record of delay and inaccuracy in transposing directives into French law and in respecting ECJ decisions. None the less, as discussed above (Chapter 2), though the French record was poor during the 1960s and 1970s the situation changed dramatically in the 1980s. The enormous potential of the Court was gradually appreciated among French economic elites in precisely the same period that the French Constitutional Council was winning wide respect – and much greater usage – by political elites in Paris.

A third change concerned the recruiting and training of senior civil servants in key economic ministries. At the institutional level, almost every significant ministry or agency has created a European office. As noted above, the SGCI, in close association with the Elysée staff, became a central co-ordinating agency for all European questions. At the personnel level, circuits of secondment are organized from ministries to the SGCI, to the permanent representative's office in Brussels and to the staff of the Commission itself in the economic Directorates General. Whereas the early years had seen attempts – conscious or instinctive – to impose the French model on the structures and methods of the infant Commission staff, the 1980s saw a growing awareness that knowledge and experience of the Brussels process were essential qualifications for senior positions in Paris in ministries and in ministerial *cabinets*. Symptomatic of the change was the acceptance in the late 1980s of English as a main working language in many parts of the Council and Commission. The 1993 walk-out by a French-speaking Director General (who was

Spanish), unable to communicate with his new Commissioner who spoke only English (and Gaelic), was revealing because not a single high French civil servant protested.

The attitudes and behaviour of private sector managers and their peak associations have also been transformed by the Europeanization of markets and economic policies. Some managers have pursued expansionist strategies to build up cross-member state firms. Other French companies have sought to compete more effectively against other EC-based firms, in France or elsewhere in the internal market, by mergers, take-overs or shared technology agreements with non-EC based firms (especially US or Japanese companies). The Bull–Zenith merger and the later agreement with IBM was one such case; the attempted Renault–Volvo link another. On the one hand, the practice of privileged relations between a small number of big firms and the Commission suggests a replication of the French pattern on a European scale. On the other hand, the peak associations are weak, but sector groups may be strong. The French CNPF was a founder member in 1958 of UNICE (*Union des Industries de la Communauté Européenne*) but that organization has remained as fragmented and weak as the CNPF itself. Its secretariat in Brussels boasts a mere 40 staff and lacks both a general research capacity and specialist researchers on particular sectors. It is further weakened by its open and mixed membership: in 1992 UNICE had 32 members, including employees' federations from all EC States but also from EFTA, Turkey, Cyprus, Malta and even San Marino. These included both public and private sector firms.

The relations of the CNPF with European institutions have evolved considerably since the Paris Treaty. In the 1950s, the leaders of French steel firms made no secret of their reluctance to accept the idea and reality of the ECSC (Ehrmann, 1992). In 1968, the CNPF president argued that the completion of the customs union and subsequent increased foreign competition reinforced the need for the French government to support domestic industry. In the 1980s, by way of contrast, the CNPF participated in drafting the UNICE declaration for a 'fresh start' in Europe (1983) and in the UNICE's action plan for eliminating financial, legal and administrative obstacles to the unification of the EC market in February 1984 (Schneider, 1992, p. 43). In October 1984, the CNPF and the Paris Chamber of Commerce jointly organized a conference on the new dynamics of integration, with 200 European industrial leaders participating. The conference demonstrated the willingness of the CNPF leaders to work with colleagues from other member states to lobby for a single market. However, apart from being generally supportive of the competitive environment of the internal market and the EC programmes for research and development, neither UNICE or the CNPF is sufficiently coherent and focused to play a major role in EC policy development.

In contrast, the trade associations of several sectors are more willing and able to do so. After the SEA there has been a rapid growth in EC-wide specialized associations at both the sectoral and sub-sectoral levels. Indeed, in 1990 there were already some 600 European interest groups of which the vast majority were industry specific associations (Greenwood *et al.*, 1992, p. 262). The development of such associations has frequently corresponded to the growth of policy initiatives of the Commission. Thus, in the mid-1980s, the Commission became active in telecommunications, linking the liberalization of the telecommunication markets – both in operational services and in equipment supply – to the internal market programme. In response to this the European Conference of the Telecommunciations and Professions Electronics Industry (ECTEL) was formed with active French participation, to represent the equipment producers (Schneider, 1992).

In other sectors, the incentive to Europeanise came from non-EC sources; hence, it was Japanese innovations and competition in the domestic electric appliances market which provoked the creation in 1983 of the European Association of Consumer Electronics manufacturers (EACEM), by nine national trade associations, including the French SYMAVELEC. None the less, in this case the association was far less important than the leading firms. Cawson (1992) shows that before the 1970s there was no European consumer electronics industry, but only a series of national markets largely supplied by nationally-based firms, or local branches of Philips, the loose conglomerate multinational. By the 1980s, the harmonization of standards and the Japanese onslaught of new products and low prices had both integrated the market and led to a shake-up of European production. Two major multinationals, Philips and Thomson (including Telefunken, Ferguson and others), dominated European domestic production. The leaders of these two firms became the key representatives of the whole industry. The fact that Thomson had the full backing of the French government certainly helped its lobbying, but, even without that, its senior managers were part of the 'chosen few', the 'insiders' of the European television policy community. The carve-up of EUREKA funding for high definition television research between Philips and Thomson appeared to show that a transformation to the EC level of the French ministry of industry's traditional role of being (in Hayward's words) 'an indulgent father whose role was to guide his frequently feckless or spendthrift sons . . . in the way of righteousness' (1986, p. 74) had taken place.

None the less, Greenwood, Grote and Ronit (1992) concluded that although most firms and business associations recognized the importance of EC economic policy-making, there was a great variety of adaptations to business strategies for dealing with the EC. Some French groups prefer their own governments to forward their interests, while others choose a 'Eurostrategy', either representing their views and demands directly in Brussels or acting indirectly through a federal association. Many big firms have agents or offices in Brussels and pursue all three strategies simultaneously.

Among small firms there are differences between sectors and member states. The French pharmacists' association is one example of a group which relies both on the national government and on a series of alliances with associations in member states (for example, Italy, Spain) where pharmaceutical distribution is regulated in a similar, highly profitable way; it is hostile to the competitive ideas of the internal market programme, and particularly the threat of inroads into the French market by low-cost British chain pharmacists. It uses the health argument as the basis for its anti-competitive stance. In contrast, associations in the high-tech sectors and in craft industries are often effective in forming European organizations and lobbying at the EU level.

If the transformation of the organization and methods of firms and employers associations have taken place in an inconsistent and varied manner, the Europeanization of the fifth group of actors, the trade unions, has been consistently slow and small. In 1972, a study by Blanpain (Gunther, 1972) concluded that there was very little general co-operation between the trade union movements in the Six, let alone an effective EC-wide union organization. Twenty years later, Visser and Ebbinghaus (Greenwood *et al.*, 1992) concluded that very little had changed, despite the Single Market programme, intensified global competition, high unemployment, technological changes and neo-liberal policies of leading governments. They found a pattern of cross-national diversity and a remarkable degree of structural inertia. OECD statistics indicate that France, with only 10 per cent of the work force in unions, has the lowest rate of unionization in the EC, far below the 30–40 per cent levels typical of Germany, Italy and the UK.

Furthermore the French unions, like those in Spain and Italy, remain ideologically fragmented. When, in 1992, Visser and Ebbinghaus compared the vertical and horizontal integration of the European union movements, the French unions came bottom of the list on both measures. When the ETUC (European Trade Union Confederation) was created in 1973, *Force Ouvrière* was a founder member, the CFDT joined in 1974, the CFTC signed up only in 1991, and the CGT remained a non-member. ETUC membership involves not only joint action by the peak associations or national confederations, but also action by different groups of individual trade unions in the same industries but in different countries as 'European Industry Committees'. Both the ETUC itself, and the industry committees have failed to take leading roles in the EU policy processes. Indeed, the level of internal cohesion in the ETUC has been compared with that of the TUC in Britain. Furthermore, although the Commission subsidizes the operations of the ETUC and its industry committees and warmly encourages trade union participation, especially in DGV (social affairs) and the Economic and Social Committee, national peak organizations and the individual unions seem to show little enthusiasm for EU activities in general.

Indeed, most unions seem to see little common interest in acting together across borders. In 1979, Northrup and Rowan identified four major obstacles to firm-level transnational collective bargaining:

- differences of national employment laws
- opposition from employers fearing higher costs
- opposition from unions fearing loss of sovereignty and 'levelling down', and
- employee opposition.

The decision by Hoover to close its Dijon factory and to transfer the jobs to Scotland provoked a storm of protest from the French workers against the British government for its refusal to adopt the social chapter of the TEU. The inability or refusal of the French confederations to work together at home or in Brussels guarantees their continued marginalization in domestic French economic policy-making and ensures their insignificance in the new Europeanized processes.

France in a global economy or EU economic policy-making with French traits?

There is no doubt that membership of the ECSC and later the EC, and the policies which flowed from the treaty obligations contributed to the extraordinary performance of the French economy during the post-war period. Even since 1975, despite the crises and recessions, many sectors of the French economy have performed impressively. By most criteria – growth of GNP, growth of exports, gains in efficiency, productivity and competitiveness, investment performance at home and abroad, improvement in real purchasing power of the average family – the economic impact of the French membership of the EU must be judged a success. The only flaw, albeit a major one, is that of unemployment, especially since 1979.

Adams (1989) stresses the contribution of the new international environment to French economic performance in five ways. The first is that of the exposure of French industries to competition and imports. In 1959, imports accounted for 8 per cent of domestic consumption. On a subdivision of French manufacturing industry into 46 sectors, only four sectors were exposed to import competition of 20 per cent or more, and half the industries had exposures of under 5 per cent. In non-manufacturing industries a similar situation prevailed. All in all, imports provided 8 per cent of consumption manufactured goods and 13 per cent of non-manufactures. Between 1959 and 1980, the situation changed dramatically. Imports accounted for 25 per cent of consumption for manufactures and 22 percent for non-manufactures. Exposure to import competition increased by 17 points in manufacturing and by 7 per cent in non-manufacturing. Many of the industries experiencing big increases in exposure to imports had been highly protected at the start of the EEC; textiles is the best example of this (Adams, 1989, pp. 155–59).

Adams' second performance indicator is that of the propensity to export. In 1959, the average percentage of the output of manufacturing industries for export was 14 per cent, but in 1980, the comparable figure was 27 per cent. These figures again hide a certain number of differences between different industrial sectors. Propensity to export increased very markedly in electronic equipment, office equipment, bulk organic chemicals and aerospace products, but in wood products, the export percentage of output actually fell. Outside manufacturing, there was virtually no change in average although that average reflected export declines in some sectors and increases in others.

A third indicator of change employed by Adams is that of inward direct foreign investment. Data from Varpel and Curham (1973) show that of 500 subsidiaries of foreign companies in France, 80 per cent had been acquired after 1958 and half after 1968. Later data show an average level of direct foreign investment of 25 per cent across the 37 sectors analysed. In general, the level of inward direct foreign investment appeared to have stabilized at a new higher level in the late 1980s. The major effect of inward foreign direct investment is that in many sectors French firms now compete with subsidiaries of their foreign rivals.

The mirror image of inward direct foreign investment – outward direct French investment – is the fourth indicator. Here, studies by Varpel and Curham (1973) and by Delapierre and Michalet (1976) both show the same trends – that French manufacturers started to control subsidiaries abroad on any scale only during the 1960s and that the process of multinationalization has grown since then, especially during the 1980s.

The fifth indicator is that of import discipline – the extent to which imports increase competition in the domestic market. This is most likely when the domestic buyers or foreign sellers do not belong to the same groups, and when the foreign sellers do not join any formal or informal price-rigging cartel. Adams concludes 'in large measure the increased exposure of French companies to international trade is attributable to increased trade within the EC'.

French economic performance has been affected by many other factors besides EC membership. Firstly, the activities of French firms, both public and private, have been considerably influenced by the decline and disintegration of the French empire. Adams shows the proportion of French exports going to French imperial territories declined from 1952 to 1984. While the total volume of French exports rose steadily during that period, the proportion of those exports going to the old empire declined steadily from over 40 per cent of the total to under 10 per cent. Other indicators, notably French investment abroad, show similar patterns of decline in respect of French overseas territories. The end of empire has not had a simple effect, but subsequent French trading and financial relations with former colonies have varied considerably according to the politics and economic policies of the subsequent rulers. In French Indochina, for example, after the defeat of Bien Dien Phu and the withdrawal of the French army, the USA replaced France as the major trading partner, and with the subsequent Communist take-over, French economic links were almost completely cut. In Algeria, there was an equally dramatic decline in exports after independence in 1962 and a further marked decline in imports when the Algerian government nationalized French oil company assets. Elsewhere, especially in former colonies which supplied France with energy, such as Gabon, trade and investment links were maintained or increased. Thus, while the ending of some colonial ties encouraged French firms and financial institutions to look for markets and profits elsewhere, this was not always the case. None the less, the political and economic instability which followed independence often meant that former colonies were regarded as high risk and therefore low priority markets, by public and private enterprises alike.

The impact of decolonization was only one element of the changing environment. A second aspect was the gradual movement towards global free trade within GATT. French membership of the EC took place in a context in which governments of most countries in the world believed in removing tariff and non-tariff barriers to trade. With governments in the USA, Great Britain, Germany and the Netherlands favourable to tariff reductions, any French government would have faced strong pressures to reduce protectionism. Within the EC, France was only one partner in decisions on the Common External Tariff, and the actual GATT negotiations were carried out by the Commission. The Dillon and Kennedy rounds led to a 38 per cent average reduction in the common external tariff of the EC. French trade and financial links with the world outside the EC grew markedly, in terms of exports, imports and investment.

The measurement of the impact of EU membership on French economic performance is also complicated by a third factor, that of the effects of the specific policies adopted unilaterally by French governments. The most obvious examples are to be found in those policy sectors outside the terms of the Treaty of Rome. In the armaments industry, for example, successive governments have pursued strategies of building up French companies as manufacturers and exporters. The high state of international tension, at least until *perestroika*, and the exemption from EU competition rules in this sector, undoubtedly facilitated this strategy. Its success had some spill-over effects, since many defence contractors were also manufacturers of non-military products, and cross-subsidization from highly profitable defence contracts was difficult to detect or to prevent. Some analysts, however, have argued that lucrative defence contracts led some firms to neglect competitive strategies in other sectors. The weaknesses of CEG and of Thomson in consumer electronics and of Schneider in machine tools have been attributed to their single-minded pursuit of defence contracts.

Most writers none the less identify an 'EU membership effect' in France of moving companies away from behavioural conservatism, altering the opportunities or goals of business enterprises, and changing relations between firms and the French government. The role of the public sector and its managers has clearly undergone a dramatic transformation, especially since the SEA. In 1982, after the Socialist nationalizations, France had a public sector which produced over one-sixth of annual GDP and absorbed over one-third of all investment. Almost all banks and most insurance companies were in public ownership, giving the government, in theory, a large degree of control over lending to industry and the services in the private as well as in the public sector. By the early 1990s, the impact of the rules of the internal market were being reinforced by the consequences of the recession: the large public debt and the high fiscal burden massively prevented the government from giving large financial assistance to public corporations, since it wished to reduce both the debt and the level of taxation, while retaining the existing levels of welfare benefits.

Under Chirac and Juppé serious efforts were begun to reduce public spending, with the aim of reducing public sector borrowing so that France would qualify as a founder member of the Euro. However, the first attempts (in late 1995), which focused on the deficits of the state railways and social security system, provoked the largest outburst of public protests since May 1968. Further efforts to reduce public spending only exacerbated the unpopularity of the government and President Chirac, especially as unemployment remained at record levels. Ironically, many labour-market specialists argued that the real problem for job creation was not the lack of public spending but the rigidities imposed by law and conventions on French labour markets. In 1997 the Jospin government inherited three economic policy goals which its predecessor had failed to achieve: joining EMU on time by respecting the convergence criteria, maintaining the rights of workers and hugely reducing unemployment.

Already in the 1980s, the Socialists had given encouragement to private investment in general and had allowed for private 'quasi shares' in public corporations. Arguably, there had been some logic in nationalization in the early 1980s – to provide counter-cyclical investment, to restructure firms and groups for more coherent strategies and to achieve economies of scale, and to increase efficiency and productivity. None the less, the idea of producing more competitive and dynamic capitalism with public sector firms 'leaner and meaner' than those in the private sector was hardly close to the Socialist dreams of the 1970s. A further complication was that many of the firms acquired by the 1982 nationalizations were already multinationals, while within the pre-existing state sector several firms had opted for strategies of growth by foreign acquisitions and mergers. However, foreign take-overs were both difficult to finance and considerably more politically sensitive – both at home and abroad – for public firms than for those in the private sector. In short, the practical logic of the internal market – fair competition between firms – ran counter to the traditional approaches: of statist leadership, at least in policy formulation and unfair competition between French firms backed by the French government.

Adams concludes that effect of EU membership has been that:

> foreign goods came to account for major shares of French consumption, French producers came to export major fractions of domestic output, and international investments came to migrate . . . in both directions across French borders.

Furthermore,

> the French government could now fend off [domestic] protectionists by claiming that Treaty obligations render it powerless to protect particular industries or companies . . . aiding the EC, in its effort to keep markets open, are rival companies in other member states. They have a national incentive to share with the EC Commission their knowledge of restrictive practices elsewhere in the Community. (Adams, 1989, p. 192)

In short, many French firms are becoming more efficient, innovative and dynamic. Business leaders, especially those from big firms, are looking increasingly to the market and to Brussels, and they take fewer leads from the French government. They are increasingly drawn by the Commission into the policy-making process in Brussels. In policy implementation, there is little to gain from close collaboration with the authorities in Paris, as their capacity to give favourable loans or derogations from regulations or profitable public procurement contracts has been drastically reduced. In general, smaller and medium-sized firms and the trade unions are less confident about facing competition within the EU, are less well organized to influence policy-making in Brussels and are more nostalgic about the lost 'golden age' of protectionism and *dirigisme*.

It is still too soon to say whether a new French model of capitalism replaced the traditional one, or a new European model emerged. The changes in France have been considerable, but even the process of privatization has been slow and remains, in 1997, incomplete. Furthermore, the precise method of privatization has discouraged take-over bids and minimized foreign ownership. Shareholder power remains weak, labour markets highly regulated and public utilities relatively protected. None the less, the impacts of the internal market and the Maastricht convergence criteria have been considerable, and the process of economic integration still appears to be incomplete.

7

Territorial Policy

The growing regional dimension of EU policies has coincided with a continual domestic re-organization of both the political and administrative machinery in the French provinces. Hence it is difficult to assess the specific impact of EU policies on centre–local government relations in France. Mitterrand saw the decentralization of power as a central theme of his first administration, and introduced a large number of measures to give cities, *départements* and, to a lesser extent, regions, more political and economic power. In addition, French governments, like others in Western Europe, have attempted to 'roll back the State' in the traditional areas of directing and financing economic development. Through the linked processes of deregulation and privatization, economic development has become increasingly co-funded by the government (EU, central and local) and by private industry. Local authorities have also adopted new tools of economic management – such as contracting-out policies and developing partnerships with private agencies and industry. Since 1988 there has been a wave of reforms to 'deconcentrate' administrative services from central ministries to local field services and prefectures. President Chirac has emphasized the on-going nature of improving public services by creating a 'Commissariat for the Reform of the State' with a special focus on shifting power to the local level. These reform processes have been shaped both by the need to remain competitive internationally and within the single market, and by the espousal of market-based economic policies by both Socialist and Gaullist governments.

The Europeanization of the policy-making process has had significant effects at all levels of territorial government in France. Firstly, EU policies have had an increasing impact on the spatial distribution of economic power within member states. Policies such as the internal market legislation, competition policy and research and devlopment policy affect regions differently, benefiting some areas and discriminating against others. The freeing of capital and labour markets and the erosion of states' capacity to protect their industries have led to new poles of economic activity, often crossing national boundaries. In some cases this has led local authorities to compete against one another to attract transnational industries. In others it has led to co-operation between regions and localities within a state, or among regions across states to try to maximize benefits.

Secondly, since the mid-1980s there has been a growing concern about the imbalance of economic growth within the EU. Hence policies aimed at social and economic 'cohesion' have become a key part of the EU's political agenda. An increasing proportion of EU funds, estimated to become 35 per cent of its budget by 1999, is now being spent on trying to reduce regional disparities. The existence of these funds has, in many cases, mobilized regions and localities into political action to exploit the economic opportunities open to them: e.g. sub-national governments increasingly use the context of the EU to argue for greater powers within their own states. Thirdly, since the SEA, regions have formal legal status within the EU, and the Maastricht Treaty gave political status to regions by setting up the Committee of the Regions. The principle of subsidiarity, outlined in the TEU, has been seized upon by sub-national governments as a working principle for the devolution of power. Finally, subnational governments are often the agencies responsible for implementing the growing volume of EU legislation in areas such as environmental protection, common standards, transport and public utilities (Mazey, 1995), and hence become key actors in European 'policy networks'.

These changes lead to two hypotheses about the possible future relationship between nation states and the EU. Firstly, that European integration and regionalism would weaken nation states both from above and below. Within this scenario, central governments would eventually lose substantial control over policy decisions and implementation. Initially, this would lead to 'multi-level governance' (Marks, 1992; Scharf, 1994), and ultimately for some commentators to a 'Europe of the Regions' (Leonardi 1993, 1995). The alternative view is that nation states would adapt to these new challenges and would continue to structure and control many areas of policy-making in the short to medium term. One aspect of this adaptation might be changing power relations within the state, defined to some extent, though not exclusively, by the EU.

An examination of the relationship between France and the EU in the area of territorial policy would seem to substantiate this second perspective. Economic activity is increasingly being shaped by EU policies and the European framework has certainly been one of the key factors in re-shaping centre–local relations in France. New policy networks are constantly evolving around sectors such as transport, the environment and vocational training, and local and regional actors play their parts in these networks. However, the central state remains important in drawing up and negotiating most aspects of regional policy and in mediating between the localities, the regions and Brussels: in short, it continues to perform a 'gatekeeping' role. Paradoxically, the more complex the sets of relationships become between Brussels, Paris and the localities, the more scope there is for a centralized state with a highly proficient administrative and political elite to control the process.

This chapter will, firstly, outline the nature of local and regional power in France and assess the nature of the relationship between local policy networks, central government and the EU. It will then examine the development of the territorial dimension of EU policies, concentrating on regional policy and its implications for France. It will be argued that, though the EU plays an increasingly important role for subnational governments, especially in funding and in setting regulatory frameworks, the benefits which are gained are unevenly spread and there are both winners and losers in the process. Furthermore, although central government now operates within the EU framework, it is still a key actor in shaping policy, in determining who participates in the policy process, and in influencing the relationship between local government and Brussels.

The territorial structure of France

The traditional model

The traditional picture of the French state was that of the most centralized country in Western Europe. The key to this centralization lay in its wide-ranging administrative and judicial powers over local authorities, and its key role in strategic economic planning and resource management. The system of prefects (originally set up by Napoleon to represent the state in each of the 96 *départements*) ensured both political control by the centre over the peripheries and the co-ordination of policy-making at the local level (Machin, 1977). With nearly 37 000 mayors and over 300 000 local councillors, France also has the largest number of local authorities per head of population in Western Europe, but until the 1980s they had few powers to raise money or to decide policy. Paradoxically, their sheer number was also a source of their weakness.

However, this much viewed snapshot of French centre–local relations never really captured the dynamics of the relationship between the centre and the periphery (Wright, 1989). Long before the 1970 reforms to 'deconcentrate' administrative control to the *départements*, the 1982 reform to decentralize political power, and the return to deconcentuation in the 1990s, local interests were quite well protected. Firstly, most deputies and ministers, and many types of civil servant, held multiple local offices and they usually took their local responsibilities very seriously by lobbying on their constituents' behalf. Until the 1960s, political parties were relatively weak at a national level and local power bases were often very important for politicians. Secondly, national civil servants working in the provinces often became spokespeople for *their* territories. Even the prefect, that key symbol of the French state, was often the advocate of his own *département* against the central government (Machin, 1977). Finally, for the system to be effective and efficient there was often an informal system of co-operation between central and local government (Mazey, 1994). The notion of informal policy networks is long-established in France for understanding the complex web of interrelationships between central and local government (Grémion, 1976).

The decentralized model

Reform of local government has been on and off the political agenda throughout the whole of the Fifth Republic. Successive governments, driven by the goals of modernization, of efficiency or of cutting public spending, have attempted to rationalize the relationship between central and local government, and to devolve functions to regional or departmental bodies. Reform in this area always proved difficult, as change inevitably disturbed the well-feathered nests of local political elites and was usually resisted by them. Therefore, the modifications that took place under centre-right governments during the 1970s tended to be incremental and pragmatic rather than strategic (Lagroye and Wright, 1979). Some progress was made in devolving powers in the areas of economic management and planning to the regional level (which was an administrative body until the 1982 reform), and in giving local authorities more financial powers and to deconcentrate key services out of Paris, but no real changes were made in the political structures of local government.

Since 1981, the process of change in centre–local relations has dramatically speeded up. There are two main sources for this change:

- the political and administrative decentralization reforms introduced by the first Mitterrand administration and
- the decrease in the role of the central state in economic planning and the deregulation and privatization of key areas of the state.

These two areas will now be examined in more detail.

Gaston Defferre, Mitterrand's first minister of the interior, hailed the 1982 decentralization bill as the most significant reform of the Socialists' first term in office. The Socialist Party was committed to decentralize power to 'democratise' France and to bring government nearer to the people. Regional councils were to be directly elected and were given responsibility for planning and socioeconomic development. New powers were also given to departmental councils and municipal councils and mayors. Elected bodies were given more financial autonomy and a new local government service, the 'territorial civil service' was created. The powers of regional and departmental prefects over local councils were largely were taken over by the pesidents of the elected regional councils and departmental councils.

However, the reforms did little to sort out the complexity of French regional and local government: 36, 700 *communes*, 96 *départements* and 22 regions now with directly elected councils. The problem of diversity of resources among local authorities, which had been exacerbated by 30 years of rapid urbanization, were not really tackled in the reform. Many small local authorities (*communes*) simply did not have the resources to undertake a new role in urban planning and poor *départements* were hard pressed to take on new responsibilities for provision of social services. Nevertheless government attempts to encourage co-operation between smaller *communes* have often met with little success (Stevens, 1996).

The centre-piece of the 1982 reform – the introduction of a directly elected regional assembly with independent financial resources and its own administrative staff – has not lived up to the hopes of the regionalists. There are numerous factors which explain the still limited strategic role of elected regional councils:

- Political decentralization was followed by a devolution of administrative resources to the regional level with new co-ordinating powers being given to the regional prefect.
- There is still considerable competition between regions and the *départements*, which were also given new responsibilities in the area of economic planning in the 1982 reforms.
- The power of the elected regional councillors continued to be challenged by well-established political elites within the *départements* and communes.
- Regions were limited in what they could do by the amount of financial transfer from central government.

The other beneficiary of the decentralization reform has been the mayors of big cities. Mayors are no longer so bound up in 'red tape' by the central administration; and the delegation of more powers to local authorities, particularly in the area of funding, has led to increasing competition for EU and government funds and inward investment at the municipal level. Many commentators (Balme, 1994; Le Galès, 1995; Mazey, 1995) have highlighted the increasingly important role played by the 'entrepreneurial mayor' in shaping public policy.

A key reason behind the growing role of mayors as an economic managers has been the shift in functions from the state to private actors and agencies. There are a number of reasons for this shift. Firstly, the economic crises of the 1980s and 1990s led governments to devolve functions away from the state to agencies or local authorities. Secondly, forces of internationalization led to an increasing lack of confidence in the indicative planning system, and in the role of the regional planning body DATAR (*Délégation à l'Aménagement du Térritoire et à l'Action Regionale*) was considerably reduced by the early 1980s. Market solutions were seen as the way to solve the economic crises. The espousal of policies of deregulation and privatization in the 1980s also opened up opportunities for local authorities to raise their own funds and establish new relationships with the private sector. Mixed ownership companies (*Sociétés d'Economies Mixtes*), jointly controlled by local authorities and private industry, have greatly proliferated since decentralization. This means that in most major cities, policy-making is much more inter-agency in character and consequently much more complex (Cole and John, 1995).

Although this 'politics of contractualization' has become a marked feature of policy-making at both a local and a regional level since the mid-1980s, it is important to remember that the state continues to have a hand in most major decisions. In contrast to the UK, where liberalization and deregulation has tended to erode even the limited power which local government held, in France the state continues to steer and back new areas of development. Central and regional civil servants often work in partnership with local politicians, bureaucrats and the private sector to ensure competitiveness in the face of international challenges. For example, in the area of telecommunications policy the state has tried to facilitate local and regional initiatives to develop 'state of the art' telecom structures. A range of institutional structures, such as the think tank *urba 2000* (bringing together telecom research institutes, DATAR and France Télécom), give help and advice to urban telematics initiatives (Graham, 1995). Another initiative is *L'Observatoire des télecommunication dans la ville* which is a project led by central government to bring together central ministries, *France Télécom* and a large number of local and regional authorities. The idea here is to provide information and technical expertise to the localities (Barré, 1990, cited in Graham, 1995). These types of partnership arrangements can also help local authorities access EU funds which provide support both for regional development in general, and for specialized sectors such as telecommunications. Although this system breeds tensions and conflicts (partly because of the overlap of functions), the typical pattern is for central government civil servants working in the provinces – such as regional civil servants or the departmental or regional prefect – to work together with local actors to 'provide funds for or to market their cities or regions' (Cole and John, 1995).

The development of regional policy

When the EC was set up, its founders were not specifically concerned with regional policy. It was widely believed that the economic growth which would follow from the setting up of the common market would, over time, benefit all areas of the Community. In the late 1950s the main regions in decline were backward agricultural areas, such as the Midi–Pyrénées in France, and these were to benefit from the EAGGF of the CAP (see Chapter 5). The other areas of hardship were regions which had been dependent on the coal and steel industries, such as the Nord-Pas-de Calais, and these were catered for by the ECSC, which gave aid for the retraining of redundant workers. The European Investment Bank and the European Social Fund also provided a small amount of regional aid. Outside these categories, the granting of aid for particular areas was seen to be within the domain of the member states.

It was not until 1975 that the Community took on some responsibility for regional policy when, at the insistence of the British, the European Regional Development Fund was set up. With the setting up of the ERDF, the European Commission devised a 'synthetic index' to evaluate regional disparities across the Community. This index (estabilished on the basis of unemployment rates, economic growth and standards of living) was largely in line with national priorities. It formed the basis for the modest aid allocation which was made by the Community to the member states. In the early years of the fund, France ranked about average in terms of regional disparities; these were less marked than in Italy but greater than in Holland and Germany. As can be seen from Table 7.1, many French regions, especially around Paris, were well above average, whereas others, such as Limousin and Corse and the Overseas Territories, were well below. Like Germany, Belgium and the UK, France suffered from areas of industrial decline, such as the north-east, and from poor agricultural areas, such as the south-west. Between 1977 and 1985, the relative ranking of most of the French regions had changed, but this can largely be explained by the enlargement of the Community to include Greece, Spain and Portugal. As Balme (1992, p. 180) observes, '[Enlargement] has transformed the more peripheral French regions, such as Brittany and Acquitaine, from the richest of the poor to the poorest of the rich.'

Regional disparities continued to grow in France during the 1980s, and the regional planning agency DATAR predicts that regional diversity will continue to become more marked into the late 1990s (DATAR, 1993). A further enduring concern of French planning bodies is the relatively small number of major cities in France and the comparatively slow growth in economic activity in all but the major French cities. Recently, only the Paris region has showed significant economic growth compared to its European rivals: Lyons, Marseilles, Strasbourg and Toulouse reached average levels of growth but lagged a long way behind Paris (DATAR, 1993c).

TABLE 7.1

EU regional policy: funding in France, by objective and region, 1994–9 programming (millions of ECUS, 1994 prices)

Region	Objective 1	Objective 2[a]	Objective 5(b)
Alsace	–	19.6	46.5
Aquitaine	–	107.1	225.3
Auvergne	–	61.1	164.7
Basse-Normandie	–	57.9	133.3
Bourgogne	–	49.4	112.7
Bretagne	–	87.7	186.3
Centre	–	24.2	84.1
Champagne–Ardennes	–	77.5	29.3
Corse	249.9	–	–
Franche-Comté	–	47.8	74.6
Haute-Normandie	–	146	11.2
Languedoc–Rousillon	–	70.5	119.9
Limousin	–	–	128
Lorraine	–	127.4	96.8
Midi–Pyrénées	–	42.6	283.1
Nord-pas-de-Calais	440[b]	318.1	–
Pays-de-la-Loire	–	135.9	122
Picardie	–	122.4	–
Poitou–Charentes	–	53.3	130.1
Provence-Alpes-Côte d'Azur	–	113.1	90.7
Rhone-Alpes	–	99.7	169.3
Overseas departments	1499.2[c]	–	–
Massif funds[d]	–	–	28.1
Technical assistance	–	–	2
Total	2189.1	1761.3	2238

[a] 1994–6
[b] Specifically to Avesnes–Douai–Valenciennes
[c] Guadeloupe 344.8, French Guyane 164.9, Martinique 329.8, Réunion 659.7
[d] Inter-regional (Massifs: Mountain ranges): Central 12.5, Alpes 3, Pyrénées 8.5, Jun 2.4, Vosgien 1.7
Sources: Commission of the EC, *The Structural Funds in 1994*; *Sixth Annual Report* (1996).

European regional policy was slow to develop and, in the early years, largely ineffective. Initially there was no clear strategy, a negligible role for the Commission and an inadequate budget. The ERDF was administered through a system of quotas decided unanimously by intergovernmental bargaining in the Council of Ministers. Money tended to be thrown, rather indiscriminately, at projects in needy areas, with little assessment of the success of the aid. The principle of additionality, whereby European money was to be spent *in addition* to *national* funds was flagrantly ignored by most states.

Finally, there was little attempt to co-ordinate regional aid with other policies, such as the CAP and competition policy, which were often pulling in different directions.

Gradually, the policy became more substantial and, with the decline in agricultural spending, benefited from modest budgetary increases. A small non-quota (5 per cent) section was introduced in 1979 (increasing to 20 per cent in 1984) which gave the Commission greater power to shape the policy by supporting projects which had not been selected by national governments. Pressures from the southern enlargement of the EC and the political support of Jacques Delors for the principle of economic and social cohesion, which he saw as essential both to the successful functioning of the internal market and to the future political stability of the Community, led to an overhaul of regional aid in 1988.

In 1988, the funding for regional policy was doubled, and the policy became much more coherent and rationalized. The principles of *additionality, subsidiarity* and *partnership* were emphasized as underpinning the new policy. The Commission was given a much greater say in the allocation of funds; instead of being given set quotas, member states were given upper and lower 'margins' for aid, which meant that to qualify for maximum funding they had to reach criteria set by the Commission, rather than just automatically receiving a set amount. Most importantly, a number of *objectives* were laid down for all the structural funds (the ERDF, the EAGGF, the ESF and the EIB) (see Table 7.2). Regions within the Community were assessed according to these objectives. The majority of regions in central and southern France were eligible for funding under Objective 5(b) and those in the north-east and in other pockets of industrial decline were eligible under Objective 2. The French overseas territories (DOM/TOMs) and Corsica have a special objective and status. Although France is not one of the key beneficiaries of regional aid (see Table 7.3) the amount of money received is still very considerable: between 1989 and 1993 French regions received a total of FF 40 million from the EC structural funds and the French government contributed FF 52 million (Mazey, 1995). There was also some attempt in the 1988 reforms to co-ordinate regional policy more effectively with other policy areas. For example, areas with support from the structural funds received some special dispensation from the normal rules of competition policy (see Chapter 6), which was trying to establish free and fair competition across the EC, but many tensions and difficulties between the two policies remain (Frazer, 1994).

TABLE 7.2

European Community structural funds, 1994–9, by objective and country

(a) 1994–9 programming (in millions of ecus at 1994 prices)

Country	Objective 1 1994–9	Objective 2 1994–6	Objectives 3 and 4 1994–9	Objective 5a 1994–9	Objective 5b 1994–9	Community initiatives	Total
Belgium	730.0	160.0	465.0	194.5	77.0	233.84	1860.34
Denmark	–	56.0	301.0	266.9	54.0	88.95	766.85
Germany	13640.0	732.9	1942.0	1142.5	1227.0	1901.42	20585.82
Greece	13980.0	–	–	–	–	1083.38	15063.38
Spain	26300.0	1130.1	1843.0	445.6	664.1	2315.07	32697.87
France	2190.0	1763.3	3203.0	1931.9	2238.0	1421.36	12747.56
Ireland	5620.0	–	–	–	–	304.02	5924.02
Italy	14860.0	684.0	1715.0	814.4	901.0	1703.14	20677.54
Luxembourg	–	7.0	23.0	40.1	6.0	13.12	89.22
The Netherlands	150.0	300.0	1079.0	164.6	150.0	231.77	2075.37
Portugal	13980.0	–	–	–	–	1410.17*	15390.17
Other	–	–	–	–	–	64**	–
UK	2360.0	2142.1	3377.0	449.7	817.0	1102.26	10248.06
Total	93810.0	6975.4	13948.0	5450.2	6134.1	11872.50	138190.20

Table 7.2 *cont.*

(b) Extra funding agreed for new member states under 1995 enlargement: 1995–9 (in millions of ecus at 1995 prices)

Country	Objective 1	Objectives 2 to 5b	Objective 6	Total
Austria	184	1439	–	1623
Finland	–	1193	511	1704
Sweden	–	1190	230	1420
Total	184	3822	741	4747

[a] Including ECU 400m for Community Initiative 'Textiles and Clothing' financed under Budget Section
[b] For co-operation networks, not allocated by country.

Sources: Commission of the EC, *The Structural Funds in 1994, Sixth Annual Report* (1996); *Summary of the 1994 report*, information sheet 15 (1996).

TABLE 7.3

EU regional aid per caput, assisted regions, 1994–9 (ECU at 1994 prices)

Country	Objective 1 population (m)	ECU PC	Objective 2 population (m)	ECU PC (1994–6)	Objective 5(b) population (m)	ECU PC
Belgium	1.3	571	1.4	113	0.4	172
Denmark	–	–	0.4	128	0.4	150
Germany	16.0	855	7.0	104	7.8	157
Greece	10.2	1369	–	–	–	–
Spain	23.3	1130	7.9	142	1.7	384
France	2.5	860	14.6	121	9.8	229
Ireland	3.5	1604	–	–	–	–
Italy	21.1	703	6.3	108	4.8	187
Luxembourg	–	–	0.1	53	0.03	200
Netherlands	0.2	691	2.6	115	0.8	188
Portugal	9.9	1417	–	–	–	–
UK	3.3	713	17.7	12.1	2.8	288

Sources: Commission of the EC, *The Structural Funds in 1994*; *Sixth Annual Report* (1996).

Perhaps the most ambitious aspect of the 1988 reforms was the attempt to make regional funding more effective. The Commission moved away from funding individual projects to programmes. A system of Community Support Frameworks (CSFs) was set up, based on the principles of *additionality, partnership* and *subsidiarity*, which in theory gave both the Commission and the regions a much greater say in the planning process for regional aid (Hooghe and Keating, 1994). The CSFs were designed to give funding to programmes, over a four to five yearly basis, which covered a range of activities such as the development of infrastructure planning and economic development. This highly complex and technical system in many ways paralleled the French model and was very well suited to the French style of local and regional planning and economic development. In addition to the CSFs, which accounted for 90 per cent of the regional budget, the Commission retained the right to set up Community Initiatives (CIs), which were often aimed at cross-border initiatives or particular sectors.

The Maastricht Treaty further reformed regional policy by emphasizing the importance of economic and social cohesion as a basis for the success of the internal market. It introduced two new initiatives, a Cohesion Fund (additional to the structural funds), and the Trans-European Networks (TENS), designed to improve transport and communication across the Union. The Cohesion Fund was to disburse significant funds to the poorest four member states – Spain, Portugal, Greece and Ireland – for capital investments in transport and environment policy. France could only benefit by 'ripple' effects from projects funded in Spain. The package, which was finally agreed in 1993, also increased funding for regional policy and produced yet another attempt to redraw the technical ground rules. A fourth principle of *concentration* was added, and the CSFs were to be absorbed into a simpler procedure under single national programmes, in which member state governments, in consultation with regional and local partners put forward proposals for funding (under EU criteria) to the Commission (Williams, 1996). In France, the national programme was to be drawn up on the basis of 22 regional programming documents (DOCUP). The Commission retained control of 13 Community Initiatives (1 per cent of which were to be reserved for new initiatives) which covered problems which were not member-state specific. Examples of community initiatives in the 1994–9 programme in which France participates are LEADER (an initiative designed to stimulate rural development based on co-operation between localities in at least two member states), KON-VER (which provides restructuring support for areas which were traditionally dependent on the defence industries) and REGIS (which supports economic development in remote areas such as the French overseas *départements*, the Azores and Madeira (Portugal) and the Canary Islands (Spain)). It is argued that the 1993 reforms probably lessened the Commission's influence (Pollack, 1995; Allen, 1996) and gave power back to the member states, particularly in the highly contentious area of defining spending categories.

The final, and much fêted, innovation of the Maastricht Treaty was the setting up of the Committee of the Regions. This 189-person body, to be drawn from local and regional representatives, was to act as a consultative committee on regional matters. It has to be consulted on a number of policies, ranging from education, youth and culture to transport, economic development and economic and social cohesion. France was allocated 24 seats: after much haggling it was decided that the French representation should be equally divided between the regions, the *départements* and the *communes*. Jacques Blanc, a leading French politician, became the first President of the Committee of the Regions.

There are several types of explanation for the emergence of regional policy. Hooghe and Keating (1994) identify three types of rationale – economic, social and political. The economic argument rests on the case that intervention is necessary to overcome the negative effects of market integration on disadvantaged regions. This argument has become more potent as the pace of economic integration has accelerated within the EU. Since the mid-1980s, the advent of the internal market has tended to exacerbate the differences between rich and poor regions, with firms tending to concentrate in areas with good infrastructure and skilled (or cheap) labour forces. This prosperous core broadly includes Germany, Benelux, Austria and Switzerland, the Paris Basin, Northern Italy, parts of Southern England, Catalonia and Madrid. These regions compete and trade with each other. Firms outside this core suffer because transportation costs are higher and the level of infrastructure is generally poorer. It is widely accepted that full EMU would tend to increase this trend towards the polarization of economic growth. Governments would no longer be able to use exchange rates or public sector deficits to stimulate markets in disadvantaged areas (Armstrong, 1994). In addition, the increasingly active role of the Competition Directorate, under the assertive leadership of Sir Leon Brittan (1989–94), and Karel van Miert (since 1994), in tackling states' use of public procurement policy to bolster their regional economies, punished countries such as France. As a reaction to these policies, member state governments may argue for an increase in regional aid, either as a compensation or to facilitate their economic adjustment. The social case rests on the argument that communities need to preserve identity and integrity. Finally, the political case rests on the premise that if integration is to be successful and legitimate all countries and regions have to experience the benefits of the Union. These political arguments have been put vociferously by Jacques Delors and some national leaders since the mid-1980s. Hooghe and Keating (1994) argue that it is the appeal of these arguments to a wide enough coalition of interests (a 'winning' coalition) that will move the policy forward.

Other commentators see the development of the EU's regional policy as a series of 'side payments' to states to encourage them to participate in other policies (where they may appear to be the 'losers') and in the process of integration. There are several examples of this. Thus, the UK pressed for the development of the ERDF, to support its declining industrial regions and offset its position as a net contributor to the Community budget. A second example is provided by Greece, France and Italy whose governments argued for the establishment of the Integrated Mediterranean Programmes (IMP) in 1985 as a compensation for the enlargement of the Community to include Spain and Portugal. A third example is the insistence of Spanish governments that the Cohesion Fund should be included in the Maastricht Treaty Protocol, to make up for Spain's economically disadvantageous position in the face of EMU. A final interpretation sees the development of a 'Europe of the Regions' as an inevitable part of the integration process, with the Commission seeking to undermine the authority of states by fostering links with the regions. The counter view to this (Jones, 1994) is that the Commission is not really concerned with the regions as a *political* entity but more with regional cohesion and the development of regions as the implementation arm of EU policies.

Assessing the role of various actors in the regional policy process is highly complicated. For the early years of the policy, states were crucial in determining the size of the budget, the allocation of the budget between countries (regional policy was decided unanimously under Article 235), and the ground rules for the allocation of funds, which were largely decided on the basis of national criteria. Even though EC funding was supposed to be *additional* to the monies which member states' governments would have spent anyway, most states, including France, used it as a substitute, much to the annoyance of their regional and local authorities. The 1988 reforms meant that member state governments had less influence in determining the detail of regional aid and were, to some extent, outflanked by the Commission in taking the credit for obtaining European funding. However, the increasing prominence of cohesion policy on the Union's agenda led to concerns among the member states which were net contributors to the budget about the size of the structural funds and the way in which money was being spent (Pollack, 1995). Governments are concerned about their domestic audiences and even the richest states have regions in crisis. French governments which felt threatened by cutbacks in the CAP and the increasing sums of money being targeted on the Mediterranean countries under the Maastricht Treaty were successful in demanding that several areas in the Pas-de-Calais region be included under the enlarged 1993 Objective 1 funding, as a precondition to their acceptance of the package.

The Commission started with a modest input into the regional policy process in the late 1980s and early 1990s. However, the 1988 cohesion reforms permitted an increasingly confident DGXVI to take a greater role in setting out the objectives of the policy, drawing up the guidelines and trying to monitor the implementation of the policy. The European Commission has tended to use regions rather than smaller local authorities as its main partner. Nevertheless it has consistently tried to bring on board most local and regional authorities at each stage of the policy process. However, the ability of the Commission to build up coalitions with local actors is often thwarted by the French central government.

Accessing EU funds is a highly complicated process, which requires both a considerable level of knowledge and technical expertise, and an ability to lobby effectively at the appropriate moment in the policy process. Regions and localities have operated with varying degrees of success in this system. Paradoxically, it is often the better organized and better resourced regions which are the most effective in attracting funds designed to iron out disparities. Poorer regions often face difficulties in providing matching funding, which is a prerequisite for most structural aid (Anderson, 1991).

An emerging problem within EU regional policy is the underspending of EU money by member states. In an era of budgetary austerity, governments are either unwilling or unable to provide matching funds for EU projects. The EU provides 75 per cent of funding for Objective 1 projects and 50 per cent of funding for Objectives 2 and 5(b). Ironically concerns over public spending and the drive to meet the convergence criteria for EMU often means that member states do not take full advantage of EU funding. In 1994–5 there was a significant shortfall in spending EU funds in France because of the inability of central and regional governments to fund planned projects (*Financial Times*, 29 July 1996).

Most evidence suggests that the structure of the national political systems also still plays a key role in determining the sets of relationships between local authorities, the state and Brussels. At a superficial level this means that in countries such as Germany and Belgium where there is a significant decentralization of power and policymaking to the regional level the regions now play an increasingly strategic role in the process. In centralized states, such as the UK and France, central governments continue to exercise a significant gatekeeping role (Mazey, 1995; Smith, 1997). This is not to deny that localities have influence but to emphasise that they will tend to exert this influence *through* the central government using the Commission as a resource.

TABLE 7.4

Structural funding in France, by purposes of each objective (in ECU millions, 1994 prices)

(a) Objective 1, 1994–9 (Total 2189[a])

	Avesnes–Douai– Valenciennes	Corsica	Overseas Departments
Simulation of economic activity	141.8	–	–
R&D	38.6	–	–
Human resources	92.5	31.0	–
Human resources, social balance	–	–	394.3
Regional regeneration	165.1	–	–
Technical assistance	2.0	2.1	16.4
Reducing isolation	–	67.9	–
Access, spatial balance	–	–	214.6
Environment	–	30.7	–
Environment and infrastructures	–	–	305.9
Universities, research	–	12.5	–
Tourism	–	–	21.1
Tourist and cultural heritage	–	15.0	–
Economic development	–	18.3	–
Production, competitiveness, industry, crafts	–	–	279.7
Agricultural and marine production	–	72.4	–
Agriculture, rural development	–	–	242.7
Fisheries and aquaculture	–	–	24.5
Total	440.0	249.9	1499.2

(b) Objective 2, 1994–6

Productive environment	710
Human resources	614
Land improvement/restoration	313
Environmental protection	103
Technical assistance	25
Total	1765[a]

(c) Objective 3, 1994–9

Integration of those threatened with long-term unemployment	705.8
Vocational integration of young people seeking employment	987.2
Integration of those threatened with exclusion	714.2
Equal opportunities for men and women	17.9
Technical assistance and pilot projects	136.9
Total	2562.0

(d) Objective 4, 1994–6

Pre-emptive measures (skills and qualifications)	32.1
Increase in training effort	227.8
Improvements to training schemes	14.6
Technical Assistance	25.1
Total	**299.6**

(e) Objective 5(a), 1994–9

Agriculture[a]	
production structures	1486.6
marketing structures	255.4
Fisheries SPD[b]	189.9
Total	**1931.9**

(f) Objective 5(b), 1994–9

Agricultural diversification	311.1
Economic development	1136
Attractiveness of rural areas	739.4
Technical assistance	51.5
Total	**2238**

[a] These totals differ slightly from those in other tables, owing to rounding.
[b] Other SPDS for fisheries and agriculture exist under objective 1, and are included in objective 1 totals.
Sources: Commission of the EC, *The Structural Funds in 1994*; *The Sixth Annual Report* (1996).

The impact of EU policy on French territorial politics

The Europeanization of key sectors such as regional aid and economic development, where the central state was previously autonomous, has created a new set of opportunities for regional and local authorities in France to participate in policies from which they were previously excluded. The internal market and environmental policy have given new powers to regional and local authorities in the implementation process, although it is the central government which is ultimately legally responsible for ensuring EU policy is successfully implemented. The decentralization process means that cities are now much freer to compete in the international market and to participate in projects such as Community Initiatives, which are collaborative projects across the EU.

TABLE 7.5

Community initiatives, breakdown of finance, 1994–9[a] (ECU millions at 1994 prices)

Initiative	Belgium	Denmark	Germany	Greece	Spain	France	Eire
Interreg II	82.00	17.70	402.20	595.00	564.70	246.00	133.50
REGIS II	–	–	–	–	214.00	262.00	–
Leader II	8.00	8.00	174.00	146.00	330.00	187.00	46.00
Emploi	32.10	11.00	156.80	64.40	366.60	146.50	46.10
ADAPT	31.20	29.50	228.80	30.10	256.40	249.70	21.20
Textiles – Portugal[b]	–	–	–	–	–	–	–
SMEs	12.10	2.50	183.00	82.20	227.70	57.70	28.40
URBAN	10.50	1.50	96.80	45.20	130.40	55.00	15.50
PESCA	2.00	16.40	23.00	27.10	41.50	27.90	3.70
Rechar II	15.68	–	158.63	1.50	27.29	33.12	–
Resider II	24.41	–	190.39	4.63	58.68	61.49	0.32
RETEX	4.40	–	68.40	74.50	74.50	24.80	9.30
Konver	11.45	2.35	219.40	12.75	23.30	70.15	–
Total	233.84	88.95	1901.42	1083.38	2315.07	1421.36	304.02

Table 7.5 cont.

Initiative	Italy	Luxembourg	Netherlands	Portugal	UK	SMEs	Total
Interreg II	347.40	3.50	69.10	339.70	99.40	–	2900.20
REGIS II	–	–	–	124.00	–	–	600.00
Leader II	282.00	1.00	7.00	116.00	61.00	34.00	1400.00
Emploi	348.70	0.30	40.70	40.30	146.50	–	1400.00
ADAPT	190.00	0.30	55.20	21.00	286.60	–	1400.00
Textiles – Portugal[b]	–	–	–	400.00	–	–	400.00
SMEs	187.80	0.30	9.80	122.30	61.30	25.00	1000.10
URBAN	115.30	0.50	9.90	43.70	75.60	–	599.9
PESCA	33.70	–	10.20	25.60	33.90	5.00	250.00
Rechar II	1.66	–	–	0.86	161.26	–	400.00
Resider II	84.08	6.87	17.42	6.91	44.80	–	500.00
RETEX	67.20	–	1.00	162.00	36.20	–	522.30
Konver	45.30	0.35	11.45	7.80	95.70	–	500.00
Total	1703.14	13.12	231.77	1410.17	1102.26	64.00	11872.50

[a] These figures show the situation before allocation of the reserve available for the Community initiatives.
[b] Initiative transferred to Budget Section 3.
[c] Small/Medium Enterprises. For co-operation networks, not allocated by country.

Sources: Commission of the EC, *The Structural Funds in 1994; Sixth Annual Report* (1996); Summary of the 1994 report; information sheet 15 (1996).

However, the Europeanization process is complex, constantly evolving and very varied in its effect across both the territory of France and across policy sectors. While some regions such as the Rhônes–Alpes are well organized and effective others, such as the Auvergne still rely heavily on central government for resources and support. Key resources for 'successful' regions include indigenous economic circumstances and opportunities, the political leverage of local elites, budgetary resources and technical expertise. The nature of regional policy-making is so complex that even the most well-resourced regions and *départements* often call on the support and advice of Prefects and the field services of the central administration. The extent to which a new set of relationships is developing between the Commission and the localities which circumvents the central government and its agents is, as Smith (1997) argues, perhaps overestimated.

The role of the central administration

The response of the French central government to the changing context of regional policy has, on the whole, been positive. The DATAR has produced a plethora of reports, and economic models to try and bring French regions and the *départements* into line with EU policy initiatives. Transport and telecommunication policies have been developed in such a way as to ensure that French regions benefit from the single market. The 1992 Joxe Law was designed to prepare local government for 1992 by encouraging territorial mergers and joint ventures.

The French traditions of indicative planning, *dirigisme* and integrated economic development synchronise well with the new EU system of regional policy. Regions are required to incorporate a 'strategic European perspective' into their planning mechanisms and also have to submit proposals for funding under the relative objectives to the central government for onward submission to the Commission. Once the priorities and funding levels have been decided at the EU level, funding is passed down to the relevant ministry to co-ordinate implementation. Within this cycle the regional prefects, field services of the central government departments and DATAR play pivotal roles. Indeed, the new structure of EU regional funding has given a new lease of life to both DATAR and more especially to the regional prefects. DATAR had become downgraded in the 1970s and 1980s with the demise of indicative planning and the role of the regional prefects had been overshadowed by the presidents of the newly elected regional councils. In the 1990s there is a new balance of influence in the regions.

The key co-ordinating role played by central government agents, such as prefects, can also be seen in the area of vocational training. Training has a territorial dimension (responsibility for it is split between regional and local authorities), a social dimension (helping disadvantaged groups) and an economic dimension (re-skilling workers for the new labour markets). It is an area of policy supported by many funds, central government monies, the European Social fund, educational schemes such as COMETT and LEONARDO and the structural funds. The agencies involved in vocational training include higher education establishments, regional and local training agencies, development agencies and the private sector. Within this labyrinth, two deconcentrated state agencies, the DRTEP (*Délégation Regionale, Travail, Emploi, Formation Professionele*) and RACINE (*Resau d'appui et de capitalisation des innovations européenes*) help to foster partnership and mediate between the various competing agencies and levels of government to maximize funding opportunities (Carmichael, 1998). Most actors involved seek technical advice from the administrative services of the regional prefect.

Region and cities

Although the decentralization reforms devolved executive and financial powers down to the regions, they have not yet become key actors in the French system of government. Regional economic strategies are, on the whole, poorly developed, and it is often major cities such as Lille, Grenoble and Lyons, run by entrepreneurial mayors, which have the political and economic resources to benefit from EU initiatives. For example Lyons has mounted a long-term campaign, Lyons 2010, supported by key private interests and an inter-communal committee, to become a major 'Eurocity'.

Most of the regions (in 1994, 17 out of the 22) run an office in Brussels and all regions and major cities are now locked into a burgeoning number of networks across the EU. There are two main types of association. The first is within a funding programme such as LEADER or INTERREG, where the Commission requires localities to enter into partnership arrangements with their equivalents in other member states. The second is lobbying organizations or 'spatial policy networks'. There are hundreds of such organizations at a European level. Some are geographically defined, such as the Atlantic Arc, a lobby bringing together the maritime regions of France, the UK, Portugal and Spain, RECITE (Regions and Cities of Europe), and *Quartiers en Crise*, an association of towns with inner city problems. Others are sectoral such as RETI (*Régions Européenes de Technologie Industrielle*). In fact, the dividing line between networks operating under EU programme objectives and lobbies is often blurred, as many lobby organizations, for example RECITE, are funded by the EU.

While it is relatively easy to map out these proliferating organizations, it is more difficult to assess their power. Clearly one of the functions of some of the organizations is to market their members cities and regions and help trade promotion. Another is to provide information for the Commission or to the EP. At best, European associations can help to set the agenda and have an input into new programmes. Williams (1996) notes, for example, that no fewer than 12 cities selected from the urban pilot projects came from the 25 members of *Quartiers en Crise*. Finally, these organizations collect information about current developments in the EU for their members. French local regional authorities participate very actively in these networks, although, as in other member states, it is often the most resourced and least needy authorities which are best represented.

Conclusion

This chapter has shown that the growing regional dimension of EU policies has had a significant impact on centre–local government relationships since the early 1980s. The European context has been one factor, among others, which has advanced the regionalization of political structures and policy networks. Regional prefects and DATAR, along with mayors, have been the main beneficiaries of this new pattern of policy-making. Regions and *départements* are now involved not only in the implementation of EU policies but also the formulation of economic planning and modernization policies, However, this chapter has argued that while the involvement of subnational governments in the EU policy-making process has changed the role which central government plays, but it has not necessarily eroded it. The central state and its agents still control many policies with a regional dimension, such as education and training, and in others continues to act as a co-ordinator. The overall effect of the increasing Europeanization and regionalization of the policy process has been to create a much more complex system of policy networks, in which local and regional authorities, the state, its agents and the private sector all interact. These new policy networks can open up new possibility for interest groups and citizens to participate in the policy-making process.

8

France without Frontiers?

In theory, public policy to set rules about who may enter, reside and work in France is a traditional function of the state, but in practice there has been surprisingly little controversy about the EU making policy in this area. This low level of debate may be explained in two ways.

The first is that the initial changes were enacted within the Community pillar of the EU as incremental steps toward the completion of the internal market. The Treaty of Rome did not raise the problem of citizenship, but only that of the free movement of workers. Indeed, only after long years of numerous measures to link national social security systems, to guarantee that access to jobs is unhindered by national educational qualifications or others' rules, and to harmonize both travel documentation and workers' rights, did the member state governments address border controls (in the Schengen Agreements) or civic rights (in the TEU).

A second explanation is that in many cases the effect of the changes has been small. Hence, for example, the existing high legal protection of workers' rights in France meant that the negotiation of common EU standards did not raise the level of that protection. Equally, too, the abolition of internal restrictions on movement was not followed by huge migratory flows from other EU states to France. Consequently, the main political criticism of the granting of European citizenship to citizens of other EU states resident in France, was that it might encourage demands for similar rights from immigrants whose origins are outside the EU. None the less, in 1997, Chirac and Juppé agreed to greater joint EU policy-making in this policy area when they signed the Amsterdam Treaty.

Article 3 of the Treaty of Rome established the free movement of persons between member states as an explicit policy goal of the Community. Furthermore, Articles 48 to 51, and 52 to 58 laid down principles concerning, respectively, the free movement of workers, and the right for nationals of one member state to set up in business in any other country in the Community. These treaty provisions were to have very far-reaching effects, since the goal of free movement implies modifications to a wide range of established public policies and policy processes, both in France and in other member states. Here we consider five of the policy areas concerned, and each of the sections of this chapter focuses on one area.

- The first section examines the delicate questions of legally defining who is authorized to move, and with what official documentation, and of determining how the practical problems of removing internal border controls between member states are to be resolved.
- The second considers the policy adjustments made to ensure free access to employment; these concern both educational qualifications and legal restrictions.
- The third section analyses the attempts to harmonize conditions and rights of workers at the workplace, including health and safety rules, consultation and involvement in management and gender equality in employment.
- In the fourth section, we address the implications of free movement on democratic and civil rights, since member state governments are slowly moving towards granting rights akin to those of their own nationals to residents from other EU states, and to making common rules of access and residence for nationals of non-EU states ('third country nationals').
- Finally, we examine the reforms of the social security system in France which have taken place in the context of agreed EU policies to allow transferability of benefits and rights across internal borders.

In France, the issues of border controls, immigration, law and order, citizens' rights, workers' rights and social protection were highly sensitive and symbolic in national politics all through the 1980s and early 1990s – but only in relation to migrants from outside the EU. Consequently, national policy-makers had to be extremely cautious in the way they handled the adaptation of policies and structures in these policy domains. The political debates and impact on public opinion are considered elsewhere in this book. Our concern here is with the nature and extent of the policy adaptations and with the relatively slow modifications of the policy-making processes and policy communities.

It is difficult to identify the exact impact of EU membership in all areas of policy adaptation. In some cases policies and policy structures in France have been modified to meet new common European norms. In other cases, however, such norms have had little identifiable impact, either because French policies or structures were already compatible, or because the EU reform processes coincided with and were inextricably interlinked with domestic policy changes. Indeed, domestic debates and ideological shifts were often themselves influenced by comparisons with changes taking place in other EU states.

There were, however, a number of specific domestic factors which had particular influence on policy reforms in France. The growing deficit of the social security system was one factor, and another was the inadequate coverage provided by that system, notably for the long-term unemployed (until the late 1980s). A third was the increasing ideological salience of both the social security issue and citizens rights. The election in 1981 of a Socialist-led government, which was firmly committed to substantial extensions of both individual liberties and workers' rights was followed by centre–right governments in 1986 and 1993, which placed a new emphasis on enforcing law and order and strictly limiting immigration and with the return to power of the Socialists in 1997, liberties and rights were again the focus of attention, although Chevènement, the interior minister, argued strongly that socialism was not 'soft' on crime.

Each of the five sections of this chapter focuses on the process of policy adaptation in one of these distinct, but interlinked, policy domains. In each case, a similar interplay between domestic and European pressures for change is revealed. In each case too, the strength of existing institutional arrangements and the national distinctiveness of the policy community emerge as major explanations of the slow, hesitant and limited Europeanization process.

Free movement of persons and border control

The transformation of the goal of free movement of persons into a legal reality was a slow process. The first major regulation on free movement (1612/68 in 1968) concerned only the mobility of workers, although it extended mobility rights to the family of the worker and gave the worker the right to remain in the member state to which he or she had moved after employment came to an end. In 1982, the ECJ interpreted European law as allowing free movement to any person 'working or wanting to work', thus including those seeking jobs and having just lost jobs, as well as those actually in work and to their families. In June 1990, the Council adopted a number of directives which extended free movement to all 'potential actors in the economy', and thereby authorized mobility for those not actually in the labour market, including students and those retired, and their families. Finally, in 1992, Article 8 of the TEU completed the process by giving 'citizenship of the EU' and the right of free movement to all nationals of EU member states. The second of the 'Declarations' made at the Maastricht conference clarified the position in respect of 'nationals', by stipulating that 'whether an individual possesses the nationality of a member state shall be settled solely by reference to the national law of the member state concerned'. Thus, in agreeing to free movement of 'nationals' the member state governments avoided, or at least postponed, the highly sensitive 'sovereignty' issue of changing established national rules which define who holds, or may acquire, nationality.

One major problem for agreeing on common policies in this area is that the premises concerning citizenship differ widely among member states. In former imperial states such as Britain and France, parental nationality, place of birth, length of residency and links derived from the Empire, have determined who could acquire nationality. In Germany, blood descendence was virtually the only route to nationality. During the Cold War, the West German government offered its citizenship to anyone of German descent, from East Germany or anywhere else in the Eastern Bloc. Until *perestroika* few could take advantage of this offer, but subsequently the flow of applications has been huge, reaching almost half a million in 1992. By similar rules, anyone with one Italian grand-parent can claim naturalization, a right which would allow entry into the EU for substantial sections of the populations of Brooklyn, Sydney and Argentina.

Three implications of the EU-defined legal reality of free movement within France were of particular importance: official identity documents, border controls and the law and order consequences of free movement. The most symbolic change in terms of identity documents was the agreement to change the colour and form of

French passports: the new standard dark-red EC passports have the words *Communauté Européenne* as well as *République Française* on the front cover. A second change was the adoption of the EC format driving licence and the recognition of the validity of EC format licences issued in other member states. Furthermore, several reforms of procedures for issuing residency permits were made; nationals of other EU member states are now dealt with by a separate, fast, procedure. In practice, official documentation now classifies nationals of other member states in a special category, akin to that of French nationals and distinct from that of *foreigners*.

The most visible change concerning border controls has been the introduction of the 'two-channels' system of passport checking, and the 'three-channel' customs control. The actual dismantling of border controls at internal borders (between France and other member states) has been a piecemeal process, involving bilateral pacts and wider agreements (notably the Schengen Agreements), linking the abolition of frontier controls with common policies to deal with the negative consequences of this suppression.

Despite the political sensitivity of common policy-making in areas concerned with traditional sovereignty functions, most French governments since de Gaulle's presidency have shown enthusiasm for the goal of making common policies to deal with the possible negative results of free movement of persons. At the end of the French presidency of the EC in 1989, when the 'Paris Declaration' of the European Council underlined the importance of free movement of persons, the interior ministers noted that free movement for persons and capital increased risks of crime across internal frontiers and possibilities for professional criminals to exploit gaps in co-operation between police agencies of member states. Ministers have also worried about large-scale immigration, both legal and illegal, into Europe during the 1980s, especially since the reduction of internal border controls has transformed immigration into a common European political problem, with shared risks of poverty, social exclusion and racism.

Some crimes – including drug trafficking, electronic-financial fraud, money-laundering, thefts of art works and terrorism – have clearly increased in number in Europe during the 1980s, and all these crimes often have transnational characteristics. The growth of international drug trafficking was an early reason for co-operation between police and judicial authorities in the EC, and has remained an essential element in the debate on developing common European

policies on law and order. The development of international computerized financial transactions, made possible by major technological
change, and authorized by the internal market programme, has
allowed the growth of criminal activities with international characteristics that are very difficult to police within any national structures.
Frauds involving credit cards, and bank computers as well as tax
evasion and insider-trading are typical examples of the recent cross-
border crimes.

President Pompidou (1969–74) was the first to recognize that
greater movements of persons across borders and looser controls at
frontiers between member states should be counter-balanced by
closer European police co-ordination, but, sensitive to the anti-EC
sentiments of many of his supporters, he decided to promote a loose
'European Group to Combat Drug Abuse and Illicit Traffic in Drugs'
within the Council of Europe. His idea met with a warm response
from other governments, and a new, consultative body, comprising
ministers and senior civil servants from 19 member countries, was
created. It became known as the 'Pompidou Group', and French
police and justice officials contributed actively to its joint studies,
notably on drug-related crimes. Reports were prepared on the control
of drug trafficking, on responses of criminal justice systems to
problems of drugs abuse, on methods to deal with 'money launder-
ing', on collecting and evaluating data for common policy formulation, and on educational initiatives against drug abuse (Bigot, 1992,
p. 48).

Under President Giscard d'Estaing (1974–81), however, the EC
was used as the framework for further police co-operation. In 1975,
the EC Council of Ministers of the Interior, meeting in Rome,
unanimously agreed to create an informal, intergovernmental body
– not strictly part of the EC – for co-operation in policing and
criminal justice, especially against terrorism. That new body, the
Trevi Group, met at three levels – ministerial, senior officials and
specialists – to analyse problems and formulate co-ordinated solutions. Responsibility for organizing the work at all levels within the
Trevi Group was given to the member state holding the EC Presidency. At the lowest tier, the working groups of specialists, officials
and detectives or examining magistrates, met frequently, often in
seminars, to prepare reports for the ministerial meetings. The first
working group co-ordinated information about, and operations
against, terrorists, other groups dealt with police equipment, football
hooliganism and aspects of public order, serious and international

crime and drug trafficking, and the crime and policing implications of the internal market. Within the Trevi framework, a European drugs intelligence unit was set up to co-ordinate the national drugs intelligence units in all the member states. A similar network, set up to co-ordinate action against football hooligans, proved very effective during the World Cup matches in Italy in 1990. Another working group dealt with problems relating to the internal market programme and the effects of the 'minimalization' of internal border controls.

In parallel with this activity in the Trevi Group, French governments have also, since 1985, played a leading role in the Schengen Group (initially France, Germany and the Benelux states) which aims to abolish all internal border controls between its members. The idea of scrapping all frontier controls within the EC has been discussed since 1958, when the Benelux states abolished checks at their internal borders. It was not until 1984, however, that the massive trans-European traffic jams provoked by lorry-drivers' protests against slow and bureaucratic controls at EC internal frontiers re-opened the question. Later that year, the French and German governments signed the Saarbrücken Agreement, providing for the abolition of border controls between their two countries (Hreblay, 1994) and, in June 1985, the treaty intended to abolish border controls between all five states was signed at Schengen (Luxembourg). Ministers agreed that before border controls were actually dismantled a second 'implementation' agreement would be signed to define the precise changes to policing, rules and procedures to deal with free movement across internal borders and immigration arrangements at common external borders.

Reaching unanimity on these crucial questions proved so difficult that the 'implementation agreement', due in 1989, was signed only in June 1990, and the implementation itself was postponed until 1993. The reunification of Germany, and changing relations between the EC and Eastern Europe were one complicating and delaying factor. Another was the demand from other EC states to join. The second agreement did allow other member states into the Schengen Group, but only on the condition that their governments accept the total package without further negotiations. In November 1990, the Italian government joined, followed later by the governments of Spain, Greece and Portugal (Blanc, 1991).

The contrast between the rapid signature of the first Schengen Agreement and the slow process of negotiating an implementation agreement reflects the difference in the contents of those two deals. The 1985 Agreement laid down goals, but the June 1990 Agreement concerned concrete measures. Agreeing precise rules for the reinforcement of external border controls, for close and effective co-operation between judicial systems, police forces and administrative services of the members and for common policies on visas, immigration and the right of asylum was a difficult, politically sensitive challenge, which involved almost all the governments concerned in changing established policies. Indeed, for the French government it meant changing the Constitution. The Schengen Agreement required French politicians and policemen to accept the standards of border policing of other member states, and old prejudices about the superiority of French methods and standards die hard.

One goal of the 1985 Agreement was the establishment of a common, central, computerized 'Schengen Information System' (SIS). Studies and negotiations for creating this system commenced in 1988. A first problem was to define the contents of the database and it was only after lengthy discussions that agreement was reached. The following categories were to be included: aliens classed as undesirable in any one of the Schengen states, asylum applications and refused applications, wanted criminals, persons under surveillance, fire-arm and vehicle ownership. A second problem was that data protection rules varied between the Schengen states; hence, a common system of protecting individual rights was eventually negotiated only with great difficulty. Very practical details of financing, and choices of hardware, software, the main-frame location and the number of access terminals had also to be agreed. The final choice for the location of the central SIS computer was Strasbourg.

A second problem area was that of 'hot pursuits', since when border controls no longer exist, police officers in pursuit of fleeing criminals must either be able to continue their chase across any border or have such excellent communications with the police forces in neighbouring states that their officers can immediately take over the pursuit. In theory, it may be logical for police officers of the first Schengen state to continue their pursuit on to the territory of the second state until the police of that state takes over the chase. However, French officials were concerned to limit the extent that a foreign police officer could continue a pursuit into France and were anxious to ensure that any foreign police officer should only apply French domestic criminal law in the pursuit zone. The 1990 Agreement included a 'hot pursuit' clause which provides the right for the

police officers of one country to pursue suspects into the territory of
another country, but arrests can only be made by domestic police
officers.

It was not until 1992 that the 1990 Schengen Agreement was
finally ratified by the parliaments of all its member countries, after
long delays and challenges to its constitutionality. In March 1993,
however, the French government announced that, as the conditions
agreed for implementation had still not been achieved, a further
unspecified delay was needed. In January 1994, on a proposal from
Paris, the Schengen governments agreed to suspend implementation
sine die. In November 1994, the governments discussed a 'trial period'
of operations, and on 22 December 1994, the nine ministers, meeting
in Bonn, finally agreed to implement the Schengen agreement on 26
March 1995. The French government, retained an option of reintro-
ducing border controls if there were any evidence that its abolition
led to an increase in crime (*Libération*, 23 December 1994). In August
1995, the Juppé government decided to re-introduce some border
controls as an emergency measure to counteract the wave of terrorist
bombing. President Chirac himself publicly declared, to the considerable disquiet of some of his European fellow leaders, that lack of
control at borders had direct effects on drug trafficking and illegal
immigration. Whatver his doubts, Chirac agreed to the fusion of the
Schengen group into the EU strtuctures and to further co-operation
in policing, at Amsterdam in 1997.

The experience of the Schengen Group, like that of Trevi, shows
that if French ministers could easily agree on broad common
objectives and principles, reaching unanimous agreement with their
partners on detailed policies and institutions, achieving those goals
was much more difficult. The need for unanimity caused frequent
delays and often led to considerable setbacks.

Since the ratification of the TEU, that same difficulty has been
experienced in relation to all 'third pillar' questions, and especially to
Europol. On the one hand, the treaty does not stipulate how Europol
and its information system link with the Schengen Information
System; Article K7 allows for the continued operation of the SIS
distinct from, but in parallel with, Europol. On the other hand, the
treaty does not specify how Europol will be organized and financed.
In November 1994, despite the determined efforts of the German
Presidency, the scope, organization and financing of Europol were
still being hotly contested, especially by Pasqua, the French interior
minister. Unresolved issues included the rights of access to informa-

tion and the role of common EU institutions (the ECJ, the Court of Audit and the EP) in supervising Europol's operations. Pasqua formed a close alliance with his British colleague to restrict the role of Europol and to minimize the influence of supranational Community institutions (*Financial Times*, 1 December 1994), but as other governments rejected this Franco-British approach, decision-making reached a deadlock during 1994. Little progress was made until the Amsterdam summit in 1997.

Though French governments remain formally committed to the success of intergovernmental co-operation in justice and policing within Article K of the TEU, the experience of the Trevi and Schengen groups indicates that reaching unanimity among the 15 will not be easy. The TEU, by establishing intergovernmental structures separate from the Community framework, ensured that French governments could both pay lip-service to the goal of joint policies in justice and policing, and delay any big changes which reduced their freedom of action. The experience of the Schengen Group, however, reveals the difficulty of producing significant policy changes, even with considerable institutional dynamics, within a strictly intergovernmental structure.

Free access to employment

The possibility for nationals of any member state taking advantage of their new mobility rights depends on such practical questions as whether or not their qualifications are accepted by employers and universities and whether they have equal rights with nationals of the member state to apply for jobs. French governments are as much concerned with amending domestic legislation to ensure that nationals of other member states can work in France as with following reforms elsewhere in the EU which allow French nationals access to employment there.

The first field in which EC measures made some difference to employment opportunities was that of establishing equivalence of qualifications between member states. By a series of directives concerning doctors (1975), nurses (1977), dentists (1978), midwives (1980), and pharmacists (1985) the mutual recognition of qualifications was established. The ECJ decision on the Heylens case of 1987 opened the prospects of a mutual recognition of all diplomas for purposes of job recruitment, and in 1988 the Council adopted a directive on the equivalence of all diplomas based on at least three years full-time education after the *baccalauréat* (or A levels). The effect of these measures, however, has been diminished by the general shortage of jobs during the 1980s and 1990s. Furthermore, the exploitation of the right of free movement to France in many professions was limited by the high level of the language knowledge requirements.

In France, the equal rights of nationals of other member states to apply for jobs were, for many years, restricted by the use of Article 48 of the Treaty of Rome, which specifically exempted posts in the public service from the mobility rule. All posts covered by the civil service status were thus closed to those without French citizenship, and in 1979 there were 2.3 million such posts – slightly less than 10 per cent of the total labour market. In 1980, however, the ECJ ruled (in case 149/79 Commission *v*. Belgium) that the application of the public service exemption to free movement and free access to jobs could be applied only to those jobs directly linked to the 'regalian functions' of the state. In 1981, that interpretation of the treaty was confirmed in the preliminary ruling given to the Paris Administrative Tribunal on the appeal by Annegret Bleis against the use of the Article 48(4) exemption by the French ministry of education, to prevent her, as a German national, from sitting the CAPES competitive entry examination to become a secondary school teacher. The Court advised that

> employment in the public service for the purposes of Article 48(4) , which is excluded from the ambit of article 48(1) to (3) . . . must be understood as meaning a series of posts which involve direct or indirect participation in the exercise of powers conferred by public law and duties designed to safeguard the general interests of the state or of other public authorities and which, because of that fact, presume on the part of those occupying them the existence of a special relationship of allegiance to the state and reciprocity of rights and duties which form the foundation of the bond of nationality.

In an eventual response to that decision the French government proposed and parliament passed the law of 26 July 1991 on the civil service, which provided free access for all EU nationals to any public post in France which fell outside the ECJ's definition. In practice, that meant all civil service status posts in teaching and research and most lower level clerical jobs in public administration had now to practise open recruitment policies and their practices could be challenged by the Commission before the ECJ. The new law did not lead to floods of applications from citizens of other EU states to join the French public administration or from French civil servants to take jobs elsewhere in the EU, because non-legal factors – language, legal knowledge and experience – remain important constraints to appointments to such posts.

Equality of workers' rights

The social provisions of the Treaty of Rome, Articles 117 to 122, established few precise goals. For most matters listed as falling in the social field – employment, labour law and working conditions, vocational training, social security, health and safety at work, and rights of association and collective bargaining – the Commission was given the task of 'promoting close co-operation' by means of studies, opinion, and consultations and of devoting a chapter of its annual report to the EP to social development. For all matters, other than social security co-ordination, the Council may, by a unanimous decision, give specific tasks to the Commission, but European legislative action is possible only by means of the general enabling clause (Article 235).

The absence of policy-making at the EC level during the 1960s reflected Gaullist reluctance to make policies through the EC framework except when it was considered essential or clearly beneficial to France rather than any French hostility to the enhancement of worker's rights. De Gaulle himself supported the creation of works councils and made several declarations in favour of greater worker involvement, both in economic planning and in the management of firms in France. It was, however, under Pompidou and Chaban-Delmas (with Delors as social policy adviser) that the first real discussion of joint policy-making in the social field took place in the EC Council. In 1972, the Council agreed that the Commission should examine what action was required. As a consequence, the Commission's proposed 'Programme of Social Action' was approved by the Council in June 1974. The 21 measures suggested in that programme were concerned with achieving three main goals – assuring full employment, creating better and more equal conditions of work and life, and involving 'social partners' in economic and social decisions.

As a result of the programme, a number of directives were introduced to deal with job protection and health and safety at work. The directives concerning the protection of jobs had little perceptible impact in France, since existing French legislation was at least equally demanding. The directives obliging firms to hold official consultations with workers before declaring group redundancies (17 February 1975), guaranteeing continuity of contract for workers when firms relocated within the EC (14 February 1977) and protecting worker interests when employers went bankrupt (20 October 1980), all made little difference either to the law or to common practices in France.

The results of the first EC measures on health and safety at work were also rather small. The directives dealing with the use and handling of radioactive materials, lead and other dangerous chemical substances brought only very minor modifications to existing French rules. The limited extent of EC legislation in this area reflected the difficulty of achieving unanimity in the Council. None the less, the addition in the SEA of Article 118a led to significant change, by allowing the use of QMV for the subsequent European legislation on health and safety at work. The framework directive of 12 June 1989 on the harmonization of safety standards at places of work was one result which had long-term implications for French industry, although little impact in the short term.

In one other area of workers' rights, that of information, consultation and participation in decision making at the workplace, French law has also been ahead of (or in step) with changes made at the European level. The creation of works councils in France dates back to the Liberation, and in the 1960s the Gaullists had attempted to reinvigorate economic planning by involving the trade unions. Hence, in 1980 and 1981 the Commission proposal (the 'Vredeling directive') for works councils, which the British government blocked, would have made little difference in France. Furthermore, in 1982, the Socialists passed the Auroux acts, which substantially extended the rights of workers and works councils. Many French multinationals even took the initiative of setting up representative bodies for workers at the European level of their group structures. By 1993, 10 French-based groups, including Thomson, BSN, St Gobain, Pechiney, Rhône-Poulenc, Elf-Aquitaine and Renault, all operated EU-level works councils. Thus, when successive French governments supported the EC Charter of basic social rights of 1989 – which did not become official EC policy due to British objections – or signed the

Social Protocol of the Maastricht Treaty, they did not do so in anticipation that French structures and policies in relations to workers' rights would be markedly changed. On the contrary, the support for these policies reflected a wish, shared by Socialists, Christian Democrats and some Gaullists to ensure that French standards were extended across Europe.

The EC measures on gender equality at work matched and corresponded to the domestic reforms undertaken by Giscard d'Estaing during the early years of his presidency. A first directive (10 February 1975) detailed the application of Article 119 of the treaty in terms of equal pay and equal rights. Subsequent directives stipulated the implications in terms of equal access to jobs (9 February 1976), equal rights to all forms of social protection (19 December 1978) and equal rights in self-employment (11 December 1986). The activities in France of the Agency for Women (under Giscard d'Estaing) and later the ministry for women's rights under the Socialists, meant that the impact of these EC measures was barely perceptible within the much broader domestic programme of reforms. None the less, in 1991, the Stoeckel case at the ECJ showed that the EC equality requirement went beyond that of domestic legislation; the Court ruled that, as a consequence of the 1976 directive on professional equality, the existing French law banning night work by women was discriminatory and, therefore, illegal.

Democratic and civil rights

Initially, the EC had very little to do with citizens' rights. Human rights were the responsibility of the Council of Europe, and although France had signed the European Convention for the Protection of Human Rights and Fundamental Freedoms in 1950, French citizens did not have the right of individual appeal to the Commission on Human Rights or the Court on Human Rights in Strasbourg until the mid 1980s. The accession of the Socialists to power in 1981 led to a series of reforms improving civil liberties, many of which reflected comparisons made between the situation in France and those in other EU states. The granting of the right for individuals to appeal on cases concerning human rights to the Strasbourg Court and the abolition of the death penalty and the suppression of the Court of State Security, are typical of those early Socialist measures by which French policies came into line with standard liberal practices in other EU member states.

The Maastricht Treaty, however, marked a step forward in terms of agreeing common standards for the defence of citizens' rights, since for the first time, it laid down as a goal of the EU 'to strengthen the protection of rights and interests of the nationals of its member states' (Article B). Furthermore, the treaty recognized 'as general principles of Community law' respect for fundamental rights, both as guaranteed by the 1950 European Convention and 'as they result from the constitutional traditions common to the member states' (Article F).

As noted above, the TEU also established 'citizenship of the EU' and granted it to 'every person holding the nationality of a member state' (Article G(c), adding a new Article 8 to the Treaty of Rome). EU citizenship carries six rights:

- to move
- reside freely within the territory of the EU
- to petition the European Parliament
- to apply to the European Ombudsman
- to have access to diplomatic representation by the embassies of other EU member states (in countries where a citizen's own state has no ambassador) and
- for anyone resident in a member state of which he or she is not a national, to vote and stand as a candidate at municipal elections and to vote and stand as a candidate at European elections.

Whereas in several member states this provision provoked few comments, since long-term residents already enjoyed voting rights, it was very controversial in France. Many politicians on the right attacked this aspect of the treaty, as they feared that it would open the door to voting rights for immigrants. The effects in France, however, are inevitably mitigated both by the importance of political parties and by domestic French law which makes non-French nationals ineligible to become mayors of municipalities. Furthermore, according to the French proportional representation rules for European elections, only lists with candidates for all 87 seats are eligible, so that any individuals can become a candidate only if selected by a party. At the 1994 European elections, these TEU changes to wider voting rights appear to have little identifiable effects. Changes to French law to comply with the treaty for local elections had not been made in time to affect the 1995 municipal elections.

Although the Treaty of Rome did not mention any implications of free movement on immigration, law and order, and visas, some modifications of existing national policies on these equally sensitive subjects soon appeared essential. Equally, while both that treaty and the SEA referred to free movement of 'persons' or 'workers' who hold the nationality of any member state, they did not consider the position of third-country nationals with rights of residence in one member state. It was only with the TEU and the Schengen Agreement that governments of all member states committed themselves to reach agreement on common rules concerning visas, political asylum, immigration policy and the conditions and rights of residents from third-countries. Agreeing and implementing such policies, nevertheless, remained extremely difficult and politically sensitive in France, as in most other member states.

In post-war Europe, rules and traditions concerning immigration were very varied. France and Britain recruited labour for their post-war booms mainly from their former colonies, and offered permanent residents the possibility of naturalization. Germany recruited its *gastarbeiter* in Turkey, and classified them as temporary residents (even after 30 or more years of residence and the birth of children and grandchildren on German soil). Political and economic developments, in the 1970s and 1980s in particular, completely approaches to immigration by all West European governments. The post oil-crisis recessions and the restructuring of industry brought mass unemployment to Western Europe, making new immigrants unwelcome. Indeed, some government policies, in Germany and France, attempted to persuade established immigrants to return to their countries of origin, although with few results, except that of stirring up resentment among second-generation immigrants.

Equally, traditions of dealing with claimants of political asylum have differed considerably between member states. Since 1945, governments of West Germany and France have proclaimed their countries to be *terres d'asile*, and have promised political asylum to all dissidents willing to respect their national laws. However, if in theory free entry into these states was possible, in practice political repression, especially in Eastern Europe, in the 1950s and 1960s, meant that the few who wished to move could do so. The Fall of the Berlin Wall in 1989, however, posed the threat of mass migration from the former Eastern Bloc to the EU. The front-line state, Germany, has faced a massive demand from asylum seekers: over 250 000 in 1991 and over 400 000 in 1992. In contrast, the French government faced less than

60 000 demands for asylum in 1991 (Stewart, 1992), a reflection of its geographical location and its stricter treatment of claims of political repression. Britain, with even stricter asylum rules, has faced far fewer demands.

In one respect however, that of granting free movements and equal rights to residents in member states from third countries, the Maastricht treaty represents only a small advance on its predecessors. The TEU implicitly recognizes that absence of common rules on the entry and residence of third country nationals poses problems, but it does not identify or address those problems. It does, however, provide a framework for agreeing common policies, in the future, on visas, conditions for asylum, rules concerning the crossing of external borders of member states and immigration, and on 'policy relating to nationals of third states'. Only one of those policy domains (that of visa rules on the entry and exit of nationals of third countries), is placed within the Community policy framework, and even here the new Article 100c (added to the Treaty of Rome) provided for qualified majority voting in the Council only after 1995.

All the other policy areas are relegated, by Article K, to the third pillar of the EU, and hence to a strictly intergovernmental framework, with unanimity in the Council and a very limited role for the supranational Community institutions – the Commission, the EP and the ECJ. None the less, the third pillar provisions remain ambivalent. They allow for the possibility of joint policy-making in judicial and domestic affairs, but make such policies dependent upon unanimous decisions in the Council.

Furthermore, Article K1 sub-divides judicial and domestic policy areas into different categories – asylum policy, rules concerning the crossing of external borders of member states, immigration policy and policy relating to nationals of third states, action against drug abuse, action against international fraud, judicial co-operation in civil matters, judicial co-operation in criminal matters, customs co-operation, and police co-operation – and deals with the different categories in slightly different ways. Only the first six of the nine policy areas listed as subjects for common action are deemed to fall within the policy competence of the Commission; the others remain in the sphere of sovereignty of the member state governments, and they alone can take initiatives for joint policies in matters of criminal justice, customs co-operation and police co-operation.

There is, however, a further complication, since Article K9 allows for the possibility, by a unanimous decision in the Council, of a shift of responsibility for policy-making in the first six policy areas to the Community framework, under Article 100c (and hence subject to QMV). In contrast, only by the signing of a new treaty can criminal justice, customs and police co-operation be shifted from the third pillar to the Community system and hence be subject to some controls by the European Commission, the EP and the ECJ. By the start of the inter-governmental conference in 1996, very little had been achieved under Articles 100 (c) and Article K. Although the special committee of national representatives ('the K4 Committee') had started discussions, there were few prospects that unanimity would be easily achieved on any of the substantive issues involved in making common policies.

Social security and mobility

The main features of the French structures of social protection to deal with old age, sickness, accidents, maternity, family, poverty and unemployment were already in place by the time the Treaty of Rome became operational in 1958. There have been a number of subsequent modifications to these structures, some related to European integration (the extension of pensions to farming as a complement to the CAP is an example), others dealing with precise domestic problems (for example, the creation of the minimum revenue in 1988 to deal with long-term unemployment).

Basically, however, France had, and still has, like Germany, Belgium and Luxembourg, a system of social security based on separate professional insurance schemes linked together and supported by the state (as opposed to national solidarity schemes, as in the UK). Individuals join the appropriate employment-based social security fund, and, in the event of sickness, old age or short-term unemployment, receive benefits which are proportional to lost earnings. Membership and contribution payment(s) are obligatory. There are multiple social security funds for various socio-professional groups, but most individual funds are grouped within the 'general regime' with roughly similar rules. Members of the different schemes can participate in the elections of the decentralized management boards. This complex, employment-based, but state-backed system was built up on insurance principles, with revenue and expenditure expected to balance on an annual basis.

Given this insurance principle, the basic costs were shared between employees and employers, with employers taking the responsibility to deduct contributions from wages and salaries. The overall rules were designed to leave a role for both mutual assistance societies (*les mutuelles*) and private insurance, since ceilings were imposed on benefits paid out by the state-backed funds. In many professions, complementary pension schemes raising retirement incomes above those ceiling levels were compulsory. Similarly, membership of a mutual society to pay costs of health care over and above social security reimbursements was also compulsory in many professions. Health care services were provided either by private doctors, dentists, pharmacists and clinics or by publicly-owned hospitals. In most cases, medical acts and pharmaceutical products were charged according to state tariffs and the patients paid their bills and claimed reimbursement from their social security funds.

In practice, from the start, the system was modified by some elements of 'national solidarity' benefits. Hence, family benefits did not depend on previous income levels but were generalized and equal for all, depending only on family size. Family allowances were deliberately fixed at rates intended to encourage large families: for one or two children benefits were small, but they rose very substantially after the third child. Indeed, for families of three or more children, benefits were the highest in the EC. Another example was hospital bills, which were broken into two parts, of which the major section (about 70 per cent in most cases) was addressed directly to the social security fund, leaving the patient to pay the remaining 30 per cent (of which a substantial amount would normally be reimbursed by the mutual society). In 1982, hospital funding was modified by the creation of a global budget for hospitals to cover all medical acts so that the patient had only to pay a fixed-tariff 'hotel bill', according to the number of nights spent in hospital.

In 1958, the main features of the French system resembled those in Germany, Belgium and Luxembourg, while the Netherlands and Italy had very different social security systems. Furthermore, even among the four similar systems, there were significant differences both on the contributions and the benefits sides as well as different professional groupings for social security funds. Thus creating rules to allow individuals to move between the different systems was a highly complicated process.

Early in 1958, the Council made two regulations under Article 51, implementing the two conditions laid down in that Article. The first was the aggregation, for the purpose of receiving a right to benefits and fixing a benefit level, of all periods of employment in all the member states in which the migrant worker had been employed. The second principle was the transferability of benefits to a worker resident in any of the member states. The two regulations stipulated that the worker, and his or her dependent family, should belong to the appropriate social security fund of the firm in the country where he or she was employed, irrespective of where the work was performed or where the worker resided.

The treaty explicitly exempted the distinct public service social security funds (which covered some two million employees in France) from transferability. Two other exclusions from the transferability principle were forms of social assistance and complementary insurance schemes which were not legally enforced. Initially, general transferability rights applied to migrant workers and their families. Arrangements for workers and their families were re-codified in regulation adopted in 1971 and 1972. In 1993, a further regulation incorporated provisions for students and the retired, following the directives of June 1990 which extended the rights of residence.

Initially, the French governments obtained the agreement of the Commission for a derogation of the transferability principle in the case of the high family benefit paid to families with three or more children. That derogation, however, was successfully challenged at the European Court of Justice in the late 1980s (Pinna Case, 15 July 1986 and 24 May 1989). A similar attempt by the French government to claim that non-contributory minimal old age pensions were a form of social assistance and hence were not exportable was also successfully challenged at the ECJ in 1974 (CRAMIF *v.* Rianson 1974). Clearly, French authorities were reluctant to allow the export of the generous pensions paid to those within French contributory pension schemes.

In the 1980s, policy-makers in France returned to the problem of how French social protection structures related to those in other member state for a number of reasons. The first was that periodically the social security system as a whole went into deficit. In the short term, governments had to meet the debt out of tax revenues, but there was then a reconsideration of benefits and contributions and an attempt to reduce the former and increase the latter. The first major crisis occurred in 1967 but subsequently every few years, a new deficit arose. During the late 1970s, in consequence, social security contributions were significantly increased several times. The second reason was that the election of the Socialist majority in 1981 led to attempts to improve the system by meeting needs hitherto inadequately covered in France. A particular problem was that the complex French system, unlike some others in the EC, provided unemployment benefit for a maximum of only 30 months (for those under 50 years of age) and the financial equilibrium of the system depended on only relatively small numbers being unemployed for short periods of time. The growth of mass, long-term unemployment destabilized the whole system and left those unemployed for more than a few months (varying according to age and length of previous employment) without any income (Dupeyroux, 1993).

There were three other problems which French governments, like those of other member states, were to face throughout the 1980s and 1990s. The first was the ageing of the population. In part as a consequence of guaranteed income and better healthcare – the result of three decades of operations of the social security system – more and more people were not only reaching retirement age but also living into their 70s and 80s. By 1994, the average life expectancy for French women was 81.4 years. Between 1980 and 1991, the proportion of the total population aged 75 or more increased from 5.8 per cent to 7 per cent (Social Protection in Europe, 1993, p. 98). The first effect was to increase the total cost of old age pensions; the second was to contribute to the escalation in health care costs as old people are particularly expensive users of the healthcare system. A second problem was the soaring costs of new medical technology, new medical techniques (including organ replacements) and new pharmaceutical products. Finally, the early successes of the healthcare system generated rising expectation from the public.

The net effect of these problems was a rising bill for social protection, which had to be faced at a time of economic recession. All the governments of member states were concerned to find cost-containment policies and there was a real interest in learning from the experience of others. The French policy conundrum was further complicated by the agreement on the internal market programme, and especially by three aspects which concerned social protection:

- distinct and complex social protection systems, and especially their retirement pension features, were identified as a significant obstacle to, or brake upon, the free movement of workers, and of other citizens including old age pensioners;

- the internal market could undermine aspects of social protection schemes in some member states, since, a priori, workers would prefer employment where benefits were highest, while employers would seek to invest and create jobs where their contributions (or social costs) were lowest;
- not only Socialists but also many Christian Democrats demanded that the freeing of the market should be balanced by a general improvement in social protection.

Viewed from a purely French perspective, the policy problems of the 1980s were doubly painful. On the one hand, the books did not balance: despite the contribution increases of the 1970s, income was not growing as fast as expenditure. On the other, there were identifiable gaps in the cover provided, which meant that additional spending was required. In 1982, with welfare expenditure substantially increased by the first Socialist reforms and the underlying problems unresolved, the deficit appeared to reach crisis proportions.

From a comparative European perspective, other problems were evident:

1. Until the early 1990s, the French system was the most dependent on revenue from contributions, or in other words, the least tax-financed of any social security system in the EU. As a consequence, the social costs directly borne by employers were the highest in Europe.
2. public spending on health was the second highest in Europe (after Belgium) and its growth was not slowing down.
3. There was a persistence of poverty and an increase of homelessness despite improvements in the system.

Within France all these issues were discussed and analysed in government publications (notably the 1983 White Paper on social protection and the Tenth Plan) and public debates (before the 1981 elections and the 1987 *Etats Généraux de la Sécurité Sociale*). The policy responses were fourfold:

- benefit increases where new needs were identified;
- cost cutting and cost containment exercises across all parts of the system;
- income increases from higher contributions; and

- the financing of some non-insurance benefits was shifted to hypothecated taxes.

By creating some special allowances for those whose rights to unemployment benefits had run out (in 1981), housing pensions for widows (in 1982), reducing the retirement age from 65 to 60 (in 1982), creating parental allowances for education and looking after children at home (in 1982 with improvements in 1985 and 1987) and establishing special allowances for unemployed school leavers (1985), the Socialists brought the French system into line with social protection schemes elsewhere in the EC. In 1988, when the Socialists returned to government, they further improved the safety net by introducing a minimum income for the long-term unemployed (*revenue minimum d'insertion* or RMI) and linked the new benefit to a scheme run by local governments for re-integrating the long-term unemployed into the labour market.

On the cost-containment front, many measures were taken. For retirement pensions, the minimum contribution period for a full pension was increased from 37.5 years to 40 years; annual pension increases to meet inflation were indexed to prices (rather than to salaries) and the level of pensions was set by the best 25 years of earnings (instead of the best 10 years as before). For those receiving benefits from multiple sources, maximum total benefit levels were set. On the health side, efforts were made to reduce the total cost of drugs by limiting the number of re-imbursable pharmaceutical products, and by encouraging doctors to prescribe generic drugs. The 1982 'global budget' reform of hospital financing set budget limits for hospital treatment. Furthermore, a complex system of 'medical control' of health spending was introduced in 1992.

The revenue reforms were equally complex and varied. From 1980, health insurance contributions were deducted at source from retirement pensions. From 1982, those receiving the full unemployment insurance benefit were also obliged to pay contributions for health insurance. In 1982 there was a general rise in the level of contributions. In 1984, the ceilings on contribution payments (which had effectively reduced payments for the better paid) were abolished. However, major changes, came in 1988 and 1990 with the introduction of a wealth tax to pay for the new RMI and the creation of a 'general social contribution' (*cotisation sociale généralisée* or CSG) payable on all incomes including pensions (except those receiving the RMI or minimum retirement pension). When the Balladur government came to power in March 1993, one of its first measures was to double the CSG from its initial rate of 1.1 per cent. The revenue from the CSG was at first directed to pay for family allowances and other non-contributory benefits.

In 1991, at Maastricht, the French government gave full support to the Protocol and Agreement on Social Policy, in the complete confidence that any minimum standards set at the EU level were unlikely to lead to any major increases in benefit payments. Equally, in 1992, the government gave its full backing to the Council recommendation 92/442/EEC of 27 July 1992. In 1997, the French social protection system ranks, with the Danish, Dutch, German and Luxembourg systems, as among the most generous in the EU. Earlier anxieties about a possible 'jobs and investment' drain from France to other EU states where employers' contributions to social insurance are lower have so far proved illusory. The new measures together with recent increases in average labour productivity mean that the total salary-cost-to-productivity ratio does not make France appreciably less competitive than most other EU economies.

None the less, the recent reforms have made a complex system even more convoluted. For those employed in France who wish to work elsewhere in the EU, as for those from other member states who wish to work in France, transferring social protection rights, especially for pensions, remains difficult.

Conclusions

The adjustments made in the five policy domains related to the free movement of persons have been made both within the Community framework and the intergovernmental organizations of the EU (Trevi and the third pillar) or distinct from it (Schengen). French governments have had to face such daunting tasks as agreeing common policies, or at least co-ordinating rules, on the recognition of qualifications, working conditions, workers' rights, border controls, asylum, immigration, law and order, visas and rights of third-country nationals. In some cases, governments have agreed to new EU norms which required modifications of prevailing policies and policy structures in France. With the 1977 Amsterdam treaty more modifications will be needed. In other cases, however, the agreed norms have had very little impact, either because French policies or structures were already compatible, or because the EU reform process and domestic policy changes took place at the same time. In practice, domestic structural factors and ideological shifts in France often paralleled those taking place in EU institutions.

Indeed, one common theme which emerges from this survey of these five areas of policy adjustments is that the exact origins of many reforms are often complex. The process of discussing and negotiating common policies at the EU level itself leads all member state governments into making efforts to understand how the rules and structures applied in other member states work in practice. Hence, there is an inevitable element of comparative learning, which involves considering all elements of costs and benefits of the various systems operating across the EU. The process also induces shared analyses of new problems, which in turn lead to the adoption of similar policy responses even when common policies within the EU framework are not needed. Hence, in the case of social security, although in formal respects the French system has not changed in structure to resemble systems elsewhere in the EU, its policy responses to rising unemployment and soaring costs have been similar to those found in other member states.

A second theme is the highly nationalistic construction of the various policy communities, a reflection of the distinctive institutional and socio-political developments in the various member states. Police and judicial structures, like social security systems, vary considerably, as do the pressure groups which operate in those policy sectors. Hence, professional standards, including, for example, definitions of 'crime' and 'evidence', are not common to all states. Hence, too, while there is a common European problem of immigration and asylum seekers, the precise nature of the daily difficulties faced by public services dealing with those problems varies greatly, even between France and Germany. Given the strength of long-established institutional arrangements, it is the distinctiveness of the national policy communities and debates that emerges as a major explanation of the slow, hesitant and limited Europeanization process. Europeanization involves not only major public agreements on goals decided in the political arena, but also many small detailed measures, which are hard-fought compromises between these different policy communities. One consequence is that solving problem issues in '*low*' politics (notably educational qualifications and pension rights) often prepares the ground for resolving those in '*high*' politics (such as the abolition of border controls or policy on asylum), and hence reduces the political visibility of potentially contentious issues of sovereignty.

Conclusion

In this book we have been concerned with processes of modernization, state-building and the modification of identities in France. Our
research has focused on three interlinked questions: the changing
contributions of French politicians to the institutional design of the
EU; the methods and results of French policy-makers within the EU
framework of shared policy-making; and the impact of EU membership on politics, policies and policy-making within France.

A key theme of the book has been that making policies jointly
within the EU structures has had a varied impact on domestic politics
and policy-making. In areas such as competition policy, the single
market legislation and industrial policy, the EU sets the regulatory
framework for national legislation, whereas in others, such as foreign
policy, the EU merely provides a forum for intergovernmental co-
operation. However, we have argued that even in highly integrated
sectors, such as agriculture, the French government continues to play
a key role in shaping and implementing policy. What emerges from
the book is the growing degree of collaboration and bargaining
between French and other European policy-makers, with the French
government, like its counterparts in Western Europe, involved in an
increasingly dense set of administrative and political processes at the
European level. Our research has revealed the complexities of the
relationships between the nation state and the EU, with numerous
and overlapping multi-level territorial and sectoral networks. A
major consequence of this shared policy-making has been to contribute to the decline in the traditional regulatory and *dirigiste* role of
the French state in recent years.

The increasing scope of EU policies has not only made the policy-
making process more complex but has also led to a re-balancing of
political power within the French state. It would appear that, in
general, the effect of EU membership has been to further strengthen

parts of the executive, notably the finance ministry and the Bank of France, and to weaken the role played by parliament and political parties. The widening of EU activity into the traditional spheres of purely domestic policy-making has made it possible for some political actors, such as regional prefects, to assume new roles. There has also been some institutional change brought about by the EU, with French courts attaining a new status within the changing legal context set by the EU. Some pressure groups, such as environmental organizations, have increased their influence, whereas others, such as trade unions, have lost out.

Throughout the book we have tried to assess the impact which EU policies have had in determining the policy agenda in France. In particular, we have been concerned to distinguish policies determined by the EU from those whose origins may be traced to domestic factors or wider global trends. Our conclusion is that in most sectors it is very difficult to unravel the impact of the European level of governance from that of domestic policy-making. Policies stem from the confluence of domestic, European and international factors: for example, the growing power of French regions and *départements* as economic actors has been shaped by the need to develop strategies to compete in the global market as well as by EU policies and funding and constitutional change. It was also found that in many sectors the EU was often used as a pretext to pursue policies dictated by other considerations.

A similar difficulty arises in trying to assess the costs and benefits of EU membership. In the 1960s and 1970s French governments were able, through their leadership role in the Community, to further national goals such as economic modernization and the rationalization of the agricultural sector through the framework of the EC. However, as the EU has grown in size and scope, a new institutional and policy momentum has been set in motion which has partly escaped the control of any one member state government. The fragmentation of the concept of a single 'national interest' in EU matters partly reflects the growth and diversity of policy competence of the EU. Sectorally diversified policy-making also reflects the growth of majority voting in the Council of Ministers, which means that 'package dealing' is now much more limited and complex. Consequently, it has become increasingly difficult for the French government to shape the policy agenda of the EU to its own advantage. French governments have tended to become more reactive than proactive within the EU. Nevertheless, the support of

France (frequently coupled with Germany) remains vital for any new major policy or institutional development. For example, in the 1996 intergovernmental conference on the future of the EU the Franco-German proposals played a key role in shaping the agenda for discussion.

Having traced this broad change in France's European fortunes we have argued throughout the book that it is important to avoid using the shorthand of referring to France as a unitary actor with a continuity of purpose. Indeed, our research has revealed how misleading the notions of unity and continuity are in the context of European policies of successive governments. A key theme of this book has concerned the changing approaches of French governments to the shaping of EU institutions. Our starting point was the efforts of successive French governments to determine the nature of the European institutions and to build the Community to French designs. In the first chapter we examined how the influence of French governments over the institutional and policy development of the EU has changed in nature and extent since 1950. Certainly, at key moments in that institutional development – over the ECSC in 1950, over enlargement in 1963 and 1969, over majority voting in 1965 and over the EMS in 1979 – decisions made in Paris greatly determined the outcome for the whole of Western Europe. Those decisions, however, were far from consistent. At other times, however, French governments were unable to impose their policies on other member states (as in the case of the Fouchet Plan) or on their own parliamentarians (as in 1954 over the EDC).

What emerges clearly is that there are a number of continuities in French European policy, such as the use of the Community framework to protect French markets and to maintain political stability in Western Europe. However, there have also been significant differences in the goals which the various post-1950 governments pursued: obvious differences when the ambitions of Schuman and Pleven are compared with the sceptical nationalism of de Gaulle; more subtle differences when the evolution of policy from Pompidou to Giscard d'Estaing, to Mitterrand and to Chirac is examined. Even in relations with Germany the goals sought from that special relationship have changed markedly – from revenge to containment, to reconciliation, to co-leadership of the EU. Similarly France and UK relations over Europe have oscillated from friendly co-operation (Heath and Pompidou) to open hostility (de Gaulle and Macmillan).

We have shown that, French politicians had a considerable impact on the initial design of the EU. Jean Monnet's ideas were critical in shaping the High Authority of the ECSC and the organization of its early administrative services. However, the further development of Community institutions did not follow the French model of state institutions. Indeed, almost all French leaders firmly opposed any attempt to reproduce the French state at the European level. All de Gaulle's successors have favoured a strong Europe with weak institutions, although in some cases, this preference has been sacrificed for wider policy goals. For example, in the area of security policy French leaders have always favoured intergovernmental arrangements but have often been pushed towards a more supranationalist position because of the constraints of the Franco-German alliance. The continuing dilemma for French leaders has been that of simultaneously making the EU system work and presenting the EU as merely an international organization dependent for leadership on France. This leads, therefore, to structural ambivalence in French attitudes to European construction.

Membership of the EU has involved not only building new institutions in Brussels, Luxembourg and Strasbourg, but also changing the state machinery in France. This domestic institutional adaptation has taken place both at the top tier of government, where policy-making for the development of the EU has been presidentialized and at lower levels in ministries and the courts. The French parliament has been relatively slow in adapting to the realities of the European context of policy-making. The co-ordination of inputs into the complex process of joint policy-making within the EU was of such importance to governments that the SGCI, initially a small agency for dealing with Marshall Aid, was transformed into a powerful co-ordinating system to ensure that France 'spoke with one voice' in every branch of policy formation. Although French positions on major issues are often more effectively co-ordinated than those in most other countries, it has become an impossible task for the SGCI to keep track of and co-ordinate all policy questions which have a European dimension. Furthermore, presidential interventions (except during *cohabitation* periods) may often weaken co-ordination. In contrast to policy input co-ordination, the problems of policy input implementation were given little serious attention until the 1980s. Since then successive French governments have attempted to ensure that EU policies are actually carried out in France, and the *Conseil d'Etat*, long suspected of institutional Euroscepticism, has become an effective partner of the SGCI in policing implementation.

We have in Chapter 3 addressed the complex problem of how political forces in France have dealt with European integration and have shown that the various steps of EU development have provoked very different reactions within the domestic arena. The most controversial steps were the plans for the EDC and the Maastricht Treaty, while the Treaty of Rome and the SEA were accepted and ratified with surprisingly few disputes. In general, the mainstream political parties have been divided over EU institutions and powers. Although over the years most Socialist, Gaullist and liberal leaders have come to support European integration, significant minorities in all these parties remained profoundly suspicious of the EU and hostile to any plan to increase the scope of joint European policy-making. Thus, despite President Chirac's commitment to the internal market, to EMU and to limited institutional reform, many parliamentarians and a large number of activists in the Gaullist Party cherish nationalist Eurosceptic ideas, which they see as their inheritance from General de Gaulle. Both the Communists and the National Front have stayed fiercely nationalistic and explicitly hostile to the present powers and policies of the EU. Only one party, *Force Démocrate*, loyal to its Christian Democrat origins in the MRP, has been consistently in favour of European federalism. Public opinion to some extent mirrors the divisions within the parties, but it is also sensitive to controversial policies coming from the EU and is increasingly likely to displace discontent with the government of the day onto the EU. This leads to considerable fluctuations in popular support for the European project. It is easy to blame the EU and its policies for unemployment, rural depopulation, immigration and even crime. EU policies have been far from perfect: the internal market is still being built, the structural funds are inadequate, often ill-targeted, under exploited and sometimes wasteful, and the CAP is characterized by conflicting goals, vast expenditure, fraud and helping the rich more than the poor. The reaction of the French public to these flaws is sometimes to pressurise the French state to retake control: hence, many farmers today see French agriculture as a 'loser' in the EU and would prefer policy to be decided in Paris. The high support for Le Pen and de Villiers, who opposed the ratification of the Maastricht Treaty, demonstrates that this populist nationalism remains a serious force.

We have traced the evolution and impact of EU policies in a number of sectors to demonstrate the interaction between on the one hand the evolving policies of the EU, and, on the other, the dynamics of domestic politics and policy-making. We have noted the paradox that while EU membership may increase the capacity of a French government to influence international negotiations (as in the Uruguay Round), that same membership has made it difficult, despite its theoretical veto powers, to resist global trends of liberalization, notably in telecommunications and air transport.

France's reluctance to give up its independent and assertive foreign policy may have been a contributory factor to the slow development of joint external policies for the EU as a whole. However, changes within the international arena in the 1990s have led to a re-positioning of international security organizations and placed considerable pressure on the EU to develop its own security framework. At the same time France has now been forced to clarify the ambiguities surrounding its own foreign policy priorities within that emerging European security framework.

In our analysis of the formulation and evolution of the CAP we have underlined the transformation of French farming which has taken place since 1962. However, the CAP has only been partly responsible for the transformation of French farming. The complementary policies to improve structures which were decided mainly in Paris, and the information system of the farmers' unions helped French farmers to maximize gains from CAP. It remains a paradox that despite the vast expenditure and many reforms Europe's agricultural policy has failed to satisfy the farmers.

Our examination of adjustments in competition, trade and monetary policies, and the decommissioning of the weapons of economic *dirigisme* and protectionism suggests that, in many respects, the changes here were potentially profound. However, disentangling EU effects from global trends is especially difficult in this sector. Here, the participation of large firms and some professional groups in joint European lobbying contrasts with the more traditional nationally-focused tactics which are still the main methods of small business groups and the trade unions.

In discussing the adaptation of the work of regional and local governments in France in response to EU regional development policies, and in the context of the Defferre decentralization reforms of the 1980s we have argued that while old habits learned during decades of centralization die hard, EU membership has become an important framework in shaping centre–local government relations.

The focus of our last chapter was on the policy adjustments necessary for the free movement of persons. On the one hand, the importance of the Schengen Agreement emerges for border controls, immigration and policing but, on the other hand, the social chapter of the TEU has had only minor effects on employment conditions, educational qualifications and social protection structures.

When the finding of all these case studies of sectoral adjustment to EU policies are combined, the overall record of these moves away from traditional macroeconomic policy practices emerges. Governments of left and right alike still often instinctively react to problems by trying to use the traditional *dirigiste* tools to help French firms, but a transfer of power from state to market has occurred within the EU. The French state no longer intervenes to the same extent in the economy, and when it tries to intervene it is sometimes (and controversially) prevented from doing so by the European Commission or by the ECJ.

As assessment of how far the French state has been 'rolled' back is no easy task, because the state no longer intervenes in the same way or by the same methods. Firstly, there has been a redistribution of power within the French state structures from the political executive to quasi-judicial regulatory bodies and, more recently to the increasingly autonomous Bank of France. Second, the sharing of responsibility between the French state and EU structures means that many important decisions are made at the EU level in Brussels. Third, the court system, both in France and in Luxembourg, plays a much bigger role than in the past, and governmental discretionary powers have consequently been constrained.

All these changes also mean that in the long run the battle which de Gaulle fought to maintain European policy in the domain of foreign affairs has been lost. Indeed, the French government no longer has its effective monopoly to represent the whole of France in the EU policy process. Sub-national governments, major firms and some pressure groups are increasingly handling their own contacts with the European Commission, the EP and the ECJ. In some cases the Commission or the ECJ is the target of an appeal by French firms, citizens or associations against some policy or decision of the French government. French authorities respond by trying to control and channel contracts with the EU but it is increasingly difficult for them to do so.

The intergovernmental conference which began in 1996 was convened to lay out the future political, institutional development of the Union. The French government, a key player in this process, stood firmly in the camp of those countries which favoured an enlarged and politically stronger Union, which, it argued was essential to secure lasting peace in Europe. Along with Germany, France favoured a structure which would permit states which wanted enhanced co-operation within the EU to move forward. However in terms of institutional development, France still erred on the side of the intergovernmentalists, favouring a re-balancing of votes in the Council of Ministers to give a greater say to the 'big five' countries, (France, Germany, Italy, Spain and the UK), a smaller and more effective European Commission (with 10 members), and a greater control of EU policies by national parliaments. The French government remains committed to the introduction of EMU by 1999 and, rhetorically at least, supported a strengthening of the EU's security policy. However, as our study has argued French positions are complex, multifaceted and fluctuating. We have shown that there are two separate and often conflicting aspects to the process of Europeanization. On the one hand, there is the dynamic of domestic politics, shaped by partisan conflicts and constitutional arrangements, which may alter the rhetoric or even the substance of European policies. On the other hand, there is the dynamic of the integration process and the politics of the EU which may provoke new challenges to the French state. It is the interplay of these internal and external challenges which continue to shape the evolution of French European policy.

Bibliography

Adams, W. J. (1989) *Restructuring the French Economy* (Washington, DC: Brookings).

Albert, M. (1991) *Capitalisme contre capitalisme* (Paris: Seuil).

Allen, M. (1996) 'Spatial Policy', in Helen Wallace and William Wallace (eds) *Policy Making in the European Union* (Oxford University Press).

Anderson, C. (1995) 'Economic Uncertainty and European Solidarity Revisited: Trends in Public Support for European Integration', in C. Rhodes and S. Mazey (eds) *The State of the European Union*, vol. 3 (Boulder, Colo.: Lynne Reinner).

Anderson, J. (1991) 'Sceptical Reflections on a Europe of the Regions: Britain, Germany and the ERDF', *Journal of Public Policy*, **10** (4) 417–47.

Anderson, M. and M. Den Boer (eds) (1994) *Policing Across National Boundaries* (London: Pinter).

Andrews, G. (ed.) (1991) *Citizenship* (London: Lawrence & Wishart).

Armstrong, H. W. (1994) 'The Role and Evolution of European Community Regional Policy', in B. Jones and M. Keating (eds) *The European Union and the Regions* (Oxford: Clarendon).

Baker, D. and A. Gamble (1993) '1846 . . . 1906 . . . 1996? Conservative Splits and European Integration', *Political Quarterly* (October).

Balme, R. (1994) 'French Regionalisation', in B. Jones and M. Keating (eds) *The European Union and the Regions* (Oxford: Clarendon).

Balme, R. and L. Bonnet (1995) 'From Regional to Sectoral Policies: The Contractual Relations between the State and the Region in France', in J. Loughlin and S. Mazey (eds) *The End of the French Unitary State* (London: Frank Cass).

Banbridge, T. and A. Teasdale (1995) *The Penguin Companion to European Union* (London: Penguin).

Baudin, P. (1994) *L'Europe face à ses marchés agricoles* (Paris: Economica).

Bauer, M. (1987) *Les 200: comment devient – un grand patron* (Paris: Seuil).

Bell, D. (1996) 'Western Communist Parties and Parties and the European Union', in J. Gaffney (ed.) *Political Parties and the European Union* (London: Routledge).

Bell, D. and B. Criddle (1988) *The French Socialist Party* (Oxford University Press).

Bigot, D. (ed.) (1992) *L'Europe des Polices et de la Sécurité Intérieure* (Paris: Espace International, Edition Complexe).

Blanc, H. (1991) 'Schengen: Le Chemin de la Libre Circulation en Europe', *Revue du Marché Commun*: 722–6.

Boussard, I. (1990) *Les Agriculteurs et la République* (Paris: Economica).

Bozo, F. (1995) 'La France et l'Alliance: les limites du rapprochement', *Politique Etrangère*, **4**.

Brubaker, R. (1992) *Citizenship and Nationhood in France and Germany* (Cambridge Mass: Harvard University Press).

Burgess, M. (1990) 'Political Catholicism, European Unity and the Rise of Christian Democracy', in M. L. Smith and P. M. R. Stirk (eds) *The New Europe: European Unity and the Second World War* (London: Pinter).

Butler, D. and D. Stokes (1969) *Political Change in Britain* (London: Macmillan).

Buzan, B., M. Kestrup *et al.* (1990) *The European Security Order Recast* (London: Pinter).

Cahen, A. (1939) *The Western European Union and NATO: Building a European Defence Identity within the Context of Atlantic Solidarity* (London: Brassey Atlantic Commentaries No. 2).

Callovi, G. (1990) 'Immigration and the European Community', *Contemporary European Affairs*, **3** (3) 17–38.

Campbell, H. *et al.* (1966) *Elections and the Political Order* (New York: John Wiley).

Carmichael, L. (forthcoming 1998) 'The Impact of EU Vocational Training Policy on Centre Local Relations in the EU: The Cases of Provence Alps Côte d'Azur and North East England', PhD thesis, Newcastle.

Carnelutti, A. (1988) 'L'Administration française face à la règle communautaire', *Revue française d'administration publique*, **48**: 523–39.

Carnelutti, A. (1989) 'La formation des Agents de l'Etat aux Affaires Européennes', *Revue Française de l'Administration Publique*, 51 (July–September) 129–38.

Cawson, A. (1992) 'Interest Groups and Public Policy-Making: The Case of the European Consumer Electronics Industry', in J. Greenwood, J. R. Grove and R. Ronit (eds) *Organised Interests and the European Community* (London: Sage).

Cerny, P. (1980) *The Politics of Grandeur* (Cambridge University Press).

Chaban-Delmas, J. (1975) *L'Ardeur* (Paris: Stock).

Chilton, P. (1996) 'A European Security Regime: Integration and Cooperation in the Search for Common Foreign and Security Policy', *Journal of European Integration*, **19**, 2–3.

Cleary, M. C. (1989) *Peasants, Politicians and Producers: The Organisation of Agriculture in France since 1918* (Cambridge University Press).

Closa, C. 'The Gulf Crisis: A Study of National Constraints on Community Action', *Journal of European Integration*, **68** (1): 47–67.

Cohen, E. (1995) 'France: National Champions in Search of a Mission', in J. Hayward (ed.) *Industrial Enterprise and European Integration* (Oxford University Press).

Cohen, S. (1980) *Les Conseillers du Président* (Paris: PUF).

Cole, A. (1996) 'The French Socialists', in J. Gaffney (ed.) *Political Parties and the European Union* (London: Routledge).

Cole, A. and P. John (1995) 'Local Policy Networks in France and Britain', *West European Politics*, **18** (4).

Costigiola, F. (1992) *France and the United States: The Cold War Alliance since World War I* (New York: Tweyne).

Coulomb, P. *et al.* (eds) (1990) *Les Agriculteurs et la Politique* (Paris: FNSP).

Criddle, B. (1993) 'The French Referendum and the Maastricht Treaty, September 1992', *Parliamentary Affairs*, **46** (2).

Culpepper, P. (1993) 'Organisational Competition and the Neo-Corporatist Fallacy in French Agriculture', *West European Politics* (July) 295–315.

Daniels, P. and E. Ritchie (1989) 'Relaunching the European Communities: The Responses of Britain, France and Italy to Proposals for Institutional Reform of the Communities in 1985' (unpublished report for European Commission).

Davesnes, J. (1989) *L'Agriculture Assassinée* (Paris, Chir).

de Gaulle, C. (1970a) *Mémoires d'Espoir: 'Le Renouveau 1958-1962'* (Paris: Plon).

de Gaulle, C. (1970b) *Discours et Messages 2: Dans l'offense 1946–48* (Paris: Plon).

de la Serre, F. and P. M. Defargues (1983) 'France: A Penchant for Leadership', in C. Hill (ed.) *National Foreign Policies and European Political Co-operation* (London: Allen & Unwin).

de la Serre, F. and C. Lesquesne (1993) 'France and the European Union', in A. Cafruny and G. Rosenthal (eds) *The State of the EC* (Boulder, Colo.: Lynne Rienner).

de Villiers, P. (1992) *Notre Europe Sons Maastricht* (Paris: Albin Michel).

Debbasch, C. (ed.) *L'Administration nationale et l'intégration européenne* (Paris: CNRS).

Delapierre, M. and Michalet, G.-A. (1976) *Les implantations étrangères en France: Stratégies et Structures* (Paris: Calmann-Levy).

Delors, J. (1992) *1st Annual Jean Monnet Lecture* (LSE: European Institute).

DePorte, A. W. (1991) 'The Foreign Policy of the Fifth Republic: Between Nation and the World', in G. Hollifield and G. Ross (eds) *Searching For the New France* (London: Routledge).

Dinan, D. (1994) *Ever Closer Union* (London: Macmillan).

Dreyfus F. (1993) 'Letter from France. After the Referendum of 20 September', *Government and Opposition*, **28** (1) 82–7.

Duignan, P. and L. H. Gann (1994) *The United States and the New Europe* (Oxford: Blackwell).

Dupeyroux, J. J. (1993) *Droit de la Sécurité Sociale*, Paris: Précis Dalloz, Mémo social 95, Liaisons Sociales (Paris: 1995).

Edwards, G. and E. Regelsberger (1990) *Europe's Global Links: The European Community and Inter-Regional Co-operation* (London: Pinter).

Ehrmann, H. W. (1992) *Politics in France* (New York: HarperCollins).

Epstein, P. (1995) 'France Agricultural Decision-Making in the GATT Negotiations (1991–1993)' (Oxford MPhil thesis).

Favier, P. and M. Martin-Roland (1990) *La Décennie Mitterrand* (Paris: Seuil).

Featherstone, K. (1988) *Socialist Parties and European Integration: A Comparative History* (Manchester University Press).

Fijnaut, C. and R. Hermans (eds) (1987) *Police Cooperation in Europe* (Lochem: van den Brink).

Fieschi, C., J. Shields and R. Woods (1996) 'The Extreme Right and the EU', in J. Gaffney (ed.) *Political Parties and the European Union* (London: Routledge).

Forster, A. (1997) 'Defence and European Integration', *Theoretical Politics*, **9**, 3, July.

Fourashé, J. (1970) *Les Trentes Glorienses: ou la Révolution invisible de 1946 à 1975* (Paris: Fayard).

Fraser, T. (1994) 'The New Structural Funds, State Aids and Interventions in the Single Market', *European Law Review*, **20** (1) 3–19.

Frears, J. (1981) *France in the Giscard Presidency* (London: Allen & Unwin).

Fursdon, E. (1980) *The European Defence Community* (New York: St Martin's Press).

Gaffney, J. (1995) 'France', in J. Lodge (ed.) *The 1994 Elections to the European Parliament* (London: Pinter).

George, S. (1991) *Politics and Policy in the European Community* (Oxford University Press).

Gerbet, P. (1975) 'Les partis politiques et les communautés européenes', in J. Rideau *et al.*, *La France et les communautés européenes* (Paris: LGDG).

Gillingham, J. (1991) *Coal, Steel and the Rebirth of Europe 1945-1955* (Cambridge University Press).

Gordon, P. A. (1993) *A Certain Idea of France:French Security and the Gaullist Legacy* (Princeton: Princeton University Press).

Gordon, P. A. (1995) *The Franco-German Partnership and the Western Alliance* (Boulder, Colo.: Westview).

Graham, S. (1995) 'Cities, Nations and Communications in the Global Era: Urban Telecommunications Policy in France', *European Planning Studies*, **3** (3) 357–80.

Greenwood, J., J. R. Grote and K. Ronit (eds) (1992) *Organized Interests and the European Community* (London: Sage).

Grémion, P. (1976) *Le pouvoir péripherique: bureaucrates ét notable dans le système politique français* (Paris: Editions de Seuil).

Grilli, E. (1993) *The European Community and the Developing Countries* (Cambridge University Press).

Gronit, J. (1995) 'Size of Territory in the Organisation of Business Interests', in J. Greenwood (ed.) *European Case Book on Business Alliances* (Hemel Hempstead: Prentice-Hall) 237–58.

Grosser, A. (1984) *Affaires extérieurs: la politique de la France, 1944–84* (Paris: Flammation).

Grunberg, G. (1994) 'Les Francais et l'Europe', *Revue politique et parlementaire*, **6** (2) 20–5.

Guillaume, M. (1992) 'Déficit démocratique et déficit juridique: quoi de neuf en France?', *Revue Française d'Administration Publique*, **63** (July–September) 435–46.

Gunther, H. (1972) *Transnational Industrial Relations* (London: Macmillan).

Guyomarch, A. (1995) 'The European Dynamics of Evolving Party Competition in France', *Parliamentary Affairs*, **48** (1).

Hainsworth, P. (1990) 'France', in J. Lodge (ed.) *The 1989 Election of the European Parliament* (London: Macmillan).

Hall, P. A. (1986) *Governing the Economy: The Politics of State Intervention in Britain and France* (New York: Oxford University Press).

Hall, P., J. E. S. Hayward and H. Machin (1994) *Developments in French Politics 2* (London: Macmillan).

Hayward, J. E. S. (1986) *The State and the Market Economy* (Brighton: Wheat-sheaf).

Hoffman, S. (1992) 'Dilemmes et stratégies de la France dans la nouvelle Elée', *Politique Etrangère*, **57** (4). Also in English as 'French Dilemmas and Strategies in the New Europe', in R. Keohane, J. Nye and S. Hoffman (eds) *After the Cold War: International Institutions and State Strategies in Europe 1989–1991* (Cambridge, Mass.: Harvard University Press).

Hooghe, L. and M. Keating (1994) 'The Politics of EU Regional Policy', *Journal of European Public Policy*, **11** (3).

Howorth, J. (1990) 'France since the Berlin Wall; Diplomacy and Defence', *The World Today*, **46** (7) 126–30.

Howorth, J. (1992) 'France and the Defence of Europe', in J. Howorth and M. McClean (eds) *Europeans on Europe* (Basingstoke: Macmillan).

Hreblay, V. (1994) *La Libre Circulation des personnes, Les Accords de Schengen* (Paris: Presse Universitaires de France).

Inglehart, S. and J. R. Rabier (1987) 'The Evolution of Public Attitudes Toward European Integration: 1970-1986', *Journal of European Integration*, **10** (2 and 3) 135–55.

Jacob, F., R. Corbett and M. Shackleton (1995) *The European Parliament* (London: Catermill).

Jones, B. (1994) 'Conclusion', in B. Jones and M. Keating (eds) *The European Union and the Regions* (Oxford: Clarendon).

Jones, B. and M. Keating (eds) (1994) *The European Union and the Regions* (Oxford: Clarendon).

Jouve, E. (1967) *Le Général de Gaulle et la Construction de l'Europe* (Paris: Plon).

Kaiser, K. and P. Lelouche (eds) (1986) *Le couple Franco-allemand et la défense de l'Europe* (Paris: IFRI).

Keating, M. (1994) Introduction to B. Jones and M. Keating (eds) *The European Union and the Regions* (Oxford: Clarendon).

Keeler, J. T. S. (1987) *The Politics of Neocorpratism* (Oxford University Press).

Kennedy, P. (1978) *The Rise and Fall of the Great Powers. Economic Change and Military Conflict 1500-2000* (New York: Random House).

Kolodziej, E. (1974) *French International Policy under de Gaulle and Pompidou* (Ithaca: Cornell).

Ladrech, R. (1994) 'Europeanization of Domestic Politics and Institutions: The Case of France', *Journal of Common Market Studies*, **32** (1) 69–88.

Lagroye, J. and V. Wright (eds) (1979) *Local Government in Britain and France: Problems and Perspectives* (London: George Allen & Unwin).

Lawsen, F. and S. van Hoonacker (1992) (eds) *The Intergovernmental Conference on Political Union* (Maastricht: European Institute of Public Administration; Dordrecht, Netherlands: Nÿhoff).

Le Galès, P. (1995) 'Regional Economic Policies: An Alternative to French Economic *Dirigisme*', in J. Loughlin and S. Mazey (eds) *The End of the French Unitary State* (London: Frank Cass).

Le Roy, P. (1993) *Les Agricultures françaises face aux marchés mondiaux* (Paris: A. Colin).

Leonardi, R. (1993) 'Cohesion in the EC: Illusion or Reality?', *West European Politics*, **16** (4).

Leonardi, R. (1995) *Convergence, Cohesion and Integration in the European Union* (London: Macmillan).

Lequesne, C. (1987a) 'L'Adaptation des administrations nationales à l'existence des Communautés européennes – le cas des ministres françaises', *Revue française d'administration publique*, **42**: 275–92.

Lequesne, C. (1987b) 'Coordonner la politique européene de la France', *Projet*, **206**: 31–46.

Lodge, J. (ed.) (1990) *The 1989 Election of the European Parliament* (London: Macmillan).

Lofthouse, A. and D. Long (1996) 'The European Union and the Civilian Model of Foreign Policy', *Journal of European Integration*, **19** (2–3).

Loughlin, J. and S. Mazey (eds) (1995) *The End of the French Unitary State: Ten Years of Regionalisation in France 1982–1992* (London: Frank Cass).

Machin, H. (1989) 'Stages and Dynamics in the Evolution of the French Party System', *West European Politics*, **18** (3) 59–81.

Machin, H. (1994) 'Political Leadership', in P. A. Hall, J. Hayward and H. Machin (eds), *Developments in French Politics* (London: Macmillan).

Machin, H. (1977) *The Prefect in French Public Administration* (London: Croom Helm).

Malgrain, I. (1965) *L'Integration agricule de l'Europe des Six* (Paris: Cujas).

Marks, G. (1992) 'Structural Policy in the European Union', in A. M. Sbragia (ed.) *Europolitics* (Washington: Brookings).

Marks, G. (1993) 'Structural Policy and Multilevel Governance', in A. W. Cafrury and G. G. Rosenthal (eds) *The State of the European Community, Vol. 2: The Maastricht Debate and Beyond* (Harlow: Longman).

Mazey, S. (1994) 'La France Saisie Par La Decentralisation: Aperçu Britannique', in R. Balme *et al.*, *Le Territoire Pour Politiques: Variations Européenes* (Paris: L'Harmattan).

Mazey, S. (1995) 'French Regions and the European Union', in J. Loughlin and S. Mazey (eds) *The End of the French Unitary State* (London: Frank Cass).

Meimeth, M. 'France Gets Closer to NATO', *World Today*, **50** (5).

Menon. A. (1994) 'Continuing Politics by Other Means: Defence Policy in the Fifth Republic', *West European Politics*, **17** (4).

Menon, A. (1995a) 'From Independence to Cooperation: France, NATO and European Security', *International Affairs*, **71** (1).

Menon, A. (1995b) 'Explaining Defence Policy: The Mitterrand Years', *Review of International Studies*, **21**.

Mertial, E. (1992) 'France and European Political Union', in F. Laursen and S. Vanhoonache (eds) *The Intergovernmental Conference on Political Union* (Maastricht: European Institute of Public Administration; Dordrecht, Netherlands: Nÿhoff).

Mesnier, S. (1990) 'Le Role du Quai d'Orsay de mai 1986 à mai 1988', *Revue administrative*, **258** (November–December) 489–98.

Meunier-Aitsahalia, S. and G. Ross (1993) 'Democratic Deficit or Democratic Surplus? A Reply to Andrew Moravcsik's Comments on the French Referendum', *French Politics and Society*, **11** (1).

Michalet, C.A. (1985) *Les Multinationales face à la crise* (Paris: PUF).

Michalet, C. A. and M. Delapierre (1973) *La Multinationalisation des Entreprises françaises* (Paris: Gouthier-Villars).

Milward, A. S. (1984) *The Reconstruction of Western Europe* (London: Methuen).

Milward, A. S. (1992) *The European Rescue of the Nation-State* (London: Routledge).

Minc, A. (1989) *La Grande Illusion* (Paris: Grasset).

Monnet, J. (1976) *Mémoires* (Paris: Fayard).

Moravcsik, A. (1993a) 'Idealism and Interest in the European Community: The Case of the French Referendum', *French Politics and Society*, **11** (1).

Moravcsik, A. (1993b) 'Preferences and Power in the European Community: A Liberal Intergovernmentalist Approach, *Journal of Common Market Studies*, **31** (4) 473–524.

Muller, P. (1992) 'Entre le local et l'Europe: La Crise du modèle français ou le politique publique', *Revue française de science politique*, **42** (2).

Muller-Gräf, P. C. (1994) 'The Legal Basis of the Third Pillar and its Position in the Framework of the Union Treaty', *Common Market Law Review*, **31** (3) 493–510.

Muth, H. P. (1970) *French Agriculture and the Political Integration of Western Europe* (Leyden: Sijthoff).

Mutimer, D. (1989) '1992 and the Political Integration of Europe. Neo-Functionalism Re-considered', *Journal of European Integration*, **13** (1) 75–101.

Myers, J. A. (1992) 'The WEU: Pillar of NATO or Defence Arm of the EC?', *London Defence Studies*.

Neveu, A. (1992) *Agriculture: Economie de l'agriculture française en Europe: Forces et faiblesses* (Paris: Dunod).

Newman, M. (1984) *Socialism and European Unity: The Dilemma of the Left in Britain and France* (London: Junction Books).

Northrup, H. R. and P. Rowan (1979) *Multinational Collective Bargaining Attempts* (Philadelphia: University of Pennsylvania Press).

Nugent, N. (1993) 'The Deepening and Widening of the European Community: Recent Evolution Maastricht and Beyond', *Journal of Common Market Studies*, **30** (3).

Nugent, N. (1995) *The Government and Politics of the European Union* (London: Macmillan).

Penaud, R. and F. Gaudichet (1985) *Séléctivité du crédit, financement, politique monétaire* (Paris).

Pollack, M. A. (1995) 'Regional Actors in an Intergovernmental Play: The Making and Implementation of EC Structural Policy', in C. Rhodes and S. Mazey (eds) *The State of the European Union, vol. 3: Building a European Polity?* (Harlow: Longman).

Rideau, J. *et al.* (1975) *La France et les communautés européenes* (Paris: LGDG).

Ross, G. (1993) 'Democratic Deficit or Democrat Surplus? A Reply to A. Moravscik's Commentary on the French Referendum', *French Politics and Society*, **11** (1).

Rudnick, D. (1974) 'An Assessment of the Reasons for the Removal of the French Veto to UK Membership of the EEC', *International Relations*, **14** (6) 658–72.

Saint-Ouen, F. (1990) *Les partis politiques et l'Europe: une approche comparative* (Paris: PUF).

Scharf, F. (1994) 'Community and Autonomy: Multilevel Policy-making in the EU', *Journal of European Policy*, **2**.

Schifres, M. and M. Sarazin (1985) *L'Elysée de Mitterrand: secrets de la maison du Prince* (Paris: A. Moreau).

Schmidt, V. (1991) *Democratising France* (Cambridge University Press).

Schmidt, V. A. (1995) 'Loosening the Ties that Bind: the impact of European integration on French Government and its relation to business', (unpublished paper) LSE European Political Research Workshop, November 1995.

Schnapper, D. (1991) *La France de l'Intégration* (Paris: Gallimard).

Schneider, V. (1992) 'Organized Interests in the European Telecommunications Sector', in J. Greenwood, J. R. Grote and R. Ronit (eds) (1992) *Organized Interests and the European Community* (London: Sage).

Shields, J. (1996) 'The French Gaullists', in J. Gaffney (ed.) *Political Parties and the European Union* (London: Routledge).

Shonfield, W. R. (1986) 'Le RPR et l'UDF à l'épreuve de l'opposition', *Revue française de science politique*, **36** (1) 14–28.

Silverman, M. (1992) *Deconstructing the Nation: Immigration, Racism and Citizenship in Modern France* (London: Routledge).

Simonian, A. H. (1984) *The Privileged Partnership: Franco-German Relations in the European Community 1969–84* (Oxford: Clarendon).

Smith, A. (1997) 'Putting the Governance Back into Multi-level Governance. Examples from French Translation of the Structural Fund', *Public Administration*, **75** (4) Winter 1997.

Smith, J. (1995) 'The 1994 European Elections', *West European Politics*, **18** (3): 199–217.

Stevens, A. (1986) 'France', in J. Lodge (ed.) *Direct Elections to the European Parliament 1984* (London: Macmillan).

Stevens, A. (1996) *The Government and Politics of France* (Basingstoke: Macmillan).

Stewart, A. (1992) 'Migrants, Minorities and Security in Europe', *Conflict Studies*, **252** (June).

Story, J. (ed.) (1994) *The New Europe* (Oxford: Blackwell).

Sutton, M. (1995) Chirac's Foreign Policy: Continuity – with Adjustment', *The World Today*, **51** (7).

Taylor, T. (1994) 'West European Security and Defence Co-operation', *International Affairs*, **70**.

Tiersky, R. (1991) 'Mitterrand, France and Europe', *French Politics and Society*, **9** (1): 9–25.

Tiersky, R. (1992) 'Mitterrand, France and the New Europe', *French Politics and Society*, **7** (2).

Tiersky, R. (1993) 'French Foreign Policy Stumbles', *French Politics and Society*, **11** (1).

Tiersky, R. (1995) *France in The New Europe: Changing yet Steadfast* (Belmont, California: Wansworth).

Twitchett, C. and K. Twitchett (eds) (1981) *Building Europe: Britain's Partners in the EEC* (London: Europa).

Urwin, D. (1991) *The Community of Europe* (London: Longman).

Varpel, J. W. and J. Curhan (1973) *The World's Multinational Enterprises* (Boston, Mass.: Harvard University Press).

Vedel, G. and E. Delvolvé (1990) *Droit administratif* (Paris: Thémis).

Vernet, D. (1992) 'The Dilemma of French Foreign Policy', *International Affairs*, **68** (4), 655–64.

Vernet, D. (1995) 'La France et l'Allemagne', *Politique Etrangére*, **4**.

Weil, P. and J. Crowley (1994) 'Integration in Theory and Practice: a Comparison of France and Britain', *West European Politics*, **17** (2) 110–26.

Wihtol de Wenden, C. (1994) 'Immigrants as Political Actors in France', *West European Politics*, **17** (2): 91–109.

Williams, R. H. (1996) *EU Spatial Policy and Planning* (London: Paul Chapman).

Wood, P. 'European Political Co-operation: Lessons from the Gulf War and Yugoslavia', in A. Cafruny and G. Rosenthal (eds) *The State of the European Community, vol. 2* (Harlow: Longman).

Wright, V. (1989) *The Government and Politics of France* (London: Hutchinson).

Zysman, J. (1977) *Policy Strategies for Industrial Order: State, Market and Industry in France* (Berkeley, California).

Official documents and cases

French sources

Ministère de la Défense *Livre Blanc sur la Défense*, 1994

DATAR (1993) *Débat Pour l'Aménagement du Territoire* (Paris: Documentation Française)

DATAR (1993b) *Les Villes, lieux d'Europe* (Paris: Aube)

DATAR (1993c) *Les Territoires du futur* (Paris: Aube)

Ligot, M. (1990) *Rapport sur l'achèvement du marché intérieur et la transposition des directives en droit interne* (Délégation pur les Communautés Européennes, Assemblée Nationale).

1995 Lettre du Matignon: Policy Statements for the Cannes Summit

European Union sources

Case c-4/91 27 November 1991, European Court of Justice

Social Protection in Europe, 1993.

Agence Europe

Newspapers

'German Hopes for Europol Dashed', *Financial Times*, 1 December 1994.

Libération, 23 December 1994

Le Point

Libération

European Voice

Other Sources

Eurobarometer surveys of public opinion
European Parliament News

Index